# LIFE SKILLS FOR

# STUDENT SUCCESS

## ACHIEVING FINANCIAL LITERACY

Bill Pratt | Mark C. Weitzel | Len Rhodes

# Kendall Hunt
### publishing company

Cover images © Shutterstock, Inc.

**Kendall Hunt**
publishing company

www.kendallhunt.com
*Send all inquiries to:*
4050 Westmark Drive
Dubuque, IA 52004-1840

To the
personal and financial
success of our students
and to our wives,
without whom this project
would not have been possible.

Special thanks to NSLP for their contributions
to our Paying for College chapter.

# BRIEF CONTENTS

# CONTENTS

## Chapter 6 THE HOUSING DECISION 121

## Chapter 7 TAXES 151

**Chapter 8**    **RISK MANAGEMENT**    **169**

Chapter **11**  **INVESTING  235**

chapter
1

# CAREERS

## Welcome to the Jungle

Two friends with the same major came to our office to share news of their upcoming graduation. The first friend was really excited over three very good job offers and wanted advice on how to go about making the best decision. Just 15 minutes later her friend came in and he was almost in tears. He too wanted advice, but it was about moving back home to his parents'. Although he spent the semester interviewing just like she did, he had no job offers, and graduation was just a few days away. As it turned out, it was not until six months later that he received his first job offer. Would you like to know what he did wrong? Let's explore.

# THE BIG PICTURE

## Why Are You Here?

For so many of us, our last two years of high school revolved around getting into a good college. There are many reasons why you are attending the college you are in now. Perhaps your parents attended this college. Maybe you have been watching their sports program for years. For some, you have decided on a specific major that this school is known for. For others, the school you wanted to get into was out of reach financially, so you came here instead.

Your answer only addresses part of the real question. The question was not "Why did you choose to attend this particular college?" The question was why are you here? Why are you in college? Why did you choose to attend any college?

Was college simply the next step for you? Did your high school counselor recommend college? Are you attending college because that is what all of your friends are doing? Maybe your parents gave you a choice right after graduation; either get a job now or go to college. Maybe you saw a value for you in obtaining a higher education.

But wait . . . there's more. Are you in college just to get smarter? To learn some new skills? Why? Do you plan to do something with that new skill? Get a job, perhaps, or maybe start a career?

What type of job or career are you planning for? Where do you want to work? What is the starting salary?

In any case, you are here now, so how do you make the most of it, and why is that important?

## *Student Loans*

Before we answer the question of why are you here, do you understand what it is costing you to be here? Do you know how much you are paying to attend this college? If you are borrowing money through federal loans or other types of student loans, have you considered what it will cost you to repay the money? The average tuition and fees for a public four-year college for in-state students in 2010 was $7,020, and room and board costs an additional $8,193.[1] The average full-time student borrows $8,000 per year,[2] which equates to nearly $32,000 for a four-year degree. Right now the cost of tuition may not be of concern to you. However, have you considered what the monthly payments will be once you graduate?

Based on interest rates of 5.1% and the standard repayment period of 10 years,[3] the average college graduate can expect monthly payments of $340.[4] Have you considered what the consequences of this payment will be to your lifestyle the first several years after graduation? In other words, are your expectations in terms of salary and lifestyle aligned with what can be expected of a new graduate in your career field? And did you include in your assumptions the payments you will be making on your student loans?

## *Job Choices*

What if your only job was at a fast-food restaurant? We'll call it McFood. Assume that you have two choices:

You can get a job now, making McMinimum wage at McFood or you can attend college for four, or five, or maybe six years, spending upward of $32,000 in tuition, and then graduate and still get a job at McFood for McMinimum wage.

Which would you choose?

Ask yourself the following questions: "Do I enjoy taking exams? Do I enjoy cramming for finals? Do I enjoy writing papers and doing research projects? Do I really like spending all night studying, then drinking tiny bottles of energy drinks, and attending class early in the morning all jittery?"

Obviously, there is no point in spending tens of thousands of dollars and four years of your life studying, taking exams, and writing papers, just so you can get the same job you could have if you never went to college in the first place.

# So What Is the Answer?

So why are you really here? You are here to get a job. More important, you are here to get a better job than you otherwise could without your higher education.

Before we can begin to really understand how we can go from being in college to getting a good job, we have to understand the employer's perspective. Something most of us never give a thought to is, "Why do businesses buy things?" Let's start with a much easier question. Why do you buy things? Look down at your shirt, your backpack, your shoes, or maybe even your cell phone. Why did you buy them? Did it make you feel good? Maybe you think it will make you look better or help keep you connected to your friends. When you purchased the item, you probably felt that buyer's high; the "warm fuzzy" connected to making a special purchase just for yourself.

Businesses do not buy things to feel good. Businesses buy things for one reason and one reason only: to make a profit. A fast-food restaurant will likely not purchase a large piece of construction equipment such as a bulldozer because it is not related to their business and cannot be used to make money. The same concept applies to employees. A business is not going to hire an employee and pay them a salary unless the business believes the employee can make them money.

Do not get too caught up on the term "business." A federal government agency, a state government agency, or a nonprofit organization also operates like a business. In fact, nonprofit organizations sometimes have to be even more accountable with their dollars because they are relying on donations to operate. If they are going to use their limited funds to hire an individual, the expectation is that the organization will get much more out of the individual than they are putting in.

Once you start searching for a job, you become a product. You are a business investment that is expected to provide the company with output greater than what they are investing. As a product, you are competing with tens, hundreds, or even thousands of others. Think of your education as a car. Your GPA is the engine. Everyone has a GPA, just as every car has an engine; some are just more powerful than others. Any other skills you acquire in college are the same as any other college graduate. Think of it as if you come with standard equipment such as the ability to compose a professional e-mail or the ability to write a professional letter. Although some of these skills may seem advanced, they have become standard over time, just as all new cars now come with power door locks, power windows, and power steering. It is your job to come with advanced equipment such as GPS or leather interior. You need to make yourself a more attractive product by picking up additional skills and experiences that make a potential employer see the added value you bring to the business.

Your diploma will make you marketable, but it will not make you successful. It is nothing more than third-party verification that you have met certain criteria. A diploma is a prescreening process that your potential employer can bypass because your college already did it for them. It says that you come with all the standard features we just discussed.

## *Get the Most Out of Your Education*

Imagine for a moment that you place an order at McFoods. You want a double cheeseburger, a large drink, and a large order of fries. The total meal costs $6.50, and you gladly pay the full amount. When your order arrives, you have a regular hamburger, no cheese, a small order of onion rings, and a small cup of tap water. How would you react? Would you just say, "Oh well, it's hard to get good help these days" and gladly eat the meal, or would you take the order back to the counter and demand to get what you actually ordered? Most of us would quickly demand to have the order corrected. In some instances, we would demand to be compensated for the error or may choose not to return to the same restaurant.

Now ask what you would do if your instructor lets you out 10 minutes early, or cancels class. Same reaction? We doubt it. As discussed, you are paying tens of thousands of dollars to get an education. You want to learn as much as you can so you can come equipped not just with the standard equipment, but also with all of the extra upgrades as well. You should always demand your money's worth. In fact, you should ask your instructors to supersize your education! Higher education seems to be one of the few instances where we celebrate getting less than what we paid for and complain when we are actually given as much if not more than we purchased. So the next time your professor lets you out of class early, stand up and say, "Heck no! Give me my money's worth. In fact, supersize me and keep me five minutes longer!"

Your degree is a big step to a career, not just a job. Your degree is an investment of time, money, sweat, and opportunity cost. Spending time going to a party is time you cannot spend studying. Spending your money on choice beverages is money you cannot spend on Ramen noodles. You should pay attention and be engaged. This applies not only to your classes in college, but also in life. The more you pay attention and the more engaged you are in your career, in your family, and in your marriage, the more you will be successful. You should learn to think about your situations or decisions and not just react. We are responsible for ourselves. Every decision has consequences. You can no longer use the excuse that "nobody told me."

Now that we understand our reason for attending college is to get a better job than we could have otherwise, the question becomes, How do we go about getting that job? There are four steps necessary to making the most of your college investment:

1. **The Attitude**—We have to think differently about our time in college
2. **The Task**—Getting a job is a full-time job
3. **The Job Market**—Know what you are getting yourself into
4. **The Plan**—To get where you want to go, you have to know where you are

### THE ATTITUDE

You have to believe in yourself. Your college already does. Your college has certain standards and criteria, such as minimum GPA, SAT, or ACT scores. They have determined that if you meet certain standards, you can be successful, which is what they want from you. A successful college graduate is more likely to give money back to the school through their alumni fund and is more likely to make a positive impression on the workforce, leading to more job opportunities for future graduates from your school.

If you think you can—you can. If you think you can't—you're right. Attitude is more important than aptitude or appearance. It can make or break a marriage, a family, a church, or a career. We cannot control the actions of others, but we can control how we respond to their actions. The most successful people are those with a positive attitude. What your employer has already figured out and is looking for is a positive attitude. You will learn how to do the work, but it is the positive attitude that will drive your success and advancement from the very first day on the job.

## Career Success Begins While You Are in College

First the bad news. You are not special. This may come as a huge shock to you, but you are not special. Again, you are not special. For the last 18+ years you have been told by your parents, teachers, and coaches that you are special. You even have trophies for coming in ninth place out of ten participants to prove it. Here is the bad news. When you graduate, along with approximately 1.6 million other students, you will not be special.[5] You will be a product. You are unique, but not special.

Now for the good news. Because you are not special, that means none of the other thousands of graduates competing with you are special either. With no special people, you are all on an even playing field. Now all you have to do is work just a little harder. A little more involvement on campus where you have a leadership role will give you a leg up. A little more effort to get an internship will help set you apart.

Once you get a job, the same rules apply. Just work a little bit harder, just do a little bit more, and you are the one who will get the promotions and pay raises during good times, and you will keep your job during the bad times.

In the business world, perception is often reality. If you are perceived to be a hard worker, then you are a hard worker in the eyes of your employer. If you are perceived to not be aggressive, then you are not aggressive in the eyes of your employer. You need to develop special work habits that will set you apart from your colleagues. It will not require an extra 40 hours at the office every week, just a little more than your competition. If you are not assigned a mentor when you start your first post-college job, then you need to seek one out for yourself. A former student told us how fortunate he was to have had a mentor on his first job and how it led to an interesting lesson in perceptions. He told us how Tom, his mentor, always seemed to work harder than him. "He was always there when I arrived in the morning and still at his desk when I left. Curious to see how hard he was really working, I started coming in earlier and earlier and staying later and later. He was always there. Finally, one evening he came to me and said, 'You have to go home.' I asked him why, and he said it was because he wanted to go home. I looked at him puzzled, and he explained that as my boss, he had to create the impression in my mind that he worked harder than I did. Once that impression was created, he could come and go as he pleased, but in my mind he would always be working harder than me."

## THE TASK

Nearly 80% of all college graduates move back home with their parents after graduation.[6] According to the National Association of Colleges and Employers, roughly 25% of students graduating in 2010 had a job lined up after graduation.[7] Why such startling statistics? After all, if these students spent tens of thousands of dollars to get an education that was supposed to help them find a job related to their field, then why were so many unable to successfully find employment? The answer is simple: They did not start preparing for their career early enough. They did not create and, more important, execute a plan. Many students who receive their diploma think they are getting an automatic job-creation certificate. Nothing could be further from the truth. A diploma is not a job offer. It is a piece of paper that certifies you have mastered a skill set, whether it is in biology, economics, management, or nursing.

Seniors should be working with their career services office already. If not, you are already behind and will have to work harder to catch up. Freshmen and sophomores are very fortunate to get this advice early. Your job search begins right now! Yes, that includes freshmen. Don't wait until six weeks before graduation to go to the career services office and say, "Get me a job." They will just laugh at you. If you spend your four (or five or six) years at college just thinking about your education and not about your career, you will be way behind in your job search. You need to think about your education as a means to an end, not as the end goal itself.

At every college, successful alumni return to campus to speak to current students about job opportunities. For instance, on our campus, we have a successful graduate that speaks about and recruits for a national health-care provider. This health-care company provides in-home care for those who may be injured or need assistance following surgery. One of the most important features the company is looking for on a college transcript is coursework in Spanish, preferably four semesters. There is tremendous opportunity for this company in serving the growing Hispanic population, so they would rather hire a 3.0 student with four semesters of Spanish than a 4.0 student with little or no foreign language coursework. If you are looking for an opportunity similar to what this company is offering, you cannot wait until your last semester to find out that you need four semesters of Spanish. Knowing what a job or company requires early in your college career gives you time to obtain and achieve those skills.

## *Job versus Career*

What is the key difference between a job and a career? A job is what you are doing right now to earn your paycheck. A career is what you are going to do throughout your lifetime. Hopefully whatever jobs you find yourself in will help you achieve your career aspirations. We all make decisions to accept certain job offers for various reasons. And no matter what job or job situation you find yourself in, there are always opportunities to learn and grow from your experiences. You may find yourself in a job that has good benefits, a great salary, and big bonuses. After working there for several years you realize that you have hit a plateau, and you want to change directions in your career. Sometimes, your job can get in the way of your career. Think about that. Other times, your job is necessary for you to keep moving forward and keep your career on track.

Pharmaceutical sales representatives can earn a lot of money and are usually hired in their early twenties. For those looking to get into a lucrative sales career with many perks, becoming a pharmaceutical representative is a great option. However, to get hired you will need a certain number of years of outside selling experience (selling to customers face-to-face). So if you want to get into this career track, you may have to sell cars or cell phones for a few years to gain experience. The point is you are going to have to do some "dirty jobs" to get to the job you really desire.

It is important to keep in mind that everything you do does count. Every class you take, every internship position you complete, and every organization you choose to join has an impact on your future. You must make sound decisions—and have good reasons for making those decisions. You must always think, "What is my next step?" What you do today determines your tomorrow. The key point is that your education is the early part of your career.

### THE JOB MARKET

Now we know our education is important to our career, but what does that really mean? In 2008 and 2009, the unemployment rate in the United States hit 20-year highs with rates moving above 10% for many states and hovering at around 10% for the nation as a whole. You may find the unemployment numbers reported every day by the media quite disheartening. Most college students assume that the picture is bleak and it will be even worse for them as they graduate because they are entering the workforce with no previous experience. But the unemployment numbers you are likely to see in the media (and the media loves to oversensationalize everything) do not reflect the opportunities available to you as a college graduate.

Let's take a look at unemployment rates and education level. When we understand this relationship, we see an encouraging trend for you. Look at the Education Pays Chart. The higher the education level, the lower the unemployment rate. In fact, the unemployment rate of college graduates is much less than that of high school graduates. More important, college graduates earn more money.

It is not as if everyone gets a degree. So just completing your college degree gives you an advantage over everyone else. You may think everybody goes to college nowadays, but keep in mind that not everyone graduates from high school, and of those who do, only 46% actually finish college.[8] In other words, if you started your freshman year of high school with 400 other students, only 182 of them will finish college. That means if you complete your two-year or four-year degree, you become part of an elite group of educated individuals that suffers very little from unemployment and earns bigger paychecks. The key point is that education pays.

## EDUCATION PAYS

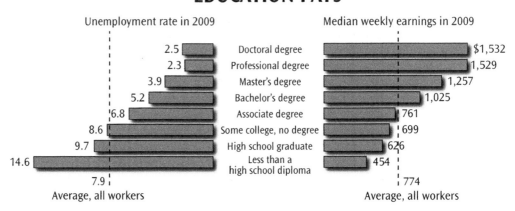

| Unemployment rate in 2009 | | Median weekly earnings in 2009 |
|---|---|---|
| 2.5 | Doctoral degree | $1,532 |
| 2.3 | Professional degree | 1,529 |
| 3.9 | Master's degree | 1,257 |
| 5.2 | Bachelor's degree | 1,025 |
| 6.8 | Associate degree | 761 |
| 8.6 | Some college, no degree | 699 |
| 9.7 | High school graduate | 626 |
| 14.6 | Less than a high school diploma | 454 |
| 7.9 | Average, all workers | 774 |

If you think about it, this is all good news. Getting a degree gives you a greater chance of getting a job, keeping your job, and earning a higher salary.

However, not all jobs are created equal. At some point you may find yourself under-employed. This refers to people who are employed, but are at a job significantly below their skill level or as a part-time employee. Starting out in an entry-level professional position right after college, despite your desire to be the president of the company, does not constitute underemployment. On the other hand, if you graduated with a degree in accounting and your friend stops by to see you at work and you have to ask him, "Do you want fries with that," then you are probably underemployed. Underemployment is okay in the short run because it is better to be underemployed than unemployed. However, you can do long-term harm to your career if you end up underemployed for an extended period of time because employers will assume you have lost many of your previous skills. Keep in mind that college degrees do have a shelf life in the business world.

## Unique Challenges and Opportunities for the New Graduate

The obstacle you will likely face as a new college graduate is your lack of pro-fessional experience. Because you are seeking an entry-level position, you are not expected to have five years of progressively increasing responsibility or previous experience in the field. You will, however, be competing against many other job applicants who have also just graduated, and in a depressed job market you may actually have to compete against those who do have at least a handful of years of experience. So how do you make yourself stand out?

Most people are hired not according to what they know, but according to who they know. We are not referring to some underhanded or unethical hiring process like you may read about in the news. We are talking about networking. Whether you are attending a four-year college or a community college, take a look at the students around you. Imagine the number of connections all of them must have. Try to name one other time in your life when you will have the opportunity to connect with as many people as you do while in college.

You are in a unique position where recruiters actually come to campus looking for students just like you. Most of your professors have either previous experience outside academia or have connections in the community. Even if they cannot help you get in touch with anyone hiring, they can offer advice and maybe serve as a reference. Most colleges sponsor at least one career fair each year or partner with the community to hold multiple events throughout the year. You may have roommates, classmates, study partners, teammates, or friends who know people or who know people that know other people. You will never have a networking opportunity again in your life the way you do right now.

Another plus for you is that expectations are low. Because you are new to the career field, most employers enjoy the pure energy and passion that recent college graduates bring to the job. You are also not seen as much of a threat to those who have been in their careers for several years because you are coming in at a different level. Most people love to help others, particularly if they do not see any potential threats to their comfort level or livelihood. Throughout your career this may change somewhat, but not drastically.

Be sure you send a personal thank-you note to anyone who helps you with your career, as you never know how many times in the future you may need their assistance. It may sound outdated to write an actual thank-you note, but this is one form of etiquette that has never gone out of style. A thank-you note is what will set you apart and will keep those friends and connections willing to help you throughout the years.

In addition, many new college graduates do not really know what they want to do. It is riskier to hire someone who *thinks* they understand an industry or a job than to hire someone who has actually seen it or done it firsthand. For example, if you want to go into banking, you could work as a teller part-time while in college. You may not be preparing stock portfolios, but you at least have a general understanding of how the industry works, which will keep your resume at the top of the stack.

What you want to do is find ways to overcome your lack of experience. Look for opportunities to lead and to serve within your existing community, most notably your campus community. Do not just join a sorority or fraternity, but seek a leadership role. Consider joining organizations that are directly related to your major or area of interest. Look for intern opportunities, even if they are unpaid. Internships give you the chance to prove your abilities, work a regular schedule, work within the industry, and make additional contacts. By proving to a potential employer that you are reliable in coming to work, have a positive attitude, and understand the industry, you make it easier for them to want to hire you. The key point is to do something!

### The Plan

We need to plan where we want to go and how we can get there. Without a plan, we will all end up somewhere eventually, but probably not where we wanted to go. Proper planning allows us to assess where we are, see where we want to go, and see which routes we can take to get there.

How do you put your plan together? A good plan has three parts:

1. The Three "W"s
2. You—The Product
3. The Job of Getting a Job

## The Three "W"s

The Three "W"s are "What," "Where," and "Who."

What kind of work do you want to do? Do you prefer inside sales? Outside sales? Management? Customer interaction? Manufacturing? Retail? Insurance? Medical? Software? The choices are endless. It helps to start broad and then narrow your selection. For instance, you may be interested in health care. From there you may decide you want to be a doctor, nurse, or physician's assistant. If you want to be a doctor, are you going to be a primary-care physician, surgeon, or some other specialty? The same applies to being a nurse or physician's assistant. Keep narrowing the field down until you have identified your career choice.

The way to begin is to ask yourself what you *like* to do. What is it that you would pay others to let you do? Choosing something you like allows you to do something that you are good at doing. You are good at doing those things you like to do because you practice them a lot. You practice them a lot because you like to do them. If you choose a career doing what you like to do, you will be good at it. It will feel like you never really work a day in your life.

Where do you want to live? Where are you willing to move to get that dream job? Do you want to live in the United States or abroad? Do you want to live on the East Coast or West Coast? Do you want to live near mountains or near an ocean? Do you want to live in a big city or a small town? It is important to narrow your choice down to one or two places that have large concentrations of jobs you like to do.

Who do you want to work for? You need to choose specific companies. Is it Proctor and Gamble, Sprint, BB&T Bank, or Target Corporation? There are hundreds of thousands of companies of all sizes in our country and around the world. You need to identify individual companies that offer jobs you like to do in the places where you would like to do them. This is important because now you can ask those companies, "What do I need to do while I am in college that will make you interested in hiring me when I graduate?" You want to find out as early in your college career as possible what those companies find attractive in new graduates so you can take the necessary classes, get the appropriate internship, or join the right organization to demonstrate that you are the right product to meet their needs. This is a win–win situation. The company gets a productive new employee, and you get a job that you like.

As you answer these three questions, it is important to prioritize them in the order that is the most important for you. Make sure that where you want to live aligns with what you want to do. If it does not, you must decide which is more important. If what you want to do is more important than where you want to do it, then identify places where large concentrations of those jobs exist. If where you want to live is more important, then you identify what is available in that location. If who you want to work for is most important, then identify where they are located and what opportunities are available there.

# You—The Product

Now that you have identified what you need to do while in college, you also need to recognize that from the employer's perspective, you are a product to be purchased. Businesses only spend money on products that make them money. Because you are a product, you will need to sell yourself to prospective employers. To sell any product, you have to first understand it.

## *Know Yourself*

To know yourself, you have to honestly and critically evaluate yourself. Ask what your strengths and weaknesses are. If you can't think of any weaknesses, then you are not being honest with yourself or critically evaluating yourself. Everyone has weaknesses, and everyone has strengths. Some people evaluate themselves emotionally instead of objectively. An emotional evaluation will never give you the proper results.

Start by asking some fact-based questions about yourself, such as what is your work experience and education. Now you can dig a little deeper and look for evidence of specific skills such as leadership and communication skills. Continue your self-evaluation based on the qualities that your potential employer is looking for in new graduates. You want to demonstrate real-life examples of how you have acquired those qualities the employer finds important.

Most likely you will not possess all the necessary skills and experience required for your future dream job. Do not panic. This is all part of the process. Remember, you are still in college. Take advantage of the opportunities available to you to improve those qualities.

## *Improve Yourself*

How can you start to improve? For starters, you can get an education. Completing your degree will bring you one step closer to meeting the minimum requirements for your dream job. Along the way, you will pick up new skills and new experiences that can also add value to you as a product. Do not just attend class and go through the motions while you are in college. Take advantage of all the resources and activities available to you. To determine where to spend your time and energy, ask "What skills do I need to acquire now based on my answers to the three 'W's?" Two skills that are universally part of any job are communication and leadership. Fortunately, you have time to work on these while you are in college.

Communication skills include writing and speaking. Both should continue to improve if you take your assignments seriously and incorporate the feedback from your professors. Your writing skills will also improve by reading books, such as textbooks, popular novels, and nonfiction. Reading comic books, text messages, and celebrity tweets does not count.

Speaking skills improve with the more presentations you give in class, but this may not be enough. Keep in mind your goal is to demonstrate that you are successful at speaking. Your employer will look for practical application of those speaking skills. Here is a prime opportunity for you to stand out from the rest of your graduating class. You can even join organizations specifically dedicated to public speaking such as Toastmasters. The key is to look for opportunities to present to groups, obtain feedback, and practice.

Leadership skills are also very important to every employer in every field. You have a great opportunity to gain valuable leadership experience while in college. By starting early with one or more organizations you will have a better chance to get elected to a leadership position. You do not have to run for president; you can be vice president, secretary, or parliamentarian or serve as the chairperson on any number of committees. You can also volunteer for community service projects or work with other students who have similar interests to create your own service project. What is important is that you have a good leadership story to tell a potential employer.

## *Position Yourself*

All successful products are well positioned. The easiest way to position yourself is to get the right kind of job experience. The better the job you want out of college, the better job experience you will need. Not all experience is created equal. Certainly a full-time position in your field is the best experience you can gain. Holding a full-time position within your field means that you understand the industry, and you understand various aspects of the job. Your knowledge and experience helps remove much of the risk that your prospective employer will have to take when hiring you. A part-time position within your field tells the prospective employer that you understand some aspects of the field and you are still interested. In fact, you have probably worked at the "grunt" level and are ready to move up to a position with more responsibility. A full-time position in any other field also provides a level of relief to a potential employer because at least you have proven that you will not have a long adjustment period as you transition from the college lifestyle into the professional world. A part-time job in any other field also indicates that you at least understand some basics such as taking direction, having a schedule, and working with a team. Finally, working in fast food with a basic job in the kitchen counts some, but certainly not at the level of the other types of experience. In general, the order of priority should be:

◆ Full-time job in field

◆ Part-time job in field

◆ Full-time job out of field

◆ Part-time job out of field

◆ Flipping burgers

In addition to, or in place of, working in or out of the field, you should attempt to get an internship or work as part of a cooperative education (coop). Try to get a full-time internship for a full semester. Many large companies offer internships, including IBM, Nortel, Marriott, banks, the federal government, and many more. The easiest time to take part in an internship is during the summer when you do not have any classes; however, the competition will be stiff. Your best bet is to seek an internship during the spring or fall semester and attend summer school. You must plan and allow room in your course schedule for both the time and credit hours for the internship. Some internship positions are paid, whereas others are not. Do not let the lack of salary keep you from accepting an internship. Do not let a few hundred dollars keep you from gaining valuable experience that will enhance your resume and may help you secure a job in the future worth tens of thousands of dollars. An internship will help you gain great experience, which will enhance your resume, generate contacts, and in many cases lead to job offers.

Moreover, you never know from where those lucrative job offers might come. A colleague of ours offered students the choice of doing a term paper or working with a local company on a specific project. Most students chose the term paper. Although the term paper was not easy, it was better than having to go off campus to a company's headquarters, meet new people, work in a group—you get the idea. One student, however, chose to work on a project for a local bank. She had to meet twice a week with a team of analysts, information technology specialists, and bank officers. She spent the whole semester developing a cost analysis spreadsheet. It was a lot of work and was all unpaid. Even though she received a good grade for the project, the real payoff came at graduation. She received a great job offer from this bank and is now a vice president in their Information Technology department. Her great job today is all due to her not taking the easy way out. When the opportunity presented itself, she took advantage of the chance to meet new people (especially people who hire new graduates), learn new skills, and impress people with her positive attitude and strong work ethic.

## *Market Yourself*

Now that you have improved yourself, it is equally important that you properly market yourself. Your resume is your primary marketing tool. The purpose of the resume is not to get you a job, but to get you an interview. Because your resume is your primary marketing tool, you don't want the first person to critique it to be your potential employer. This is one of those times where you want criticism from your teachers, your career services office, your parents, etc.

Your first and maybe only chance to impress a potential employer or hiring manager is through your resume. If you do not pay attention to details on something this important, it gives the impression that you will not pay attention to details in other areas of your work, so they certainly will not want to hire you.

If that seems unfair, it is only because you have not yet been on the other side of the hiring process. Imagine you are a hiring manager, and you have a job opening posted in the newspaper, on the Web, and so forth. Now you have 250 resumes to sort through to select five candidates to bring in for an interview. Keep in mind that you still have your other work to do. How in the world are you going to narrow a pile of 250 resumes down to just five or ten? You start looking for ways to eliminate candidates, such as any resume with a misspelled word or of unnecessary length. No manager wants to read a four-page resume for an entry-level job. So after removing these applicants from further consideration, they finally have a reasonable number of resumes to sort through. You do not want to be eliminated from consideration because of a silly mistake on your resume.

Your resume has to be perfect. You need to read it and read it again. Have at least three other people review it. Then read it again. Utilize your career services office and ask them to review it for you. Remember, your resume is a critical document. You need it to get an interview with a specific employer; therefore, it must be tailored to that specific employer. This means if you are applying for different jobs, you will have a different resume for each job application. For example, if you are looking for a job in sales, then you need to emphasize your experience in sales or dealing one-on-one with other people. On the other hand, if you are applying for an accounting position, you would emphasize your accomplishments in business and math-related areas.

Once you are ready to submit your resume, make sure you print the final version. For any electronic submission, make sure the file is clearly named so you will easily be able to attach the correct version. If you are submitting to an online posting, make sure to avoid all formatting other than simple text and indents. Bullets, lines, and other advanced formatting features do not always transmit well. If you are submitting via e-mail, make sure you attach the correct file and review any text within the body of your e-mail message for misspellings. Then double-check that you attached the correct file by opening the attachment. Your resume and e-mail must be perfect before you hit "send."

# The Job of Getting a Job

## *Cover Letter*

Although your resume is the tool that will help you get an interview, it is your cover letter that will get your resume read by the potential employer. If you just send a resume without a cover letter, it will be ignored, set aside, or trashed. The cover letter is your first opportunity to introduce yourself to a potential employer. You can illustrate that you are a real person behind the information about your skills and education. In other words, without a cover letter, your resume is just a list of classes and job tasks. The cover letter brings it all together and allows you to say, "I am a real person who you want to consider hiring so go ahead and look through my resume and then call me to set up an interview and learn more." You do not literally write that on your cover letter, but you need to understand what your cover letter represents.

Whenever you are creating a cover letter, it should be customized for each individual job for which you are applying. All the research that you have been doing on your potential employers will come in handy at this point. You want to start the letter by directing it to an actual person. Use the contact information on the job application or find out who is the hiring manager. If you are unable to determine an actual person's name, then use the phrase "Dear Sir or Madam:" as your greeting.

Your cover letter should be brief and concise. It should be three paragraphs long at the most. The first paragraph should say who you are. The next paragraph should explain why you are the best person for the job. The final paragraph should tell the reader how to contact you. You want to leave plenty of white space on the page and resist the urge to fill the page. Keep in mind that the people who will be reading your cover letter are very busy, and you want to illustrate that you value their time. With a lot of white space, your letter will be easy to read. Nobody wants to read a small font on a page filled to the brim with text. It stresses the eyes and seemingly takes forever to read. You do not want to bore the reader. You want to whet their appetite so they want to review your resume.

Once you have completed your resume and cover letter, it is finally time to start sticking stamps on envelopes and applying for jobs. Not only will you stick stamps, but you will also spend many hours completing online job applications. Regardless of the way you apply what is important to remember is to not become discouraged. You will hear the word "No" much more often than you will hear the word "Yes." That is the nature of the game. Keep in mind that it only takes one "Yes" to land an interview.

## *The Interview*

Congratulations, you made it through round one! The hiring manager read your cover letter and resume and is interested enough to schedule an interview with you. Now the real work begins. There is much more to an interview than just showing up and answering some basic questions. You have to prepare.

Before you even get off the phone when you are being offered an interview you must ask the caller for their name, title, and telephone number. Try to catch the name of the company as well or delicately ask at the end of the conversation. You do not want to just say, "So which job was this again?" That type of response indicates that you only care about getting "a" job as opposed to wanting to work for "them." Everyone likes to feel special, even your future employer. It is a good idea to keep a file on each of your job applications so you can match the caller with the job. The only time you may find yourself in a bind is when you have applied for multiple positions with the same company. If the caller is within a specific division, you can use that to narrow it down. If the caller is from the human resources division, then you may simply have to indicate that you had applied for two positions within the same company and ask for which position you will be interviewing.

You need the contact information of the caller in case you need to call back and ask for directions or to double-check the interview date and time. If you are scheduled for a telephone interview, it is nice to have a phone number to call in case you want to ask them to use a different number (home phone vs. cell vs. office).

Preparing for the interview is like cramming for an exam. You need to find out as much as you can about the company. One of the worst things you can do is walk into the interview totally unprepared with little or no knowledge of the company. Start with the basics and find out what the company does and how they make their money. Find out how the company did last year and what their goals and objectives are. Research how many employees the company has, in how many countries, who their competitors are, and what the outlook is for their industry. You can see if they have received any awards recently or if they have received any bad press. Listen to the chairman's address to the board of directors to determine what seems to be the current priorities and direction of the company. You should Google the company to track down the most recent annual report, which contains more information than just sales figures. Read the company Web site for important and recent news. The key is to show that you actually have an interest in the company and not just in the job.

It has been said many times that practice makes perfect. Although perfection may be a standard hard to achieve, practice does certainly lead to improvement. The only way to get better at interviews is to practice. If you don't want your practice to be at the first real interview where mistakes can blow your chances at getting a job, then you need to practice mock interviews with other people such as friends and family. You can also utilize your college's career services office, which will offer not only resume writing tips and assistance, but also help with interviews.

Of course, the only way practicing will actually help is if you accept the criticism and work on improving your weaknesses. This also includes the manner in which you should dress for the interview. If you simply try to defend everything you did wrong ("I only slouched because this is not the real interview" or "I only said 'um' so many times because it is early in the morning" etc.), then you will defeat the purpose of the exercise and probably anger those who are trying to help. The more you practice, the more confident and polished you will become. A confident person is more likely to get selected than a timid interviewee. You do not want to go in and act like you own the world, but you do want to act and look like you belong.

Freeze in the position you are in at this very moment. Are you biting your lip or your fingernails? Are you twirling your hair? Is your knee bouncing? Do you notice yourself doing any of these things while you are in class, while you are working, or when you are nervous? Any of these small habits may not seem like a big deal to you now, but they can be very distracting during an interview. A few years ago, a product advertisement featured a man in an interview with a stain on his shirt. The whole time he was trying to answer the interview questions his stain kept yelling, "blah, blah, and blah." The interviewer kept looking at the stain and clearly was not paying much attention to the job candidate. While the commercial was funny, it is also very true. If you display a behavior that continues to distract the interviewer, they will not remember anything about the interview except the distraction, and you will clearly not get the job.

Before your interview, you will also need to practice your "elevator speech," which can come in handy on many different occasions. An elevator speech is a 20-second summary of who you are and what you are looking to do. The theory is that if you get on an elevator and the hiring manager or the CEO gets on the elevator with you, then you will be able to confidently look him or her in the eye and say, "Hello, my name is Pat Doe and I will be graduating this May with a bachelor's degree in underwater basket weaving. As an active member of XYZ International Honor Society I have successfully participated in many leadership roles, and I am now ready to take what I have been able to accomplish in college and translate that into success in the private sector. I am looking forward to speaking with someone at your company about job possibilities in your aquatics weaving department." Of course, you will have to make the speech your own but you get the idea. Your 20-second elevator speech can be used at career fairs, networking events, and other occasions where you could run into a potential employer or potential contact.

Now that you have practiced interviewing several times and have researched the company, you can go into the interview with confidence. You will need to arrive at the interview early; otherwise you are adding stress to an already stressful situation. If you show up late for an interview, you are already done before you begin. With very few exceptions, such as a major traffic issue so severe it actually makes the news, you may not even get a chance to have the interview. In the event that you are running late due to unforeseen circumstances, it is time to dial that phone number you wrote down when you scheduled the interview. Call and calmly explain the situation and ask if there is any way you can still be seen or in extreme circumstances, you may have to ask if they can hold the interview over the phone because traffic is not moving, your airplane was delayed, etc. Remember, they do not know what is going on if you do not tell them.

To avoid any last-minute surprises, you will need to drive to the place where the interview will be held at least one day in advance and at the same time as the interview, if possible. You are testing the amount of time it will take to arrive, confirm where you can park, and possibly even confirm the exact floor and office number within the building. Keep in mind that during rush hour in major cities it is not uncommon to spend 30 minutes or more traveling a total of three or four miles. The more prepared you are when you walk into the interview, the less stressed you will feel.

Now that you have done all your preparations and arrived 30–60 minutes ahead of time, you can relax in your car and review your research about the position and the company until it is time to walk in the building. Do not drink coffee or anything with caffeine or anything that can spill and stain your clothes just before the interview. Drink only water to keep your throat from getting dry. When it is time, just relax and be confident that you can do this. You are about to convince a handful of professionals that their company, as good as it already is, is still lacking because they do not yet have you as one of their employees.

When you are first introduced firmly shake the other person's hand. Do not try to break any knuckles, but also avoid the "dead fish" handshake. A firm handshake indicates confidence. Because you are relaxed, your palms will not be too sweaty either, which is another plus. Keep a smile on your face because you want to look enthusiastic, not scared or unsure of yourself. Look the interviewer in the eye while they are speaking and when you are responding, but do not have a staring contest with them. Eye contact indicates confidence and sincerity. Lack of eye contact indicates that you are hiding something or you are scared.

Once you answer a question during an interview, shut up. Silence is an interview tactic designed to get you to reveal much more about yourself than you ever intended. For instance, after answering the question, "Why did you apply for this position?" with a simple explanation of your high regard for this company and how well it aligns with your background, you may be done, and the interviewer may be satisfied with the answer. But if a few seconds of silence makes you nervous, then you may continue to ramble and say, "I have already applied for many other jobs that actually are a better fit but because I have not heard back from any of them I figured even though sales is not really my main focus I could give it a try because it is better than nothing." At that point you can just use the rest of the interview as practice for your next one because you have just lost this job opportunity.

You also have to pay very close attention during the interview and rely on your research so you can ask some intelligent questions of your own. Intelligent questions are ones that indicate to the interviewer that you have done your homework, you understand the job and the company, and you are generally interested in this job and not just anything with a paycheck. Again, you need to make the interviewer(s) feel special in some way. You want to avoid questions that will turn off the employer. If you start asking about salary, vacations, etc., then you are indicating that salary and time off are more important than actually doing your job. Salary and benefits will come in due time, after the offer has been extended. If they are not interested in offering the position to you, then those things will not matter.

At some point during the interview you will want to either get a business card from each interviewer or at least get their name and title. In most cases, you can get the correct spelling and title from the receptionist or from the person who escorts you to the interview. If all else fails, research the company directory on their Web site.

Now that the interview is done and your deodorant has been pushed to its breaking point, you can finally walk out knowing you did everything you could to get the job. Now it is time to relax and wait . . . or is it? You now have the perfect opportunity to critique yourself. Replay the interview in your head. Did I stumble during the initial handshake? Did I sit up straight during the interview and look everyone in the eye? Did I answer every question thoroughly? Were there other examples I wish I would have used or was there a better way to answer one or more of the questions? You do not have to have a perfect interview to get a job, but if this is not the one for you, at least you are more prepared to make a better impression at the next interview.

## *After the Interview*

So why did you have to collect the correct spelling of everyone's name and title? You are now going to write a personalized thank-you note to each individual that interviewed you. Everyone loves to feel special, and receiving a personalized note does help in that regard. On the flip side, getting a personalized note with a name misspelled is annoying, shows lack of detail, and also makes people feel like they have been somehow insulted or diminished as a person. "Everyone knows Madonna's name and President Obama's name, and they should know mine as well." It is simply human nature. You also want to get their title spelled correctly because sometimes people will forward thank-you notes or display them on their desk, but nobody wants to display a thank-you note that has their title wrong. Because the whole purpose of the thank-you note is to keep your name in front of the hiring committee, you do not want to give them a reason to throw it away or delete it.

The best time to write your thank-you letter is within 24 to 48 hours after the interview. If you are sending a thank-you via e-mail, you need to think about when the person will receive it. If your interview is on Wednesday or Thursday afternoon, you do not want to send it to them on Friday. The last thing they want to do is read someone's message that is not directly related to what they have to do before they can get out of the office. You also do not want to send it over the weekend because Monday mornings are all about digging through all the e-mail that came in over the weekend or cleaning up the last few things that got put off on Friday. Monday afternoon or Tuesday morning would be the best time to send your thank-you e-mail in most instances. It will have the most chance of actually being read and not just glanced at and then deleted.

## Thank-you "Do's" and "Don'ts"

There is a fine line between high levels of exposure and getting burned. In other words, you want to write a thank-you note to get your name out in front of the interviewer(s) again, but if you do it wrong it can actually hurt your chances of being offered a position. A thank-you note consists of more than simply, "Thank-you for interviewing me on Monday, August 7th. I look forward to hearing from you." A computer could produce something that boring and impersonal. You want to hit the high notes of the interview focusing on specific questions or topics that resonated with each interviewer. This way each person receives their own individual thank-you, which is critical in the event that they share with each other. An e-mail thank-you is easily forwarded to others. Although each person may be happy to receive an e-mail thank-you addressed to them, if they realize you sent the exact same one to each person, once again you have attacked their integrity and made them feel less special. Your goal is to get your name back on the top of the pile by making each person feel special. You want to keep your note brief and concise, so you should only hit one or two high points. You will need to use proper grammar and spelling. Read the e-mail or letter again and again and have someone else read it at least once. You would be amazed at how easy it is to mentally add a word or letter to your own work even though it does not exist on the page.

## Career Stoppers to Avoid

In the working world there are few things that will end your career or your job search as fast as not showing up for your interview. When you interview, you are meeting with people who are very busy. When they have multiple qualified candidates, they sometimes have to look for ways to eliminate candidates. If you show up late for an interview then you have just indicated that you do not respect the interviewer's time and you are also not reliable.

Coming unprepared for an interview tells the potential employer that you do not respect their time, you do not respect their company enough to do basic research, and you obviously do not see them as special. Most interviewers spend a lot of time reviewing resumes and creating a list of questions. If you are not willing to put in at least as much work for the interview as they do, then you have just indicated that you are lazy and cannot be responsible on your own without being given a lot of direction. That sounds like extra work for the employer if they hire you. "Don't call us, we'll call you."

If you are going to make a statement with your body, then you better think before you speak. You might be proud of all 33 facial piercings that you have endured, which really reflects the true independence of who you are, but your potential employer may not like you displaying that much of *your* free speech at *their* workplace. If you have visible tattoos or piercings, particularly ones that may seem offensive, you may be hired only on the condition that you keep them covered. In many instances you are the face of the company, particularly on a sales force, but also in district meetings and other instances. During the interview, the employer is evaluating if you can positively reflect the company's image. What you do not realize is that the interview does not end when you walk out the door.

The Internet is perhaps the most unforgiving entity ever created. Every picture posted, every e-mail sent, every tweet or Facebook update is now somewhere floating around cyberspace and may be used by your potential employer to screen you out. If you want to be hired by a school to teach high school students and there are 50 pictures of you partying at various states of consciousness, then your online profile or digital tattoo may prevent you from getting a job offer. The worst part is that you may never be told why you did not get hired. Your digital tattoo can haunt you for many years into the future, so be careful what you post and where you post it. You also need to be aware that others may actually post pictures of you and then tag you in their picture, which could also come back to haunt you. If it is on the Internet, assume anyone can see it or read it, and it's fair game.

# THE COST OF  FINANCIAL IGNORANCE

At the beginning of this chapter, we asked, "Why are you here?" The answer is to get a better job than you would have without a college degree. This chapter gives you the tools to get the most out of your time in college. If you start early, you can graduate on time and find your dream job. If you miss by just one semester, it could cost you $18,000.

The average cost of one semester of college tuition is around $3,500. Now you know the importance of having a plan, utilizing your time wisely, making good decisions with your time, and choosing a major. If you do not plan properly, you may have to attend college for an additional semester or two.

Most students understand the additional costs involved with paying tuition for one additional semester. Perhaps not as obvious to you is your lost income during that same time period. Assume you have to delay your graduation by one semester, which is six months. You have also delayed your paycheck by six months. If your starting salary is $30,000, you lost $15,000 worth of income. Your total cost of making poor decisions in college is $18,500.

| | |
|---|---|
| Cost of one additional college semester | $ 3,500 |
| Salary lost with one semester delay | $15,000 |
| Total Cost of Financial Ignorance | **$18,500** |

# PAYING FOR COLLEGE

## Plan Before You Spend

A student had just left the campus bookstore with his cap and gown in his hand when he stopped by our office to talk about his upcoming graduation. It was just a couple of days before his family was due in town, and he was busy getting ready for their arrival. Everyone that he was close to was coming to see him walk across the stage and graduate. You see, he was the first person in his family to attend and graduate from college. He had done well in school, and everyone was extremely proud of him. However, he was in our office to talk about his school loans. He showed us the financial aid exit interview sheet that clearly laid out his options to pay back over $48,000 in school loans. Yes, that's right. The college degree everyone was so proud of came with a price tag of more than $48,000 in school loans. When he started college more than five years earlier, neither he nor his parents really had any idea how much college would cost, how they would pay for it, or the consequences of borrowing so much money. What should they have done before he started college? What do they do now?

# COLLEGE COST

What is the real cost of college? Is it just tuition, fees, books, room, and board? Is it the factors used in determining your scholarship or financial aid award? Do we include what our family contributes? What about our own savings and earnings? The truth is that it is all these things and so much more. There are so many hidden costs to college that if we do not recognize and understand them, and more important, do not plan for them, we are destined to spend many years after graduation paying for them.

It does not matter if we are a freshman or a senior, or if we are in a four-year university or a two-year community college. We cannot change what we spent in the past, but we can start to change our behavior now to minimize the cost of college in our future. The most important thing we can do is to recognize all our college expenses now to begin planning for them. In the financial planning chapter, we focus on creating a cash flow statement so we can see the actual dollar amounts we spend each month. For now let's identify the obvious and not so obvious costs to college and discuss the best ways to pay for them.

Tuition and fees are often the first costs considered, and rightly so. Unfortunately, all too often they are the only costs considered. However, there are "hidden" fees to college that do not show up on your tuition statement. For example, the privilege of parking on many college campuses can cost hundreds of dollars each year. Textbooks are excessively expensive. It is common to spend $150 or more on a single textbook and more than $200 per class on required materials. It is common for students to spend $600 to $800 on books each semester. In addition, don't forget about the specialty supplies for class. These may include financial calculators, art supplies, portfolio cases, and special software, in addition to the basics like book bags, notebooks, pens, paper, etc.

Housing is also an obvious expense, yet many of us never account for all the real expenses of living on our own. Total housing costs go far beyond the residence hall fees charged each semester or the monthly rent check we write to our landlord. Even in the residence hall we still need a small refrigerator and microwave, linens for the bed, and a lamp for the desk. If we live off campus we need a bed, furniture for the living room, perhaps a small dining room set, and pots and pans for the kitchen. Not only do we forget about our move-in expenses, but we also often underestimate them. In addition, if we live off campus we tend to underestimate our recurring monthly expenses such as Internet, cable, electricity, and so forth.

Most of us also underestimate our car and health-care expenses. These include not only our monthly payment and gas, but maintenance and insurance as well. Car insurance is not the only insurance we should consider. Health insurance is extremely important and often overlooked by college students. In fact, many colleges now require that you either buy health insurance from the college's provider or prove that you have coverage from another plan. Don't forget to take into consideration money for prescriptions and other medical supplies. Renters' insurance is also essential if you plan to live off campus. This insurance covers your personal possessions while renting and is discussed in greater detail in the risk management chapter.

There are many other costs that, although they are not directly related to our education, we must take into consideration. Some are unavoidable, whereas others are a lifestyle choice. Just the bare necessity of food can be a major cost that many of us fail to incorporate into our budget. Many colleges have a variety of meal plans available to all students—commuters and those living on campus. However, even with a meal plan, we will want snacks and drinks on hand and want to eat out from time to time. Let's also not forget about clothing. You may think your wardrobe is complete, but every college student wants the occasional T-shirt and sweatshirt bearing their school colors and logo.

Of course, there will be some expenses that you cannot predict but will need to include. If you move far from home, travel expenses could add up quickly if you want to visit home over holidays, vacations, and breaks. In addition, you could experience sticker shock simply from living in a more expensive city. Finally, do not overlook or underestimate the cost of entertainment and other miscellaneous expenses.

## The Real Hidden Cost

We just listed some obvious and not so obvious costs to college that we should think about when planning for our expenses. The purpose is not to provide you with an exhaustive list of college costs, but to get you thinking in the context of the total cost of college and how expensive it really is. Don't worry; we will spend the rest of this book discussing how to manage your finances. However, there is one critical cost to college that no one really talks about. What is it? The amount of time it takes to graduate.

The reality is that the chance of graduating within four years is slim. Most students end up paying for an extra semester or an additional year or two to obtain a degree. Roughly one-third of college students graduate in four years. Slightly more than half will graduate in six years.[9] The average tuition and board at a public four-year college is $9,000 per year, whereas at a private college it is $35,000 and $2,713 at a two-year college.[10] Delaying your graduation by just one year gets very expensive. It's not just the added tuition, board, and other living costs. Each additional year you spend in college is another year you are not working and earning money.

### College Transfer

One big gotcha is the added expense of transferring between schools and the effect on your academic plan. Even though it may make sense to attend a community college for two years and transfer to a four-year school, it can be costly if you do not plan wisely. More often than not transferring to one or more schools extends the length of time it takes to get your degree.

Make sure you are transferring to a new school for good reasons. It is a bad idea to transfer because your classes are too hard, you are homesick, you do not like your roommate, you do not like your professors, or worst of all, for love. Every college has challenging classes, and almost every student struggles with homesickness at some point. In addition, every college has demanding professors and problem roommates.

Expectations in college are much higher than in high school, plus you are learning to live on your own. If you want to succeed at school, you cannot run away. Remember the advice from the careers chapter—be proactive. Seek out the services on your campus to help you with your particular problem. Check with your advisor for programs that help you enhance your study skills or speak with your resident advisor about a room change to help with a lousy roommate. Visit the college counseling center if you seem to be paralyzed by homesickness. Talk to other students for suggestions on choosing classes and professors.

Most important, do not base your decision to transfer to a new school on love. Although love is not bad, it is a bad reason to change schools. If you change schools for love, will you still be happy at the new school if the relationship ends? Because a normal college year is really only two 15-week semesters, you can see each other over spring and holiday breaks plus the summer. A strong relationship can survive the distance.

Good reasons for transferring to a new school include finding a better school or major, family obligations, social situations, and of course financial necessity. You may find that you are not challenged by the course work or that your current major is no longer a good fit. You might need to move back home to take care of an ailing loved one or because the culture of the college is not what you thought it would be. You might find that you can no longer afford your current school, especially if you are paying out-of-state tuition rates.

If so, a transfer to a school that better fits your current circumstances is in order. The important thing is to recognize and plan for the costs associated with that decision.

## Transfer Credit

Many four-year colleges and their academic departments are very particular about the classes they accept from other universities and community colleges. College curricula are not standardized. An intro to computers class at one school may not transfer in as an intro to computers class at another school. Transfer credits can be even trickier within specialized majors. In addition, you may find that you receive elective credit only. You earn credit hours toward graduation but your transfer courses do not fulfill specific requirements for your major at your new school.

It is a mistake to assume transferring will not cause disruptions in your academic path. Most transfer students will experience some hiccup in their overall academic plan. Before submitting a transfer application, have a detailed conversation with an advisor at your current school and discuss your options. You should also make an appointment to speak with an admissions counselor at the new school as well as an advisor of your new major to ask if you will receive credit for the course work you already completed.

## Financial Aid

Many new transfer students suddenly find that they are low on the financial aid priority list. It is common for the best merit scholarships to go to new incoming freshmen students. In addition, many schools accept transfer applications much later than freshman applications. Financial aid tends to be awarded until the funds dry up. Beginning in the admissions cycle later than other students will make it more difficult to receive grant aid. If a transfer is in your future, apply as early as possible and do not submit your enrollment deposit until you know exactly what your financial aid package will look like.

## *GPA Is Important*

Make sure you are academically prepared if transferring from a community college to a four-year school. Community colleges have fewer and less-rigorous admissions requirements than four-year schools. They also tend to be more general in subject matter. In fact, don't be surprised if you are asked to provide a syllabus from your community college class so that your new school can make sure all the appropriate content was covered before granting you credit. The point is that after transferring, you might find that your work receives more scrutiny and you are held to a higher standard than at your old community college. You will be shocked to earn a C when you used to earn straight As. You do not want to find yourself in a situation where you are no longer in good academic standing. This will result in losing your financial aid and will affect your graduation plans and future job prospects.

## *Social Cost*

Do not underestimate the social cost to transferring to a new school. It is common to feel isolated when you arrive at your new college. Unlike the students that began as freshmen, transfer students usually do not start off with a strong group of friends and have not had time to connect with faculty, and student organizations or develop a social network. If your isolation leads to depression, poor academic performance, or problems in lining up internships or reference letters, it could cost you in the end. You should take advantage of every academic and social support service for transfer students to acclimate yourself to your new school and make friends.

Not all four-year schools are "transfer friendly," and you need to do your homework on which school is right for you. Planning and research are crucial if you want to avoid many of the hidden costs to transferring to a new school.

# COLLEGE IS AN INVESTMENT

Before you think college is not worth the time and money, remember why you are here. You are here to get a better job and advance your career further and faster than you can without a college degree. Over your lifetime, you will earn about $1 million more than a high school graduate. That should easily be enough to repay your student loans and then some. The payoff for a graduate degree is even higher. If you go on to graduate school you can earn as much as $2 million more than people without a college degree.[11]

Of course a college education is about more than just money. Your college degree makes you a more rounded person, increases your critical reasoning skills, and gives you amazing experiences that you will cherish the rest of your life. There are countless ways that a college degree has value that cannot be measured with numbers.

Yet, it is imperative that you fully understand that you, your family, and Mr. and Mrs. Taxpayer are investing a lot of money, hard work, time, and emotion into your college education. With all this investment being made by you and on your behalf, it is now up to you to figure out how you can maximize your return on this investment.

## Maximize Your Return

The first step to maximize your return on investment is to finish your degree. The second step is to finish quickly. The third step is to choose your major wisely. The fourth step is simply to minimize your costs. Remember why you are in college in the first place: to get a better job with a bigger paycheck. Staying focused on the bigger picture will keep you on the right path.

Finishing college and graduating with your degree is critical. Nothing is worse than shelling out thousands of dollars for a couple of years of college only to apply for jobs with nothing more than a high school diploma.

Finish as quickly as possible for you and your situation. We mentioned earlier that only a third of students finish in four years; there is no reason why you cannot be one of them if you plan wisely. Taking five or six years to get your degree can mean 25 to 50% more in costs as well as losing out on one to two years of earning a paycheck.

Choose your major wisely. Consider how much you will earn with your degree compared to how much you will spend or borrow to obtain that degree. We are not suggesting that you choose your major solely on the size of the paycheck. It is critical that you choose something you like to do because no amount of money can make you happy in a job you do not like. You need to know what the financial consequences are of choosing a major in a lower-paying profession and plan for them accordingly. Are you choosing a major that will allow you to afford a decent place to live, have a car, and manage your student loans?

Hold down your costs while you are in college. The less money you pay to earn your degree, the higher the return will be on your investment. Let's discuss a few ways to minimize the amount of money you have to pay to earn your degree. We can begin with a few of the larger expenses and work our way to some of the smaller ones.

## Community College

Completing your first year or two at a community, junior, or technical college saves you money not only on tuition, but also on room, board, and transportation by staying close to home. According to finaid.org the average community college tuition cost is just 40% of the average tuition charge at a four-year public college.

If your intention is to ultimately earn a four-year degree, then spending the first two years at a community college is one of the most cost-effective ways to do so. To make your community college experience cost effective, it is important to map out your entire four-year plan. What you take at a community college needs to clearly work in conjunction with the specific degree requirements at your intended four year college.

If you are already at a four-year school, take a summer class or two at your local community college while home on summer break. Why pay thousands of dollars for a course when you can take the same course and receive the same credit for just a few hundred dollars? Plus it keeps you on schedule to graduate in the shortest amount of time possible.

The real key to getting the most bang for your buck in any community college system is to make sure your credits are transferable to the four-year college of your choice. Check with your advisor that the courses you take or plan to take not only transfer to your college or university, but also are applied to your specific major.

## Credit for Nothing

Make sure that if you completed any college courses while in high school that you get credit for them from your college and from your major. If you took Advanced Placement (AP) classes and scored high enough on the corresponding exam, you may be entitled to college credit. Check with your college registrar or course catalog for requirements. Double-check with your advisor that the credit satisfies the degree requirement for your major.

Ask your advisor if you are eligible to take a CLEP (College Level Examination Program) exam. Each school determines its own acceptable minimum score. You receive college credit for very little cost (usually around $100). Plus you do not have to sit in class for an entire semester for those three or four credits.

Check to see if your university or college offers any type of credit by exam for your specific major. Typically you must have the permission of the dean or chairperson of the department in which the course is offered. Be warned; the grade you receive on the exam usually becomes part of your academic transcript and is included in your grade point average. Once the exam is taken the grade must be recorded and cannot be removed.

## Live Off Campus

Of course, living at home is your cheapest room and board. If that is not possible, do not assume that living on campus is the next best option. In addition to the room charge each semester, you may be required to buy an expensive meal plan. Combine this with the cramped quarters of a residence hall and renting an off-campus apartment can be an attractive alternative. Not only are the living accommodations usually roomier, but if you share an apartment you cut your rent, utilities, and some other expenses in half.

Although not for everyone, you might ask your family to buy a townhome or condo. This is not as crazy as it might sound. If you rent the other bedrooms to your classmates the income could easily offset the monthly mortgage payments. In many college towns there is an abundance of relatively inexpensive homes for sale close to campus. Of course, the purchaser of the home should fully understand the real estate market of the area and the financial consequences of such a choice.

## Textbooks

You can easily spend more than $1,000 a year on textbooks, sometimes even in a single semester. However, there are some cheaper options for purchasing textbooks than just going to the campus bookstore. You can find used books online through chegg.com, craigslist.org, half.com and Campus Book Swap. Consider purchasing electronic textbooks if possible. In some instances, E-books can cut your textbook cost in half.

You can even find some free textbooks. Textbook/Media Press (www.textbook media.com) provides some electronic texts but includes advertisements within the books. Other sites, such as Bartleby.com offer classic literature that can be downloaded for free.

You might consider sharing books with your classmates or see if there is a library copy. A side benefit of this approach is forcing you to be more efficient with your time because you will have to be disciplined enough to do your work before the last minute.

Make sure to resell your nonessential books when the semester is over. Do not limit yourself to the campus bookstore. To get the most for your used book, remember to handle them with care and with as few marks as possible. Keep in mind that textbooks are updated frequently and new editions released. You will have better luck selling your books if you act quickly after your classes are over.

## Little Things Add Up

You would be surprised how much your small personal expenses add up while at college. Cutting each expense just a little can add up to big savings over your time in college. In the financial planning chapter we will spend a lot of time developing a cash flow statement so you can see exactly where and on what you spend your money. For now let's list some ways to save on some everyday expenses to start you thinking in the right direction.

A car is a killer expense if you are paying the bill out of your own pocket, especially if you live on campus and have to pay for parking. Leave the car at home. You might even consider getting rid of it, depending on the public or student transportation system at your college. Walk, bike, or ride the bus. It is a great way to save money while in college.

Pay attention to your tuition bill to determine if you are being charged for health insurance by the college or university. Many colleges have a hard waiver policy, which means that you are automatically covered and charged for health insurance. You have to opt out to get the charges waived if you already have your own plan or if you are covered on your family's plan.

Do not underestimate the cost your social life while at college. Restaurants, bars, and theater expenses can eat up a lot of money. Try socializing on a budget. Take advantage of the free on-campus concerts, movies, or other events provided by your student union. You can also check out the local museums or art galleries as well as the nature parks for hiking. Many local businesses and parks offer student discounts.

Check with your bank to make sure you are taking advantage of your student status. Many banks offer discount or free checking and savings accounts for students. Do a little research to find the best fee and rate structure for you. Make sure to keep track of your balance once you start using your debit card. Banks charge relatively large penalties for bounced checks.

Shop secondhand. Secondhand furniture is much less expensive than new items. Look for desks, tables, dressers, couches, chairs, lamps, reconditioned appliances, and carpets at local garage sales, flea markets, and charity shops. You can also search for used items online or in the classified section of your local newspaper.

Use open source software when you can to save on expensive software. For example, the OpenOffice suite (www.openoffice.org) can be a great alternative to Microsoft's Office Suite and is absolutely free.

# PAYING FOR COLLEGE

Now that we are in the right frame of mind—that college is expensive and we should work to maximize our return on investment—we can get to what is really important. What is the best way to go about paying for college? The truth is that you will use a combination of ways to pay for school that include grants, scholarships, family, jobs, and even loans. How do you know what the best combination is for you? Before we can begin to discuss the best to worst ways to pay for college, you have to educate yourself about the options and the process, which all begins with your FAFSA (Free Application for Federal Student Aid).

## Your FAFSA

Your very first step in determining how you are going to pay for college is filling out and submitting your FAFSA. You can complete a paper form or submit an application by phone, but the easiest way is to complete the form online at www.fafsa.ed.gov. This is a free application. You should never be asked for any kind of fee. If you ever are asked for money when submitting your FAFSA you are on the wrong site or talking to the wrong people.

*Steps to Federal Student Aid[12]*

All federal and state financial aid and almost all other financial aid programs use the FAFSA to determine your eligibility. It is important that you complete the application early, accurately, and completely. You can file as early as January 1 for the fall semester, and you must file each year. Each college has somewhat different filing deadlines. It is important that you meet with your school's financial aid office or at least visit their site to understand their rules, regulations, and deadlines to ensure financial aid is in place to cover your tuition bill when it comes due.

The application process is not difficult, but it is not completely painless. Both you and your family need to gather some basic information such as Social Security numbers, birth dates, and tax returns before beginning the application. Once you finish your FAFSA, you receive your SAR or Student Aid Report. Your SAR summarizes the information you included on your FAFSA and provides you with your EFC (Expected Family Contribution) that colleges use to determine your financial aid package.

Next your college financial aid office determines the type and amount of aid options available to you. They will contact you with the types and amount of aid for which you qualify. The information that you are receiving at this point does not necessarily represent your best way to pay for college, only what you are eligible to receive through the college. They will explain your eligibility for grants, scholarships, and loans, but it is up to you to determine the best combination of options for you.

## How FAFSA Determines Financial Need

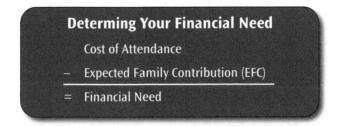

In the financial aid world, the term "financial need" may not necessarily reflect your true need. It is based on how much your college is *expected* to cost minus the amount of money you and your family are *expected* to contribute toward that cost.

In financial aid terms, it is the cost of attendance (determined by your school) minus your Expected Family Contribution (EFC) as determined by your FAFSA. Your school's cost of attendance includes tuition and fees, room and board, books and supplies, transportation, personal expenses, and even student loan fees. Your EFC is based on a formula set by the Department of Education and uses both your and your parents' contributions from assets (the things that you and your parents own) plus your and your parents' contributions from income (how much you and your parents make).

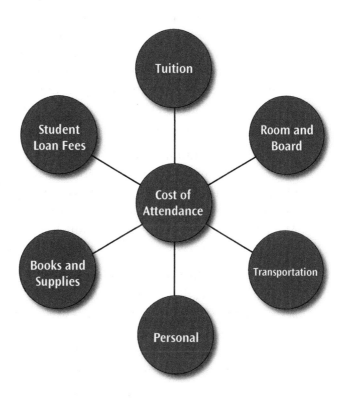

*Cost of Attendance*

For most of us getting our first undergraduate degree, we are considered dependent. Even if we are completely on our own, we still have to include our parents' information on the FAFSA. The government's philosophy is that if you are under 24 years of age, Mom and Dad have the primary responsibility of paying for your undergraduate education. Only in unusual circumstances are you considered independent if you are under 24.

You can never fully represent your particular situation in numbers and forms. If you have a special situation or something unexpected happens, you need to talk to your financial aid counselors first and certainly before you take any action or make any decision. Never withdraw from college for financial reasons without first speaking to your financial aid counselor. The financial aid office is there to help. They can use their professional judgment to help you, but only if you let them know what unique situation you and your family face. A financial aid counselor should be one of your first friends on campus. They will do whatever is within their power to help.

Now let's turn our attention to the multitude of ways to pay for college. We will begin with the best ways (free money) and work our way down to the least desirable ways (have to be paid back).

## *Grants*

Finding and applying for grants should be the first place you look for financial aid because grant money is like a gift and does not need to be repaid. Most grants come from the state and federal government, such as the Pell Grant and the Supplemental Educational Opportunity Grant. However, there are also college specific and private grants. Most grants are need-based with eligibility determined by your FAFSA.

You do not have to repay grant money as long as you remain in good standing and are successfully progressing in the completion of your degree. Failing to meet all the requirements of the grant could result in having to pay it back. Typically this includes dropping below a minimum GPA, withdrawing before the end of the semester, or failing to maintain full-time or half-time status. Some grant requirements are determined by the college or university and vary from school to school. It is very important to apply before all deadlines. Applications submitted after the posted deadlines are rejected.

There are a large number of federal, state, and private grants available for students. The most common federal grants include the Federal Pell Grant, the Federal Supplemental Educational Opportunity Grant (FSEOG), Teacher Education Assistance for College and Higher Education Grant (TEACH Grant), and even the Iraq and Afghanistan Service Grant. Each grant has its own criteria for eligibility. You can find out more at www.studentaid.ed.gov and your school's financial aid office.

There are other institutional grants in addition to the ones from the federal government listed earlier. Some are merit based and are awarded for high academic achievement. Others are need based, either on you or your family's finances. Many of these types of grants come with specific obligations. If you do not maintain your eligibility you may have to pay it back. You will have to ask your financial aid office for any institutional grants specific to your school and your state.

## *Scholarships*

Like grants, scholarships typically do not require repayment as long as you maintain eligibility. Many are need based, but there are also scholarships that center on specific criteria such as academics, athletics, community service, the arts, or a whole host of other things. The scholarships can be from your university, your major or program, private donors, or other organizations. There are scholarships for bringing a specific talent to your school, such as athletics, music, or the performing arts. There are state-sponsored scholarships, scholarships for students whose parents work for particular companies, or scholarships sponsored by your church or civic organizations.

You must be persistent in finding scholarships. Sometimes all it takes is to apply. You just need to fill out the application or interview by the deadline. The tricky part is finding them. The two best places to find scholarships are your financial aid office and the Web. Your financial aid counselor can point you to specific scholarships offered from your state or your school. Studentaid.ed.gov and fastweb.com are great Web sites with links to numerous scholarships. Finally, many scholarships from small, local organizations in your hometown may not show up in any database. Even though you are already in college, your high school is still the best source of information on local scholarships.

Scholarships have very early deadlines and come with strings attached. Some deadlines can be as far as a year in advance. If you fail to maintain eligibility you may lose the scholarship and be forced to pay it back. If, for example, you cannot play your sport, you would lose your athletic scholarship, or if your GPA falls you would lose your academic scholarship. You need to fully understand the ongoing requirements of the scholarship so you do not lose it or be forced to pay it back.

It is unnecessary to pay someone to help you search for grants or scholarships. Your financial aid counselor is already paid by your school to provide some assistance. In addition there are plenty of free resources on the Web to help you find grants and scholarships.

## Tax Credits

Tax credits can save you, or your family, thousands by reducing your tax bill at the end of the year. Although tax credits are not thought of as financial aid in the traditional sense, it can mean additional money to help pay for school. Any money you do not pay in taxes is money you can use to pay for tuition, books, or meals.

The American Opportunity Credit can reduce your or your parents' tax expense by up to a maximum of $2,500 per student per year. Likewise, the Lifetime Learning Credit can lower your tax expense by up to $2,000 per year, or for your parents up to $2,000 per year for each of their children in college. There is no limit on the number of years the Lifetime Learning Credit can be claimed. However, you or your parents cannot claim both the American Opportunity Credit and Lifetime Learning Credit for the same student in the same year.[13] Although you are entitled to the credit, you have to ask for it. It is not automatic.

A few states also offer state tax credits for tuition expenses. Search your state's department of higher education Web site to determine if your state offers these educational tax credits.

## Pay As You Go

After finding all the free money you can (grants, scholarships, and even tax credits), the next best way to pay for college is to work. Make no mistake. College is hard. That is why more than a third of students never finish. However, it is possible to find an appropriate balance between school and work while still getting good grades.

Earning your own money goes a long way in establishing your independence, building your self-esteem, and paying a few college bills at the same time. However, some jobs are better than others. The best part-time jobs pay well, provide you valuable career experience, and are flexible around your class schedule. Let us start with work study.

## Work Study

Federal College Work Study is one of the most overlooked forms of financial aid. You work for the college or university but are paid with federal financial aid dollars. This is different from being a university employee and being paid with their dollars. Federal work study is part of your federal financial aid.

There are several advantages to work study. First, work study earnings do not impact your eligibility for financial aid the following year. If you work a part-time job off campus you have to include those earnings on your next year's FAFSA, and it is used in determining your expected family contribution. Second, you get to learn new skills and gain experience, which you can include on your resume. Third, because you are working at the university, your supervisors tend to be more flexible when it comes to working around your class schedule.

While the school may offer you work study as a part of your financial aid package, you are not required to accept this portion if you do not have time to work. However, any work study financial aid that you accept is money you do not have to borrow. Plus, if you must work to pay for college there is no job better than work study because of all the advantages.

It is important to let your financial aid office know that you want work study. Funding is limited, and your school wants to make sure the money is there for students who do want to work.

## Cooperative Education

The next best thing to work study is cooperative education (coop). Many schools and departments offer paid cooperative education programs. These are typically available regardless of whether or not you qualify for a work study position. The best coop jobs are paid and in your major. You might consider an unpaid coop job for the experience and job contacts, but if your goal is to finance college then you should only consider paid coops. In addition, many coop jobs pay higher wages than work study jobs. Talk to your career services office and your advisor to find coop jobs that are best suited for your circumstances.

## Good Deeds

A number of not-for-profit agencies offer some sort of tuition reimbursement or forgiveness program in exchange for your commitment to work with them for some length of time after graduation. AmeriCorps, Peace Corps, and Teach for America all offer educational service awards that help you pay for school while you do something that makes a difference in the world. Unlike scholarships and grants, a service award from one of these organizations usually does not affect your federal financial aid eligibility. That is the good news. However, most of these programs require you to successfully complete one or two years of service before you get any money. You must use the money to pay for costs related to your degree or your school loan.

Other groups to check out include the National Health Service Corps, the Army National Guard, and the National Institutes of Health. Each of these have student loan forgiveness programs that help you pay off your school loans in exchange for going to work for them for a year or more after graduation. Volunteers in Service to America (VISTA) and the Reserve Officers Training Corps (ROTC) not only have these programs, but also have programs that provide you cash while in school if you commit to some service time immediately after graduation. Visit each of these groups' Web sites for details on their programs.

## Get Paid to Live on Campus

Earlier we stated that living off campus is usually cheaper than living on campus. Here is the exception. Be a resident assistant (RA) or resident director (RD). Keep your grades up and stay out of trouble and then after your freshman year you can apply to be an RA or an RD. Generally you live in the residence hall for free (or at reduced cost) and work by being on call or planning and organizing activities for your residence hall. In addition to a free room, other perks can include free meal plans, a stipend (paycheck), and even free T-shirts. It is a job that allows you to put your academics first, plus you get to develop leadership, facilitation, management, and team-building skills that will enhance your resume.

## Get a Real Job

After you exhaust all the grant, scholarship, and on-campus job opportunities, you may still need additional money to help pay for college. Working a part-time job could be the final piece of this puzzle. A part-time job is a great way to close the gap if you are a little cash strapped. Plus, if you do it right, a part-time job can give you very valuable job experience you can add to your resume. Find a part-time job that is related to your major, or even better, with the company you would like to work for after you graduate. You will be one of their prime job candidates once you finish that degree.

What you have to guard against is letting the part-time job negatively affect your grades. Ultimately, it is up to you to balance the demands of your studies with the demands of your job. Build your job schedule around your class schedule, not the other way around. Always prioritize your studies over your job. The key is to balance your job with your course work. If you do it well, you will have extra money in your pocket as well as hands-on experience that will be invaluable to you.

Although part-time jobs can be beneficial, we do not recommend working full time while trying to attend school full time. Rarely does this work out well for students. The added stress of working full time while in college is immense. It is better to find some other solution so you may focus on school work, even if it means taking out a student loan.

# Parents and Family

Now that you have exhausted all the grant and scholarship opportunities you can find, and you are working part time, it is time to ask your parents and family for help. Remember, the government expects them to help you pay for college as long as you are less than 24 years old or you are considered a dependent. Some parents will do almost anything to make sure their kids have the money to go to school. Yet it is unlikely that they have the expertise to navigate the financial aid minefield. You need to help them help you.

## *Time for the Talk*

Just as there are good and bad options for you to pay for college, there are good and bad options for your parents and family as well. You do not want your parents spending all their money and savings on you and your college education. Although that may sound like a good deal to you right now, you are getting a small short-term benefit for a big long-term sacrifice. One day you may have to take care of your parents. If they spent their retirement account to send you to college, they may have to move in with you. Just as important, you do not want them doing something with their money that would result in less financial aid to you. So what do your parents need to know about financial aid?

## *Early Birds*

Help your mom and dad start planning early. Your financial aid is based on your and your parents' previous year's income and assets for each year you apply for financial aid. It is important to plan early every year so that everybody can put their money in the right place to make sure you get the most financial aid possible. In the college financial aid world, the early bird gets the worm.

## *Whose Money Is It Anyway?*

As a general rule, it is better to keep any savings and any income in your parents' name rather than yours whenever possible. In the financial aid or needs analysis formulas, certain types of incomes and assets count more than others. Typically, income and assets in your name count against you more than if they are in your parents' names.

In addition, you want to carefully read the instructions on how to fill out the FAFSA. It gets really technical, but certain assets, such as retirement accounts, do not have to be included so they will not count against you. The mistake of including an asset when it should not be included can cost you a lot of financial aid.

The next part you are going to love; your parents not so much. Income in your name counts more against you than income in your parents' name. Many financial aid experts advise that if at all possible you should try to keep your annual income from any job other than work study to $3,700 or less. This gives you the greatest chance of maximizing your financial aid award.

## *Retirement or College*

Let your parents know it is a very bad idea to borrow against or take money out of their retirement accounts to pay for your college. Retirement funds are special tax-sheltered accounts. If your parents take money from these accounts before they are supposed to, they have to pay income tax on the withdrawals. On top of that, they have to pay a penalty unless they can clearly prove that the money paid for a qualifying educational expense. They would be lucky to keep two-thirds of what they withdrew to pay for your college. Even if they simply borrowed against the account, all the aforementioned penalties would still apply if they lose or quit their job.

In addition, retirement accounts are not included in the financial aid formulas. However, if they take the money out of the retirement account and put it in their regular savings or checking account, or even worse give it to you, it counts in the financial aid formula and reduces your financial aid award. Tell your mom and dad that taking money out of their retirement accounts is one of the worst ways to help you pay for college.

## *Home Equity Loans*

If you or your parents do not qualify for a federal student loan, they may consider a home equity loan. Equity, by the way, is the difference between the value of your mom and dad's home and what they owe on it. Home equity loans often have lower interest rates than loans from private lenders and certainly lower rates than credit cards. Plus the interest paid on a home equity loan is usually tax deductible. Keep in mind that a home equity loan is still a loan, and it does cost your parents interest. Plus interest rates for home equity loans usually vary with economic conditions and can be higher than federal student loan interest rates.

The biggest mistake your parents can make with a home equity loan is to put the amount borrowed in a checking or savings account. It would then be included in your expected family contribution and count against you in the financial aid formula. Before you have your parents rush to the bank, caution them to make sure that they do not qualify for a federal student loan first. Home equity loans should be one of the last resorts to helping you pay for college.

## *PLUS Loan for Parents*

Your parents may also apply for a federal loan to pay for your educational expenses. PLUS loans are available to your biological, adoptive, or step parent if they have an acceptable credit report. Your mom or dad must complete a FAFSA, a PLUS loan application, and sign their own master promissory note (MPN). Just like you, they only need to sign one MPN for as long as you are in school. Your school will use your parents' PLUS loan to pay for your tuition, fees, room and board, and any other school expenses first. Anything left over is sent to your parents in the form of a check or direct deposit. Your parents do have the option of authorizing any leftover amount be transferred directly to your account if they wish.

It's important to recognize that the relatively high interest of 7.9% was set many years ago and is paid on the loan from the date of the first check. More important, PLUS loans also charge a fee of 4% each time a disbursement is made. Yes, that's right, 4% is deducted from your parents PLUS loan check each time financial aid is disbursed. Are you beginning to see why loans are one of the worst options to pay for college?

## Private Student Loans for Your Parents

Private student loans can be very tempting to your mom and dad. Remember, they will do almost anything to make sure you can go to college. Private student loan companies can give almost instant approval using quick, easy-to-use online forms. However, they usually have much less favorable repayment terms and higher interest rates than federal loans. Plus, unlike federal loans, private student loans are based on your parents' credit score, so their credit report must be pristine. If their credit score is questionable, your parents will wind up with a loan that has less-than-favorable terms. Some even have variable interest rates that reset monthly. Private student loans are one of the worst possible ways to finance your college education.

## Grandparents

Do not forget about your grandparents. They love you and want to help you get a college degree. Even if they do not have any money they can still help you pay for college in many ways. You may be eligible for scholarships based on your grand-parents' affiliations (Kiwanis, Lions Club, UAW etc.). Ask them to give you a list of all their affiliations, including past and present employers, unions, military service, memberships, hobbies, and other activities. Begin by looking for legacy scholar-ships, military scholarships, and scholarships based on ancestry and ethnicity.

## Bottom Line

The bottom line is that your financial aid award is dependent on both your and your parents' financial picture. All of you should work together to present the best picture to your school's financial aid office so that you get not just the most, but the best type of financial aid available to you.

# Student Loans

Finally, there are student loans. We intentionally listed student loans as your last choice when looking for ways to pay for your college education. That is because student loans will have a greater impact on your long-term financial health than any other financial aid you can use. In 2010, total student loan debt surpassed total credit card debt for the first time.[14] Most students do not realize how much they are borrowing for college or how big their payments will be after they graduate.

Yes, you have to begin paying back your student loans very soon after graduation. The more you borrow, the larger your student loan payment will be. The larger your student loan payment is, the less money you have available to spend on other things. The point is that your student loan debt takes away your choices. That $250 per month payment you make on your student loan is $250 you cannot spend on rent, food, a car, and other personal choices.

Having said that, most of us will still have to use student loans to help pay for our college education. As much as we discourage students from taking out student loans, if you have to choose between borrowing money and not going to college, then by all means borrow the money. Earning a college degree is the single most valuable action you can take to ensure your long-term personal financial health, so don't be afraid to make the investment. Just make sure you know what the impact of your student loans will be.

It is important that you know how to manage your student loans properly. Let's begin with the most borrower-friendly student loans available.

## Perkins Loan

A Perkins Loan is a low 5% interest loan that you apply for through your school's financial aid office. The money comes from government funds, but you borrow them from your school and you pay your school back after you graduate. If you demonstrate exceptional financial need, you can borrow up to $5,500 per year and pay it back at a low interest rate. The amount you get depends on when you apply, your financial need, and the funds your school has at its disposal. Once the money runs out at your school, there is no more to award. It is important to apply early to be awarded a Perkins loan. You must begin to pay this loan back nine months after you graduate, drop below half-time, or leave school altogether.

## Stafford Loan

Stafford loans are low interest loans to you—the student—where you borrow directly from Uncle Sam; specifically the U.S. Department of Education. There are subsidized and unsubsidized loans, and it is important to understand the distinction between them.

Subsidized loans are need-based, and your school determines how much you get after reviewing your FAFSA. You are not charged interest while in school or during your grace period after you graduate. (Uncle Sam pays for the interest or "subsidizes" this loan while you are in school.)

Unsubsidized loans do not require you to show financial need. Like the subsidized loans, your school determines how much you get. However, unlike the subsidized loans, your unsubsidized loans start charging interest from the moment the money is available to you. You get the option of paying just the interest while in school or deferring it until after you graduate. Of course, waiting until after you graduate to pay the interest increases your loan amount and your monthly payment.

You could qualify to get both a subsidized and an unsubsidized loan in the same year. If your subsidized loan does not cover all your expenses, you may be able to get an unsubsidized loan to cover the rest up to the maximum annual borrowing limit. As with all federal financial aid, you must complete your FAFSA first so your school can determine the amount of loan you will receive. Your Stafford loan is included as part of your total financial aid package, and you have the option of accepting or rejecting any loans in that package.

Do not be surprised when your financial aid office requires you to sign a master promissory note (MPN) the first time you accept a Stafford loan. The MPN is the legal contract where you promise to repay your student loan to the Department of Education. It spells out in excruciating detail all the terms and conditions of your loan. In most cases you will only need to sign one MPN for all your Stafford student loans while you are in school. Your school can give you a copy of your MPN or ask you to complete one online at studentloans.gov.

### Private Student Loans

No discussion of student loans would be complete without talking about private or alternative loans. These are available from a variety of sources ranging from well-known and reputable banks and credit unions to the less-than-reputable private loan sources. The terms of these loans vary by lender, but all are credit-based, have high and sometimes variable interest rates, and typically require a cosigner. Unfortunately, there are also many scam artists out there. Our best advice is for you and your parents to be very cautious when considering private educational loans. Federal student loans are the best alternative. However, if you must consider a private student loan first speak with the financial aid office at your school to see if they can help you find one with the best terms.

### Tuition Payment Options

Unfortunately, even after looking under every rock you can find for grants, scholarships, jobs, and loans, you still may be a little short on tuition money. Fortunately, your college probably has a number of tuition payment options available, including monthly installment plans or payments. The point is that even after accepting all your financial aid, if you still are unable to pay the balance of your tuition, there are options. Go talk to your financial aid office. Chances are that your school offers a plan that will let you spread out the balance of your bill over a number of months or years.

Keep in mind that there is almost always some sort of fee or interest charged for deferment, extended, or installment payment plans. It is your responsibility to understand all the terms and requirements of any contract. However, it is always better to stay in school, graduate with your degree, and owe a little extra interest rather than not graduating at all.

# AFTER GRADUATION

Before we leave the world of paying for college, we need to spend a little time talking about life after graduation. The reality is that despite all the alternatives to paying for college, most of us borrow in some fashion to go to school.

To make the best financial aid choices while in school, you need to know exactly what managing your student loans will be like after you graduate with your degree. Whether you like it or not, once you graduate, your student loans become a very big reality. Making good choices while in school will have a huge impact on the quality of your financial life after school.

## *So What Do I Need to Know?*

In spite of the fact that you want to avoid student loans to pay for college, the good news is that if you do have to borrow then at least federal student loans are some of the friendliest loans you will ever have. There are many repayment options available to you for almost every situation. No job yet? Income way below what you expected? Want to pay off your loans early? Want to consolidate your loans and make one payment every month for all your loans? Every repayment option is designed to make sure you can afford your payments. The key is to know what loans you have and what your options are. Ultimately, you want to manage your loans so that they do not manage you.

WARNING: We are going to get just a little bit technical in our discussion. The rules and options are very complex, but it is important that you understand them so that you make good decisions when it comes to your student loans. It is up to you to initiate the conversation with the financial aid counselor at your school based on your specific needs.

## *Know What You Owe*

Just before you graduate, ask your financial aid office to provide a list of all your student loans that were processed through their office. While it is a good idea to monitor your loans each year while in college, it is imperative that you know the total amount you owe before you graduate. If you attended other colleges or universities, contact their financial aid office as well. Your goal is to collect as much information as you can about how much and from whom you borrowed money to attend college.

After you have all your lists from your financial aid offices, take a look at the National Student Loan Data System (NSLDS) at www.nslds.ed.gov. The NSLDS is the U.S. Department of Education's central database for federal student loans. All your federal student loans along with all their details will be listed in this database. For each federal loan you will see the type of loan, the lender, the loan servicer, the loan amount, the date the loan originated and was disbursed, if the loan was cancelled, the outstanding principal, and any outstanding interest on the loan. Keep in mind that nonfederal student loans will not be listed in the NSLDS, which is why you want to get a list of all loans from your financial aid office.

Add up the total disbursements according to your financial aid offices and make sure it matches what you find in the NSLDS. If it appears that you borrowed more than what the NSLDS indicates, then you probably have some private student loans as well. If it appears the other way around, then you should contact the Department of Education to verify your loan information.

Now make a list of who you owe, how much you owe, what your interest rates are, what your monthly payments are, when your payments are due, and the contact information of your loan servicer. Keep your list readily accessible and not packed away in a box with your college souvenirs. At some point you are going to need it. We can almost guarantee that over the life of your student loans you will have a question or something will go wrong.

At some point you will talk to someone about your loans. This person is called a servicer. The servicer is a person that is hired by the lender to oversee the repayment process, including collecting your loan payment. Rarely if at all will you ever talk to the people that actually loaned you the money.

You are going to hear your classmates talking about something called a grace period. On your federal student loans you are granted a six- or nine-month period after you leave school before you need to begin making your loan payments. This does not mean you have six or nine months before you have to contact your loan servicer or start making arrangements to pay back your loans. In addition, most private loan lenders offer no such grace period. It is important that you meet with your financial aid counselor before you graduate to determine exactly what you owe and what the best repayment options are for you.

## Choose Your Repayment Plan

Remember when we said federal student loans are borrower friendly? You get to choose the repayment plan that fits your particular situation best. You have several options, but if you do not make a choice, you are automatically placed in the standard payment option. So what are your payment options?

## Standard Payments

The standard repayment plan is for 10 years. You make 120 equal monthly payments at a fixed interest rate. At the end of the 10 years the loan is paid off.

## Graduated Payments

The graduated payment plan begins with smaller payments than the standard repayment plan, but increases your monthly payment every few years. By the end of the loan period, your payment is larger than what your standard monthly payment would have been. This plan works well if you begin your career in a low-paying job, but expect to quickly move up the income ladder. Typically the loan period is 10 years.

## Extended Payments

The extended repayment plan has a fixed monthly payment (it does not change) but the loan can last up to 25 years. You have smaller monthly payments but they last much longer and you pay more in interest. This plan is available only if you have more than $30,000 in federal student loans. There also is a graduated extended payment option under this plan where your monthly payment increases every few years.

## *Payments Based on Income*

Three payment plans consider your income when determining your monthly payment amount. The income-sensitive repayment option bases your monthly payment amount on your annual income for a maximum of 10 years. Income-contingent repayment plans and income-based repayment plans consider your annual income, family size, and the state where you live to determine the maximum amount you can afford to pay each month. An advantage of the income-contingent and income-based plans is that any remaining portion of your loan at the end of the repayment period MAY be forgiven (you do not owe any more money even if the loan is not totally paid off), but this is not guaranteed.

The disadvantage to these plans is that your loan could end up lasting much longer than 10 years. In fact, it could be stretched out as long as 25 years, which means you pay interest over a much longer period. The longer you make payments, the more you end up paying in interest. Plus you are required to reapply for this option every year and submit documentation to verify your income.

The best source for information on these options is in the "Repayment Plans" section at www.studentaid.ed.gov.

## *Comparing Your Repayment Options*

Confused? Let us take a look at an example. If you were to graduate with a $35,000 federal student loan and your interest rate is 6.80%, your monthly payment amounts and the total amount you pay can vary a lot based on the payment option. Remember that in each case you borrowed $35,000. Pay particular attention to the total amount paid column.

### Sample Student Loan Repayment Options[15]

| | MONTHLY PAYMENT | INTEREST PAID | TOTAL AMOUNT PAID | YEARS IN DEBT |
|---|---|---|---|---|
| **Standard Repayment** | | | | |
| All Payments | $403 | $13,334 | $48,334 | 10 |
| **Extended Fixed Repayment** | | | | |
| All Payments | $243 | $37,879 | $72,879 | 25 |
| **Extended Graduated Repayment** | | | | |
| First Payment | $198 | $43,939 | $78,939 | 25 |
| Final Payment | $347 | | | |
| **Graduated Repayment** | | | | |
| First Payment | $277 | $15,944 | $50,944 | 10 |
| Final Payment | $604 | | | |
| **Income-Based Repayment[16]** | | | | |
| First Payment | $172 | $37,135 | $72,759 | 21 |
| Final Payment | $403 | | | |

You want to choose the repayment option that is the most practical for you and not just the one that has the smallest monthly payment. If you look only at the monthly payment amount, the extended payment plan is much better than the standard plan. However, you are in debt for 25 years and pay almost $79,000 for that $35,000 loan. You will be 47 years old when you finally pay off your school loan. That is old! At least with the standard plan you are only 32 years old when the loan is paid off, not to mention that you paid less in interest and kept more money in your pocket.

## Change the Plan

Once you choose a repayment plan you are not locked into that plan for life. You can switch from one repayment plan to another at least once a year. You also can pay off your student loans early in any amount at any time with no penalty.

## Forgiveness

Although you may hear or read something about having your student loans forgiven, it is possible that you may never meet the qualifications or receive any real benefit. In most cases, by the time you get to the point that you qualify for loan forgiveness your loan should have been paid off long ago. You can find out more about this option for federal loans at www.studentaid.ed.gov in the "Repaying Your Loans" section.

## Consolidation

Consolidation simply means combining all your different loans into one big loan. Instead of having multiple loan payments to different servicers, you can consolidate your federal student loans so you have one payment. However, consolidation loans do not have a grace period. If you consolidate your loans during the six-month grace period after you graduate or leave college, your first payment begins 60 days after the consolidation takes place. If you want or need to take advantage of your six-month grace period, then wait until the last month of your grace period before consolidating.

Even though your different federal student loans have different interest rates, consolidation loans have a single fixed rate. The government will use a weighted average formula, which basically means there is no interest rate advantage or disadvantage to consolidation except they round up by one-eighth percent. The advantage to consolidation is that you make only one student loan payment.

So you can consolidate all your student loans to have just one single payment, right? Not so fast. You can only consolidate your federal student loans together. You cannot consolidate your private student loans with your federal student loans. Your private student loans have to be repaid separately. The good news is that you may be able to consolidate all your private student loans together as well, so that you have just two consolidation loans (and just two payments).

Be careful! Although federal student loans have various protections, including no consolidation fees, you have to look carefully at the fine print for any consolidation you do with your private loans. Private lenders calculate your interest rate any way they choose, and they will have more requirements and penalties.

## No Money, No Payments

Despite your best efforts you have been unable to find a job, your job does not pay very well, or your employer "no longer needs your services." What can you do if the bills keep coming but the paychecks stop?

Contact your servicer and explain your situation before they contact you. This is why you made a list of all your loans and contact information and kept them easily accessible. Your servicer will explain your options and help you select the one that is best for your situation.

Whatever you do, do not ignore your servicer if you receive calls or letters about your payments. It is your responsibility to stay in touch with your servicer. Your student loans do not go away. In fact, they will come back with a vengeance with much harsher penalties. Because there are so many ways to work with your servicer no matter what your situation, there is no reason to avoid them. Instead, explain your situation and see what they can do to help.

## Deferment

A deferment is a period of time where your servicer will allow you to stop making payments. Servicers will defer your student loan payments for reenrolling in college at least half-time (e.g. graduate school), unemployment, economic hardship, or military service. Deferment simply extends the amount of time it takes to pay off your student loan debt. If you have an unsubsidized loan, your interest will be added to your balance when your deferment period ends so you end up owing even more money.

## Forbearance

If you are not eligible for deferment but you still cannot make your payments, you may be eligible for forbearance. Forbearance means either you temporarily make smaller payments or stop making payments all together. Your loan continues to charge interest, even if it is a subsidized loan, but you have less drain on your cash flow. In almost all cases, you must contact your servicer to request forbearance. The forbearance period and payment amount are based on your particular circumstances. Only use the amount of forbearance time that you truly need to use.

## There Are Consequences

Not paying or defaulting on your student loans negatively affects everything you want to do in life. It will hinder you from getting a good job, buying a car, or leasing an apartment. Most important, it is unnecessary. Regardless of your situation, there are loan repayment options available. It is your responsibility to put forth the effort and contact your servicer to explain your circumstances. There are payment options to help you avoid unnecessary interest charges, bad credit, and unnecessary financial stress, but it is up to you to make sure you know the ones that best fit your particular situation.

The important thing is to not bury your head in the sand and hope the issue will go away. Your university, the lender, the state government, and the federal government all will take steps to get you to pay. For starters, your lender will report your delinquent loan to the credit bureaus, which will destroy your credit. The negative information remains on your credit report for seven years. Any federal payments, such as a tax refund, can be withheld to pay off your loan. In addition, extra fees and interest charges are added because of your failure to pay. As if that is not enough, your wages may also be garnished. That means your paycheck can be reduced as your employer sends a portion of your paycheck to your student loan lender. The lesson here is to not default on your student loans, ever.

One final warning: do not assume that you can get rid of federal student loans through bankruptcy. The current law makes it extremely difficult to do so. In many instances, you may not be able to wipe out private student loans either. Thus, bankruptcy will destroy your credit for many years, and you still have to make student loan payments. Instead, it is always better to work with your servicer to work out an arrangement for your student loans. Keep in mind that nobody wants to see you default on a loan. They want to help you find a solution so that they get their money back.

College is expensive. There are obvious costs and hidden costs. It is an investment in your future. We should do everything within our power to maximize the return on that investment. Simply understanding these facts will go a long way toward ensuring good personal financial health.

# THE COST OF  FINANCIAL IGNORANCE

Our student mentioned at the beginning of the chapter with $48,000 in student loan debt changed majors three times while he was in school. He also had a number of course credits from a community college that did not transfer because he neglected to check with his advisor before taking the classes. The result is that he spent an extra year getting his undergraduate degree and used student loans to pay for it. He was borrowing $9,600 per year in student loans. That extra year pushed his total student loan amount up from $38,400 to $48,000. Plus he delayed earning a full year's salary.

| | |
|---|---|
| Extra year financed with student loans | $ 9,600 |
| Interest expense on student loans | $ 3,600 |
| Lost wages from graduating one year late | $36,000 |
| Total Cost of Financial Ignorance | **$49,200** |

# FINANCIAL PLANNING

## Where Does All the Money Go?

As would happen, two of our students stopped by on the very same day a few years after their graduation and talked about their school loans. The first student was excited. She had paid off her school loans in just three short years and now was ready to buy her first home. The financial planning process she learned in class helped her track her everyday expenditures and put some additional money toward paying off her school loans. She paid off $28,000 in three years rather than the ten it usually takes.

The second student was not as happy. He was looking for advice on how he could better manage his expenses. He had never implemented a financial plan or even created a cash flow statement and was having trouble making his school loan payment.

The difference between these two students is big. What did our first student do that allowed her to pay off her school loan so quickly that our second student did not do?

# FINANCIAL PLANNING PROCESS

Ask this question: "Do I have enough money, or would I like to have more?" Everyone who understands that money is what it takes to buy more stuff wants more of it. It does not mean you are being greedy. In fact, maybe you would like to have more money because there are so many great things you would like to do with that money, such as build a shelter for abandoned animals or sponsor cancer research for children. Businesses always want more money, but so do nonprofit organizations. You may even be part of a group on campus that tries to raise money for various projects or causes. No matter how noble the intentions, everyone focuses on getting more money.

But more money is not the answer. That is the fallacy that most people buy into. The purpose of this chapter is not to help you earn more money, but to help you learn the financial competencies necessary to make the most of whatever money you do earn. Financial success is not about how much you make, it's about how much you spend.

If you think financial success is tied to income, look at Michael Jackson. When he passed away, he was preparing for his "This Is It" tour. He wasn't going back on the road because he missed the crowds and adulation. "This Is It" was happening because *he was broke.*[17] Reportedly worth $400 million at one time, Michael's home (Neverland Ranch) had been taken from him, and he was on the verge of bankruptcy.

Michael Jackson is not an isolated example. It was rumored for several years that Lindsey Lohan was broke. She had allegedly gone through over $7 million. She had to sell her apartments in Los Angeles and New York to help cover expenses, which included 24-hour chauffeur service, $1,200-night stays at the Chateau Marmont, tanning and salon services, and clothing and partying, which also led to several stints at rehab clinics.[18]

If people who have a seven-figure income going back to their early childhood can go broke, what hope is there for the rest of us? You cannot outearn financial ignorance.

You have heard the term *financial literacy*. The term tends to get thrown around quite often these days. You hear teachers, parents, news reporters, and even members of congress use the phrase. So what is financial literacy anyway? Is it reading the *Wall Street Journal?* Do you have to get up every morning and sip a cup of coffee, browse the paper, and repeat phrases such as "commodity futures are down and the euro has gained on the dollar," all while spilling jam on your pressed, white shirt? Perhaps financial literacy is simply the ability to make more money? We discussed careers in the previous chapter with hints and tips on how to be successful in your field. Maybe just being able to understand your credit card bill makes you financially literate. Or maybe financial literacy can be demonstrated by making sound financial decisions.

Although many people may have a slightly different definition of financial literacy, most would agree that a combination of all the above would make for a strong case of financial literacy. So why is it so important to increase your financial literacy?

Everyone knows that literacy is important because if you cannot read and write, it will be difficult to get a decent job. But why is *financial literacy* so important? Before we can answer that question, we have to understand the pitfalls of poor financial literacy.

# PITFALLS OF POOR FINANCIAL LITERACY

Every day people walk onto car lots and believe everything the car salesperson tells them and drive off the lot with a brand new car. In the process we break nearly every rule about smart car shopping, and the worst part is we feel good about it. When we buy our first home, we make the same mistakes. Instead of doing it the right way and protecting our finances, we do it the way an industry wants us to, much to the demise of our own financial health.

What you will learn throughout this book is that entire industries are designed to take advantage of your financial illiteracy. They will not do anything illegal, unethical, or immoral, but they will separate you from as much of your money as they possibly can. You will drive off a car dealer's lot paying $5,000 less than the sticker price. You will think you got a good deal but did you really? Do you know what you should have paid? Do you know that the dealer, the salesperson, the insurance agent, and the bank all want you to get that new car? It must be nice to have so many people on your side. But why are they on your side all of a sudden? Is it in your best interest that you buy the car today or is it in *their* best interest? It is all in the way that they are compensated.

Even before the most recent financial crisis that resulted in high unemployment and skyrocketing home foreclosure rates, Americans were averaging nearly 1.5 million personal bankruptcies per year.[19] You might be thinking that bankruptcies are like the reset button on your Xbox or Wii. If you just reset it before you lose, then that game does not count. That could not be farther from the truth. You hear that bankruptcies stay on your record for seven years and then go away. What record are they talking about? Are they referring to your credit score or your public record? Bankruptcies continue to affect you well beyond the seven years that it stays on your credit report. Bankruptcy is a public admission of failure. It is a very emotional process, and the feelings that go with declaring bankruptcy stay with you for the rest of your life.

After graduation, you start a full-time job. Your first couple of days on the job involve filling out a lot of paperwork. Much of that paperwork affects your wealth, your ability to retire, your health insurance, and more. If you do not understand the paperwork, you are likely to make some serious financial mistakes that will have lifelong consequences.

It is too easy to get ripped off if you do not have a firm grasp of basic personal financial principles. Financial "experts" give all kinds of advice, and it is up to you to discern what advice is good and what is bad. For instance, one financial "expert" says not to buy disability insurance while you are healthy. Well, who in their right mind is going to sell disability insurance to you once you become sick or disabled? That would be like selling car insurance to you right after your car is totaled. Investment "experts" sell seminars and software to teach you how to get rich with no money down or how to get rich as a day trader. If it was really that easy to be a day trader, then everyone would already be doing it. What they fail to explain to you is that although you can achieve annualized returns of 300% in the short term, there are high costs involved as well as high risk that could lead to losses of 300% or more. They also fail to include the high costs of brokerage commissions, tax consequences, and the fact that you will be a nervous wreck as you are constantly watching the ups and downs of the stock market by the minute. If it was easy to make $5,000 per month from home working part time, then why would anyone work outside the home full time at a job for less than $5,000 per month? As you begin to understand the basics of personal finance, you will be able to know the right questions to ask to determine who is right and who is simply misleading you for their own personal gain.

Poor financial decisions spill over into our personal lives as well. For instance, nearly half of all marriages end in divorce.[20] The number one reason marriages fail is not infidelity but money issues and arguments. It is not the lack of money that causes the problems, otherwise only the poor would get divorced, whereas the wealthy would have long happy marriages. It is the disagreement and stress involving money that can contribute to a failing marriage. In many cases the wealthy are at greater risk. In some cases one spouse is a spender and one is a saver, and instead of talking about money, they simply work against each other until the resentment builds up to the point that the two just cannot stand each other anymore. After all, we talk more openly about sex in our society than we do about money. A couple who understands personal finance can work together, even if one is a saver and one is a spender, because they know how to communicate with each other and let their strengths complement each other.

# GOALS

So how do we achieve personal financial success? We set goals. If we do not have any goals, then how can we ever determine if we are heading in the right direction? The key is to set realistic goals. Do not set a goal of making one million dollars your first month of summer vacation unless you have a real plan on how to accomplish it. Think about a sports team that comes in last place. The very next season they are going to set new goals to improve their record, but if the coach simply says the team is going to go from last place to winning the national championship in one season without a plan, nobody on the team will be able to get behind the goal because it is not realistic. On the other hand, if the coach says they are going to rebuild and have a winning record the next season and work their way to the national championship over the next four years, then that is a realistic goal that the fans and the players can support and believe. You want to set realistic, achievable goals. For instance, your goal may be to graduate in four years or to make a certain amount of money within two or three years after graduation. The key is to give some thought to your goals because this is the very first step in your financial plan.

# Timelines

Our goals can be short term, mid range, or long term. Although there is no exact cutoff point, short-term goals tend to be less than three years, mid-range goals three to five years, and long-term goals five years or longer. A short-term goal may be to save enough money over the summer to cover your expenses during the next school year. A mid-range goal may be to have enough money for a good down payment on a car in three or four years. A long-term goal may be to purchase a home within the next ten years or save enough money so you can retire when you choose.

# SMART Goals

Now that we can differentiate between the different time periods for our goals, we need to make sure we are choosing the correct types of goals. The easiest way to remember how to set goals is to use the acronym SMART. SMART refers to goals that are Specific, Measurable, Attainable, Relevant, and Time framed.

**Specific:** Avoid general terms such as, "I plan to graduate from college." Instead, choose something specific such as "I plan to graduate from this university with a Bachelor of Science degree in Biology."

**Measurable:** Emphasize how much. For instance, "I will have a very good semester," is not measurable. Instead use something measurable such as, "I will get three As and one B this semester."

**Achievable:** Your goal must be realistic and achievable for you or your organization. You need to be able to look at the goal and say, "I can do that." For instance, if you start a new organization on campus and your goal is to have every student on campus join your organization, not only is that highly improbable, but you will also have a difficult time motivating the other members in your group. Instead, choose a more realistic goal, such as getting a certain percentage of the campus to join each semester over the next few semesters until a reasonably sized group has been achieved.

**Relevant:** The goal must be relevant to you. It needs to be yours and not your parents' goal for you. If the goal is your own, then you are more likely to succeed. If your parents' goal for you is to become a lawyer, and you want to be a school-teacher, you will be hard pressed to really do what is necessary to be a successful lawyer because it is not your goal.

**Time Framed:** You need a time frame in which to measure progress. For instance, if your goal is simply to obtain a college degree, then you could take one class every other semester for the next ten years or more. On the other hand if your goal is to earn your degree within the next five years, you can now measure your progress each semester by seeing how close you are to your goal and how well you are doing to keep yourself on pace to achieve it. The time-framed concept is one of the reasons why milestone birthdays are so difficult for some people if they have not achieved certain goals. For instance, most of us make goals or promises for ourselves such as "I want to have my first novel written by age 30," or "I want to own my own business by age 35."

## Good Goals for Everyone

Although everyone has different goals based on their own personal situations, goal setting may be new to you. To help get you started, here are some goals that are good for just about everyone.

- *Build an emergency fund*—An emergency fund is a reserve or cushion to get you through the hard times, whether it is a period of unemployment or unexpected repairs for your car. Building an emergency fund may be your first SMART goal after college.

- *Save for retirement*—Time is on your side. The sooner you start saving for retirement, the less you will be required to save to reach your goal.

- *Save for a house*—Homeownership is the American dream, but it does not come cheap.

- *Save for big purchases*—If you make all of your large purchases on credit instead of saving ahead of time everything that you buy will be significantly more expensive.

- *Pay off school loans*—The sooner you pay off your loan balance, the sooner you have more money left at the end of the month.

## Net Worth

Assume for a moment that you are going on a trip. You know exactly where you want to go, so you go to Google Maps and type in your destination. If you click on 'Driving Directions,' Google does not plot out your plan for travel right away. Google cannot tell you how to get to where you want to go without first knowing your starting point. If Google cannot do it, then it is probably safe to assume that we cannot do it either. We cannot plan how we want to reach a destination without first knowing our starting point. The same logic is true with our personal financial situation. We just finished discussing setting our financial goals. That is our destination. To understand how we are going to get there, we first have to know where we are. It is our net worth statement that tells us where we are now.

Your net worth is the difference between your assets and your liabilities—the difference between what you own and what you owe. The net worth statement is a snapshot of a moment in time. The snapshot may occur at the end of the year, quarter, or month. The important point here is that we always choose the same moment in time. We don't calculate our net worth as of the end of the month one time and the middle of the month the next. Our objective is to track our net worth over time to see if we are moving toward achieving our financial goals. One common mistake is to include our monthly bills on our net worth statement; after all we "owe" that money. But regular monthly bills do not belong on your net worth statement unless you fall behind and end up owing a past due amount. We will account for our monthly bills on another financial statement.

## Net Worth Statement Worksheet

**Assets**

| | |
|---|---|
| Cash on Hand | $ _____ |
| Checking Account Balance | $ _____ |
| Savings Account Balance | $ _____ |
| Money Market Account Balance | $ _____ |
| Market Value of Your Home | $ _____ |
| Estimated Value of Household Items | $ _____ |
| Market Value of Other Real Estate (i.e., investment, rental property, timeshare, vacation home) | $ _____ |
| Investment Accounts (Outside Retirement) | $ _____ |
| Market Value of Vehicles | $ _____ |
| Current Value of Retirement Accounts | $ _____ |
| Estimated Value of Personal Items | $ _____ |
| **Total Assets** | $ _____ |

**Liabilities**

| | |
|---|---|
| 1st Mortgage | $ _____ |
| Home Equity Loan or Line of Credit | $ _____ |
| Other Real Estate Loans | $ _____ |
| Auto Loan | $ _____ |
| Credit Card Balances | $ _____ |
| Student Loans | $ _____ |
| Personal Unsecured Loans | $ _____ |
| Other Liabilities | $ _____ |
| **Total Liabilities** | $ _____ |
| **NET WORTH** (Assets minus Liabilities) | $ _____ |

Can your net worth be negative? Absolutely. Many college graduates, especially those who graduate with professional degrees such as attorneys and medical doctors, will graduate with a large amount of debt and little or no assets. That is okay for now because it is related to your student loans. However, it should be a temporary situation because the purpose of acquiring the debt was to earn a degree that allows you to earn more money. Over time, you will reduce what you owe (your liabilities) and increase what you own (your assets) until you eventually have a positive net worth.

What is important is that you use your net worth to track your progress toward achieving your goals. You can regularly track your progress using a net worth statement. If your net worth is increasing on a regular basis it is a good indication that your financial plan is working. On the other hand, if your net worth is decreasing, then you know you need to make some changes in your financial plan to reverse that trend.

Keep in mind there is absolutely no connection between your net worth and your worth as a person. Just think about the number of wealthy people who have committed crimes against other people. Meanwhile, teachers, social workers, and volunteers with very little, if any, net worth, do good for their communities and other people. Just think about Mother Theresa, the humanitarian nun with no net worth, compared to Bernie Madoff, the billionaire who ran a pyramid scheme and robbed thousands of people of their entire life savings. It should not be about comparing your net worth to somebody else's net worth. It should be about tracking your net worth over time to make sure you are on pace to achieve your goals.

# Cash Flow

Many times the changes on our net worth statement are directly affected by our cash flow statement.

So now we need to focus on cash flow, which deserves a rather lengthy explanation. That is because most of our short-term monthly or weekly actions are driven by our monthly or weekly cash flow. The cash flow statement allows you to look at what you make compared to what you spend.

Most of us have some bills that we need to pay. If you do not have any bills yet, do not worry because your time will come. Cash flow statements show us how our money moves in and out of our banking account over a period of time, whereas net worth statements show us how much we actually have at any one point in time. A personal cash flow statement typically spans a month because most bills are due monthly. Car payments, student loan payments, cell phone bills, and rent are all due monthly. To understand if we make enough money to cover all of our expenses, we generally look at how much money we make during a month and compare that to how much we have in expenses during the month. We need to track every dollar that comes in and goes out the door.

A real eye-opener for most people is to fill out a projected cash flow statement and then compare it to reality. In other words, first fill out a cash flow statement based on where you believe you spend all your money each month. Then the next month fill out your statement as you actually spend the money so you can compare your projection to where you actually spent your money. The purpose of doing this comparison is actually to point out where you spend your money so you can make positive changes. The earlier you take corrective action, the easier it will be to get back on track toward achieving your financial goals.

Cash flow analysis consists of looking at your income and expenses. We mentioned at the beginning of the chapter that financial success is achieved by controlling your expenses, not by increasing your income. Thus, we will spend most of our time with cash flow statements focusing on understanding our expenses.

## Cash Flow Statement
For Period Ending
MM/DD/YY

### Monthly Income

| | |
|---|---|
| Net Wages (His) | $_____ |
| Net Wages (Hers) | $_____ |
| Bonuses | $_____ |
| Investments | $_____ |
| Alimony | $_____ |
| Child Support | $_____ |
| Gift | $_____ |
| Other | $_____ |
| **Total Income** | $_____ |

### Monthly Expenses

**HOME:**

| | |
|---|---|
| Mortgage or Rent | $_____ |
| Homeowners/Renters Insurance | $_____ |
| Property Taxes | $_____ |
| Home Repair/Maintenance/HOA Dues | $_____ |

**UTILITIES:**

| | |
|---|---|
| Water and Sewer | $_____ |
| Natural Gas or Oil | $_____ |
| Telephone (Land, Cell) | $_____ |

**FOOD:**

| | |
|---|---|
| Groceries | $_____ |
| Eating Out, Lunches, Snacks | $_____ |

**FAMILY OBLIGATIONS:**

| | |
|---|---|
| Child Support | $_____ |
| Alimony | $_____ |
| Day Care, Babysitting | |

**HEALTH AND MEDICAL:**

| | |
|---|---|
| Insurance (Medical, Dental, Vision) | $_____ |
| Unreimbursed Medical Expenses, Copays | $_____ |
| Fitness (Yoga, Massage, Gym) | $_____ |

**TRANSPORTATION:**

| | |
|---|---|
| Car Payments | $_____ |
| Gasoline/Oil | $_____ |
| Auto Repairs/Maintenance/Fees | $_____ |
| Other Transportation (Bus, Taxis) | $_____ |

**DEBT PAYMENTS:**

| | |
|---|---|
| Credit Cards | $_____ |
| Student Loans | $_____ |
| Other Loans | $_____ |

**ENTERTAINMENT:**

| | |
|---|---|
| Cable TV/Videos/Movies | $_____ |
| Computer Expense | $_____ |
| Hobbies | $_____ |
| Subscriptions and Dues | $_____ |
| Vacations | $_____ |

**PETS:**

| | |
|---|---|
| Food | $_____ |
| Grooming, Boarding, Vet | $_____ |

**CLOTHING:** | $_____ |

**INVESTMENTS AND SAVINGS:**

| | |
|---|---|
| 401K or IRA | $_____ |
| Stocks/Bonds/Mutual Funds | $_____ |
| College Fund | $_____ |
| Savings | $_____ |
| Emergency Fund | $_____ |

**MISCELLANEOUS:**

| | |
|---|---|
| Toiletries, Household Products | $_____ |
| Gifts/Donations | $_____ |
| Grooming (Hair, Make-up, Other) | $_____ |
| Miscellaneous Expense | $_____ |

### Total Investments and Expenses | $_____ |

| | |
|---|---|
| Surplus or Shortage (Spendable Income minus Total Expenses and Investments) | $_____ |

# Income

As you can see from the cash flow statement, the income portion is the easiest to complete because, unfortunately, most of us have few sources of income. Make sure you only include the net amount of your paycheck because we want to track the dollars you actually receive, not the dollars you earn. It is important to include all sources of income. Perhaps certain months each year you get a bonus or extra hours at work or maybe money for your birthday. You have to include these extra sources of income for those months they are received to track how you spend the extra money. If you do not include these extra sources of income, you will not truly understand your finances. Ultimately we want to know how much we get and when we get it.

# Expenses

At some point everyone asks, "Where did my money go?" There are many ways that money seems to leak out of your budget. For instance, if you have a moni-tored security alarm, you may pay around $50 to $75 per month. In addition, you may have a home telephone line, which could cost $15 to $45 per month. Perhaps you have a magazine subscription or a gym membership that you do not use. Cable expenses can easily jump to more than $100 per month if you have high-speed Internet and HDTV. Add a few premium channels, and you could be up to $150 per month. In addition to recurring monthly payments, you will also find that your income is attacked by impulse purchases, hunger, and time restraints all at the same time.

## *Expenses: Home*

Be sure to track your rent or mortgage payment. In addition, any other expenses incurred for your home in a particular month should be included in this category. For instance, if you have to call a plumber to fix the toilet, you would list the plumber's bill under home repairs.

## *Expenses: Utilities*

Most utilities are covered for students living on campus and in many private student housing complexes. However, some of you may be paying utilities (electricity, water, trash removal, etc.) now or at least a portion of them, and the rest of you will be paying them soon enough. Some of your expenses are the same amount every month (such as your cell phone bill) and others vary from month to month (such as your electricity bill).

## *Expenses: Food*

People under age 25 spend nearly 8% on prepared foods outside the home. For someone making $30,000 per year, that translates to $200 per month. That is why it is a good idea to separate your food category into groceries and dining out. As we will see later, adjusting how often you eat out is one of the easiest ways to reduce your expenses. In addition, do not forget to account for those small stops to buy bread and milk throughout the month, which usually result in picking up a few other items as well. Many adults will tell you that the average bread and milk trip to the grocery store costs around $25 to $40.

## Expenses: Family Obligations

Although most of you may not be thinking about this category at the moment, it is important to consider these expenses once they become relevant to your life. This includes things like alimony and child support.

## Expenses: Health and Medical

Even if you are young and healthy and on your parents' health insurance you still have medical expenses. Any time you pay copayments for doctor office visits or prescriptions, make sure to include these expenses.

## Expenses: Transportation

The obvious expense that should be included in transportation is your car payment. Do not forget to include other expenses related to your car including gasoline, oil changes, and other maintenance costs, as well as potential repair bills. Another transportation-related expense includes auto insurance. If you pay monthly, then include your monthly payment amount in this category. If your payments are every six months, then be sure to include the insurance amount in the month you pay it.

Other transportation costs should be considered as well. If you take public transportation, such as a subway, bus, or train, this is part of your transportation expense. If you have to pay for a monthly parking garage permit or a parking pass, then include these expenses in the transportation category as well.

## Expenses: Debt Payments

Include all your debt payments, except for your mortgage and your car payment, because those are included in other categories. For now you want to include the amount you actually pay toward your debt.

Included in this category are credit card payments, student loan payments, and any other debt you may have acquired. Perhaps you have a personal loan, or you owe some money on unpaid utility bills. If you have any accounts that are in collections and you are making payments, then those expenses should also be included in this category.

## Expenses: Entertainment/Recreation

Include your cable or satellite television service, the amount you spent on movies during the month, which could include subscriptions to services such as NetFlix.

Your computer-related expenses, such as high-speed Internet (which may be part of your cable bill) or other related subscription services, should be included. If you have any hobbies that have a cost to them, include those expenses as well. Include all your subscriptions or dues to magazines, clubs, or other organizations. You may want to include your gym memberships under medical or you can include them here, whichever you decide.

## Expenses: Pets

Although pets may come to you for free or for a very small fee from a shelter, there are costs associated with caring for a pet. The obvious expense for all pets is food. Whether you have a dog, a cat, a hamster, goldfish or some other animal, you have to feed it. Taking good care of your pets' health is also a must, so you must include the costs for trips to the veterinarian's office. You need to consider other expenses such as grooming, litter for your cat, or bedding for your hamster.

## Expenses: Clothing

Although you may not buy clothing every month, you will spend money on clothes sometime during the year. Do not forget to account for shoe purchases in your clothing category.

## Expenses: Investments and Savings

Money that you set aside for your personal savings, a college fund, an emergency fund, a retirement account or other investments should all be included in this category. Keep in mind, just like with medical expenses, if you already accounted for your retirement account through work, which lowered your net income, then do not repeat it again in this category. You may ask why investments are listed as an expense. You should remember to pay yourself first. You are going to be working really hard for the next several years, and as you can see, there are a lot of expenses that are draining your income. If you do not make it a priority to pay yourself first, then you are unlikely to ever have enough left over for you.

## Expenses: Miscellaneous

What else was missed? Where else do you spend your money? You may include gifts or donations in this category. Think about how many birthdays and anniversaries you help celebrate. During the first few years after graduation, you will likely be invited to several weddings or you may actually be part of the wedding party. Do not forget about haircuts, hair coloring, and other grooming activities, such as manicures, etc. You will probably have toiletry expenses and other household product expenses as well. Any other expenses that were not accounted for at this point should be included in this category. If your miscellaneous category begins to grow to a significant portion of your overall budget, then you may want to split some of the expenses out and create a new category.

# WHAT DO THE NUMBERS MEAN?

Now you will need to add up all your expenses and subtract that number from your total income. You will have one of three results. If your number ends up at zero, then your budget is very tight because you have absolutely no wiggle room. If your number is positive then you have a surplus. A surplus means that you have extra money you can redistribute to your expense categories (including savings). If your number is negative then you have a problem because you have a shortage that must be covered. A shortage means you either went into debt this month to cover some expenses or you reduced your savings account. If the shortage was due to a one-time event that was covered by your savings account, then you are probably okay. Replenish the savings account over the next few months. If the shortage was due to a one-time event that you covered with debt, then you need to save more in the future to avoid going into debt. If, however, the shortage was not due to a one-time event or emergency, then you need to make some adjustments to your spending as you go forward. Understanding your cash flow statement allows you to identify areas that you can immediately save on to take corrective measures before you completely destroy your finances.

Now we can use what we have tracked in the past to project our future income and expenses. This is the real power of the cash flow statement. We can begin to align our cash flow statement to our financial goals.

Over time you can take the average of the bills that vary month to month. For instance, you can estimate your monthly fuel expenses, utility bills, and so forth. By setting aside the average amount each month, you will have extra money from the cheaper months to use to pay the bills during the more expensive months.

Set aside money for unanticipated or nonmonthly expenses as well. This will help you avoid running up large amounts of debt each time one occurs. For instance, you probably do not change your oil every month, but if you treat it as a monthly expense, then you would set aside a small portion each month to cover it instead of having to come up with the full amount every three months or so. Another example is six-month insurance premiums. For six-month insurance premiums, you need to put aside one-sixth of your premium each month to avoid getting hit with a large bill every six months that you cannot afford. For instance, if your 6-month premium is $600, then your monthly expense is $100 ($600 / 6 = $100). In this example you should put $100 in your savings account each month so you will have the full $600 available when the payment comes due.

What about unknown future expenses such as clothing, veterinary bills, gifts for birthdays and holidays, or vacations? For some items you average the actual expenses you tracked, such as clothing, gifts, and vet visits. For other items, such as vacations or spring break, you simply need to decide how much you want to spend and divide that amount by the number of months remaining until your vacation or spring break begins. You should save that amount each month so you can afford your trip without going into debt.

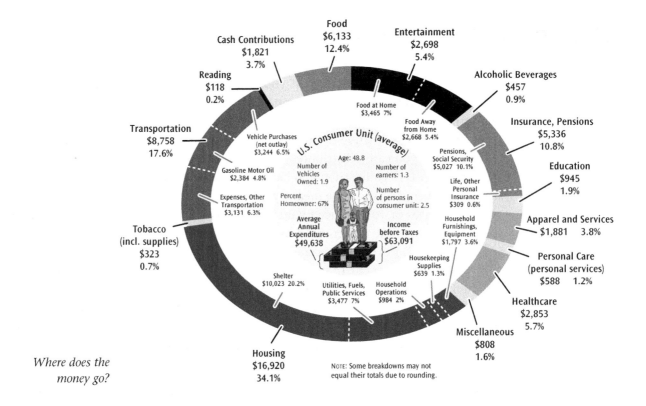

*Where does the money go?*

## Surplus

The great news is that a surplus on your cash flow statement can lead to an increase in your net worth every month. You can choose where to allocate your surplus by going through the categories and deciding what areas are your greatest priorities. Perhaps you want to focus on getting out of debt first, which will quickly increase your net worth and lead to additional surpluses in the future as you eliminate some monthly debt expenses. On the other hand you may want to save more for retirement, educational expenses, or other investment or savings. Increasing the investment and savings categories will also quickly increase your net worth. Another option is to increase funds to areas such as entertainment or clothing, which will give you a little more money to work with. The key is that having a surplus at the end of your cash flow gives you more options and choices.

## Shortage

If your cash flow statement indicates you have a shortage, which means your expenses are greater than your income, you will have to make some adjustments. You have two options; you can increase your income or you can decrease your expenses. Because increasing your income may be more desirable, yet less likely to be done quickly and easily, we will focus on decreasing your expenses. For the time being, ignore fixed expenses that cannot be adjusted such as your current rent or mortgage payment, health insurance, child support, and other fixed expenses. Now look at the remaining categories, such as telephone, eating out, subscriptions, grooming, etc. You will have to start looking for opportunities to save in some of these categories. If you can, reduce your utility expenses by making adjustments to your habits such as turning off your electric water heater when you are not home, or adjusting your thermostat. The point is that you cannot bury your head in the sand and hope everything will somehow work out. We have a word for people who try to live that way: Bankrupt.

# FINANCIAL PLANNING IS A PROCESS

Because you want to avoid the fate of the celebrities we discussed at the beginning of the chapter (at least the part where they went bankrupt), then you want to follow the financial planning process. The process is really a cycle—do it and review it!

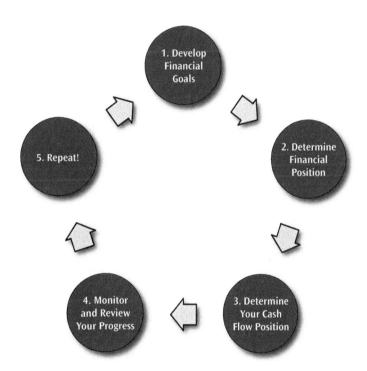

Develop your financial goals—Remember to use SMART goals and include short-term, mid-range and long-term goals.

◆ *Determine your financial position*—Use the net worth statement and take an assessment of your current situation, including your education, marriage, and family plans.

◆ *Determine your cash flow position*—Use the cash flow statement to cover your expenses and properly allocate any leftover dollars.

◆ *Monitor and review your progress*—Track your increased net worth and your progress toward achieving your goals. If you are on track, then keep on doing what you are doing. If you are not, then look to see what you can do to improve your situation.

◆ *Repeat*—The financial planning process is a cycle. As you achieve your goals, replace them with new ones and begin the cycle again.

# WHY DO MOST FINANCIAL PLANS FAIL?

Now we have these great financial tools available to us. If we use all of these tools the way we are supposed to, then why do financial plans still fail? That can be summed up in one simple phrase: life happens. More importantly, we can use the acronym L.I.F.E.

**L**—Listed expenses are underestimated

**I**—Impulse buying

**F**—Forgotten bills

**E**—Emergencies

**Listed expenses are underestimated:** It is one thing to guess how much you spend on grooming, gifts, and clothing, but it is another thing to guess correctly. Most people do not realize how much they actually spend on each category until they really start to pay attention to where their money goes. You may come up shorter each month than you realize simply because you have underestimated how much you actually spend on certain categories. This highlights the importance of accurately tracking your expenses for several months so that your future estimates are based on a period of actual spending.

**Impulse buying:** Grocery stores place candy bars right at the checkout line. Department stores place their magazines, batteries, and other impulse items near the registers. Even an innocent evening where you plan to just "go out" can result in hundreds of dollars of items that were on sale or clearance that you had not planned to purchase. The point is that impulse buying is when you make purchases that you had not planned and particularly ones that were not taken into account on your cash flow statement.

**Forgotten bills:** Because most people do not put together a cash flow statement for each month, they may forget to take into account bills that do not come due every month. For instance, many automobile insurance policies are due every six months. It is much easier to set aside $100 per month to make your insurance payment than it is to come up with $600 at one time when the statement arrives in the mail three weeks before the due date. Other forgotten bills could include tax bills, homeowner's association annual dues, or other annual or semiannual dues. Without accounting for these irregular payments, you may think you are achieving your financial goals when in fact you are falling short.

**Emergencies:** Perhaps you have been very responsible with your money and you never spend more than you make. What happens when your transmission goes out on your car, the refrigerator breaks, or you have a medical emergency? Keep in mind almost all insurances require you to pay a deductible up front. That means you could be responsible for the first $500 or even $2,500. Establishing an emergency fund and setting aside some money for medical expenses will protect you from these situations.

# DOES MONEY BUY HAPPINESS?

It would seem from our conversation so far that it is all about the money. The real trick, however, is that it is not about the money. It is about getting to the point where you can stop focusing on the money and start focusing on those things that really matter. A good financial plan means you no longer have to be stressed when you are spending money because you don't have to wonder if you are spending too much.

Does money buy happiness? After asking this question in class, a student responded by saying, "No, but it sure makes for a good down payment." As funny as that is, he missed the point. Think about some of the best moments in your life. What you will find is that the people in your life, including family and friends, are what determine your happiness, not how much money you spend. Even if you spend a lot of money to have a family reunion or go on an expensive trip, you have the most fun when you are not alone. It is all about the people and the relationships, not the money. Money should be seen as a tool or as a way to provide choices and options. Debt takes away your choices. On the flip side, money gives you choices.

Once you understand that money is a tool and not a goal, you can keep the accumulation of wealth in perspective. If you simply build your wealth for the sake of building your wealth, then you missed the point entirely.

When trying to balance our cash flow statement, most people only focus on making more money. The problem is that expenses rise to meet or exceed our new, higher income. Think about the fact that there are plenty of people making $50,000 per year who seem to be just a few hundred dollars short every month from being able to comfortably balance their cash flow statement and save enough for retirement. On the other hand, there are also plenty of people making $60,000 per year who seem to be just a few hundred dollars short every month from being able to comfortably balance their cash flow statement and save enough for retirement.

Continuing this illustration, there are plenty of people making $75,000 per year who seem to be just a few hundred dollars short every month. As you can see, we find a way to buy more expensive homes and more expensive cars and so forth as our income rises, so we continue to outspend our income by a few hundred dollars each month. Remember, you cannot out earn financial ignorance.

# THE COST OF  FINANCIAL IGNORANCE

The real power of the financial planning process is that it forces you to write down your goals and gives you a concrete way to track your progress toward achieving them. Once you see it on paper (or computer), it is easy to spot specific things you can do to reach any goal. Ask any person you know how they achieved any of their goals. Their answer will not be that they are smarter than you or that they started with more money than you did, but their answer will be that they clearly identified their goals and wrote them down.

That was the difference between our two students at the beginning of the chapter. The first student had paid off her school loans way early and now was ready to start shopping for her first house. She followed the financial planning process she learned while in class. She developed clear SMART goals and created a cash flow statement to identify expenses she could eliminate or reduce and put the savings toward paying off her school loans. That's how she paid off $28,000 in school loans in just three years. Without a financial plan in place, our hapless second student will continue to barely make his loan payments and take the entire 10 years to pay off the debt.

By focusing her efforts on one goal and putting a plan in place, our first student saved a lot of money. At the typical student loan rate of 5.1%,[21] by paying off her loan in three years it saved her $18,000 in interest expense over the student that was taking the entire 10 years to pay it off.

| Total cost of student loan payments over ten years | $48,000 |
|---|---|
| Total cost of student loan payments over three years | $30,000 |
| Total Cost of Financial Ignorance | **$18,000** |

# TIME VALUE OF MONEY

## Now or Later?

A student from our very first class ten years ago stopped by our office to ask us about two different retirement plans his company was offering. Now that he had been out of college for 10 years he had decided it was time to start saving for his retirement and had questions about small differences between his two options. He wanted to make the best choice for himself. We were dismayed that he had waited 10 years to start saving for retirement. Obviously, we did not do a good job the first time we taught our class.

# THE CONCEPT OF TIME VALUE OF MONEY

Take a look at a penny. What do you see? Most people see something of little value. By the end of this chapter you will see that penny as the beginning of financial freedom. If your instructor handed you a penny, could you come back to class the next day and bring two pennies? In other words, could you double it in value? Can you continue to double the value of that penny every day for an entire year (one cent, two cents, four cents, eight cents, etc.)?

Perhaps doubling the penny every day for an entire year may be a bit much. What about six months? That still might be a bit much. Let's try just four weeks. Double the value of the penny every day for 28 days. Do you know how much money you would have? Maybe $1,000? What about $10,000? Try $1,342,177.28. That's right; you would have over $1.3 million starting with the one little penny you doubled in value every day for just 28 days.

How is that possible? How can one penny become more than $1.3 million in 28 days? Think about it this way; how much would you have on day 27? You would have a little more than $660,000. What about day 26? That would be just over $330,000. On day 25 you would only have a little more than $165,000. You can see here how quickly the dollar amount was reduced by just going back three days. You can quickly follow that amount back down to one penny.

You may be asking, "So what is the point? It's not like I can actually invest one penny and have it double every day." You would be correct. What we illustrated here was an exaggerated interest rate (100% per day) for a very short time period (28 days) and a very small initial investment (one penny). Now imagine if you take that same concept, but make the interest rate much smaller such as 10% per year, but stretch the time frame out to 65 years and start with a larger dollar amount.

For example, let us assume that when you were born, Grandma was so excited because you were her first grandchild (or maybe you were just the last hope for your family . . . if you have lots of cousins, you understand). Because of her excitement, she decided to deposit $2,500 one time on the day you were born, into an account that earned a 10% average rate of return over your lifetime. When you turn 65, you find out about this account from Grandma and decide to retire and withdraw the money. How much do you think it is worth when you are 65? Remember, she only put $2,500 in one time when you were born and did not add or remove any money.

How much is Grandma's account worth when you turn 65? $10,000? $100,000? One million dollars?

If Grandma puts $2,500 in an account the day you are born and you withdraw the money when you turn 65 (assuming 10% average annual returns) you will have about $1.2 million. That means Grandma guaranteed that you would retire a millionaire!

So let us assume that Grandma was excited when you were born and wanted to put money into an account for you, but despite the 9-month heads up she did not prepare very well. Instead of putting the $2,500 into an account when you were born, she took five years to save up the money. When you turn 65 and you excitedly withdraw your funds, there is only $761,204 in there! Grandma cost you half a million dollars by waiting just five years! Sure, you will still gladly take the $761,000, but wouldn't you rather have had the $1.2 million?

What if things did not go well for Grandma? Although she wanted to put money away for you when you were born, she was living on a fixed income, and her prescription costs and heating bills kept going up. Instead of putting money away when you were born, she put money in the account on your tenth birthday. Now when you go to check your account at age 65 there is just $472,648 in the account. By waiting 10 years, your account was worth less than half of what it could have been. Think about that. Shaving off just 10 years from 65 years total cut the value in your account by more than half.

If you are like most people, your Grandma did not put that kind of money away for you, so it is all up to you. Sometime after graduation when you turn 25, being a smart personal finance student, you decide to put away $2,500 to begin your retirement account. To your surprise, when you turn 65 and look at the account, it is only worth $113,148! What good will $100,000 be to you when you are 65? That will probably buy two movie tickets and a large tub of popcorn.

The point is that waiting to start saving costs you a lot of money. You lose the opportunity to earn interest every year that you wait to get started. Waiting until age 25 results in losing 90% of your possible retirement account. Ouch! Most students have time on their side. There is no reason why you cannot become a millionaire. All you have to do is follow some basic principles and understand the relationship between time, money, and interest rates.

Okay, waiting until you are 65 years old seems like a dozen lifetimes away right now. But imagine if your grandmother had put $2,500 in an account earning 10% per year when you were born and gave it to you when you turned 16. You would have $11,487 to buy a nice used car.

Maybe Grandma makes you wait until you turn 18 so you can use the money for college. You would have $13,900 and not have to borrow nearly as much money for college. Not enough to pay for an Ivy League degree, but it could definitely get you through a couple of years at most in-state schools.

How about if you wait until you are 25 years old? You would have $27,086; that would make for a very nice wedding plus a honeymoon. If you wait until you are 30, you would have $43,623 to use for a down payment on a house.

How do you grow a small amount of money such as a one-time deposit of $2,500 into a million dollars or more? Not only does the $2,500 earn interest, but the interest earns interest. This is called compounding. Each year you earn 10% on the amount you have in your account. The first year you would earn $250 in interest on your original $2,500 investment. Now you have $2,750 in your account. The second year you earn $275 in interest. Now you have $3,025 in your account. The third year you earn $302.50 interest giving you $3,327.50. Your money continues to grow like this for as long as you leave it in your account. This is time value of money.

Understanding time value of money is fundamental to making good financial decisions. It is however, one of the most difficult concepts for most people to grasp. This is why many smart people make poor financial decisions. It is like when you learned to ride a bike. It was scary and difficult at first, but by continuing to practice, you mastered it, and now it is second nature. *The only way to really gain an understanding of time value of money is to practice.* Before we can start practicing, we have to know what tools to use and how to use them.

# FINANCIAL CALCULATORS

A lot of different tools are available to aid us in time value of money calculations. You can use a spreadsheet, you can use different Web sites, you can find an app for your phone, or you can use a financial calculator. Although there are many different calculators to choose from, we will use the Texas Instrument BAII Plus calculator in our examples. We prefer this calculator because it is relatively inexpensive and easy to use.

What distinguishes a financial calculator from any other calculator? There are five buttons that set it apart. You can use any financial calculator or even any graphing or scientific calculator, but only if it has these five buttons or functions. The buttons are N, I/Y, PV, PMT, and FV. They stand for **N**umber of time periods, **I**nterest per **Y**ear, **P**resent **V**alue, **P**ayment, and **F**uture **V**alue. Once we choose our financial calculator, in our case the Texas Instruments BA II Plus, we are ready to learn how to use it.

To answer any time value of money question, we must have at least three of five pieces of information. What we are doing is solving a puzzle. Our puzzle consists of six pieces. The first five are the Present Value (PV), the Future Value (FV), the Payment (PMT), the Interest Rate (I/Y), and the Number of Time Periods (N). Given any three of the five pieces of information, we can always solve for one of the other two pieces and ignore the remaining piece. We will use the sixth puzzle piece to display the answer.

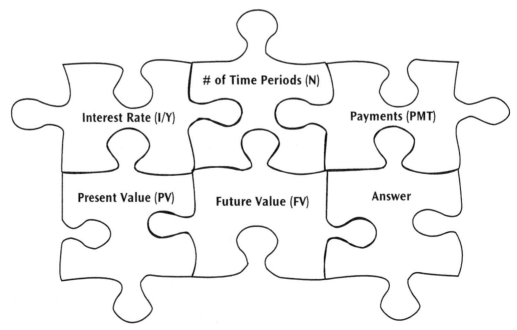

The time value of money (TVM) keys on your calculator hold memory. That means if you enter data into the PMT key for one problem, the next time you use your calculator, whether it be two minutes later or two months later, the calculator will remember the previously entered amount. To avoid using the wrong numbers, you want to clear the memory before you begin each problem. This does not mean simply pressing the CE/C button. The CE/C key only clears what shows up on the display but does not clear the memory. You must press the "Second" key and then the "FV" key. Pressing the "Second" key changes the function of the key to what is written above it. Above the "FV" key is written "CLR TVM". That stands for "Clear Time Value of Money." It clears the memory so you can begin the next problem. If you forget to "CLR TVM" then you may get the wrong answer on your next problem.

The way you assign a value to the calculator keys is to first enter the value, then press the corresponding TVM key. For instance, if the present value is $100, you would press "1", "0", "0", "PV". You enter "100" on the screen, then press the "PV" key to tell the calculator that $100 is to be used as the present value in the calculation. The screen will now display "PV = 100.00". After you enter your other numbers, such as the "N" and the "I/Y", you have to tell the calculator what you want it to compute. To do so you press the "CPT" key and then press the key to the corresponding piece of the puzzle you are trying to compute. For example, if you are solving for the future value you would press the "CPT" key, then press the "FV" key.

When you enter the amount from the "I/Y" puzzle piece, the calculator knows it is an interest rate. Your interest rate is entered as a whole number instead of a decimal. So 10% is entered as "10" on the calculator. It is not entered as ".10" nor is it entered as "10" with the "%" key. It is simply "10". Of course, if the interest rate is less than 1%, then it must be entered as a decimal. For instance a 0.5% interest rate is entered as "0.5". It is not entered as ".005". Let us take a look at an example to get comfortable with the calculator.

You deposit $100 in the bank and leave it there for two years. Your account earns 10% compounded annually. At the end of two years how much is in your account?

First we identify the puzzle pieces that we are given. Always identify three solid pieces of information.

We can identify the present value is $100 because that is what was deposited in the beginning. Next, we can identify that the account earned 10% compounded annually. Finally, we know that it earned interest for two years. Looking at the puzzle pieces from earlier, you can see that we filled in the numbers from the example.

Next, we identify which of the remaining two TVM puzzle pieces we are trying to compute. Because the problem asks how much we will have at some point in the future, and it does not mention anything about making or receiving payments, we can conclude that we are trying to find the future value.

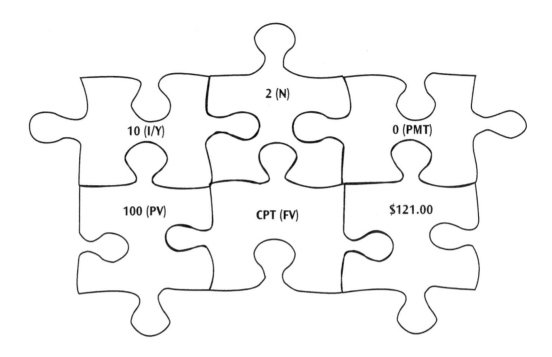

Now we can enter the data into the calculator using the following steps:

◆ Press the "Second" key.

◆ Press the "CLR TVM" key (you have now cleared the memory).

◆ Press the "CE/C" key (just to clear the display).

◆ Press "1", "0" to enter 10 onto the display.

◆ Press the "I/Y" key. The calculator will now display "I/Y = 10.00".

**NOTE:** We did not enter ".10" for the I/Y. Nor did we press the "%" key. The calculator understands that if we press the "I/Y" key it means interest rate, and it will handle that for us.

◆ Press "2" to enter 2 onto the display.

◆ Press the "N" key. The calculator will now display "N = 2.00".

◆ Press "1", "0", "0" to enter 100 onto the display.

◆ Press the "PV" key. The calculator will now display "PV = 100.00".

◆ Press the "CPT" key.

◆ Press the "FV" key. The calculator will now compute the future value for you. The calculator will display "FV = –121.00". The answer is $121.00.

So why did the answer display as a negative number? The financial calculator is designed to think in terms of cash inflows and cash outflows (money coming in or going out). If you put money into the bank, then at some point you will take money back out. Thus one number will be negative, and the other number will be positive. For our purposes in this book it will not matter which number is negative and which is positive, but if you try to solve problems later on and enter both numbers as positive, you will get an error message. "ERROR 5" means that you forgot to enter one of your numbers as negative.

For the preceding example we entered the "PV" first, then entered the "I/Y", then entered the "N". We could have entered them in any order. The calculator just needs you to enter all three numbers before you try to compute the answer. It does not matter the order you enter the numbers. Entering the numbers into your calculator is no different than entering data into a field on a Web site and clicking "Submit". On a Web site you can enter your information in any order because the Web site will not process the information until you click "Submit". We use the "CPT" key on the calculator instead of a "Submit" button.

Although there are many different kinds of time value of money questions that can be answered, there are really only four types:

1. Future Value of a lump sum
2. Present Value of a lump sum
3. Future Value of an annuity
4. Present Value of an annuity

The Future Value of a lump sum looks at what a given amount of money today will be worth at a certain point in the future. Just like in our earlier example, a one-time dollar amount that Grandma put in the bank was worth a much larger dollar amount several years later.

The Present Value of a lump sum allows you to calculate what a future dollar amount is worth today. For instance, if you win a $5,000 college scholarship as a junior in high school, you can figure out what it is worth today. It is not really worth $5,000 in today's dollars because education costs go up every year. That $5,000 will not buy as much education in a few years when you graduate because the cost of college will have increased.

The other two types are present and future value of an annuity. Annuity is a scary financial term, but it just means equal payments at equal time intervals. An annuity is simply the same amount of money invested or paid on a regular schedule, such as weekly, monthly, or annually. An amount of $100 a week every week is an annuity. An amount of $150 a month every month is an annuity.

The Future Value of an annuity will let you calculate how much a regular investment will be worth at some point in the future. For instance, if you put $50 per month into a savings account that pays 5% per year, how much money will be in the account at the end of five years? To solve that problem, you would use a Future Value of an annuity function.

The Present Value of an annuity will let you determine what a series of regular payments is worth today. For instance, if you buy a car and the dealer says they will let you drive away today for $250 per month for five years at 9%, you can calculate exactly what they are charging you for the car by using the Present Value of an annuity function. Another popular example is the lottery. If you win $100 million, you will not receive a check for that amount. What you have really won is the right to receive a check for $5 million per year for each of the next 20 years. If you want all the money up front, they will write a check for much less than $100 million.

The best way to answer time value of money questions and to feel comfortable with them is to practice. Let's walk through some examples together. When we are done we will understand time value of money and how to use the calculator to answer specific questions.

 Let's go back to Grandma. Instead of her giving you $2,500 on the day you were born, she deposited $10,000 in an account that has been earning 12% for 20 years. How much is in the account now?

Before we can answer the question using our calculator, we have to determine the three solid pieces of information and fill in our puzzle pieces. We know that Grandma deposited $10,000 in an account. Which puzzle piece does the $10,000 represent? Clearly it is not the interest rate or the number of time periods. You may think that $10,000 is a payment that Grandma made, but in time value of money payment means more than one. Because this is a one-time deposit, we do not want to put it in the payment (PMT) puzzle piece. That only leaves the present value (PV) and future value (FV) puzzle pieces. We call these present value (PV) and future value (FV) in the puzzle pieces so they match the calculator keys. What they really mean are beginning value (PV) and ending value (FV).

So where does the $10,000 go in our puzzle? Because Grandma put the money in the account 20 years ago the $10,000 is our beginning value and goes in the present value (PV) puzzle piece. Which puzzle piece does the 12% represent? We always put the interest rate in the (I/Y) puzzle piece. Which puzzle piece does the 20 years represent? We always put the length of time in the (N) puzzle piece.

Having filled in three pieces of the puzzle, we have to determine which remaining puzzle piece represents the question and which puzzle piece can be ignored. Because Grandma put the money in 20 years ago, the question, "How much is in the account now?" represents our ending value (FV), and we ignore the payment (PMT) puzzle piece.

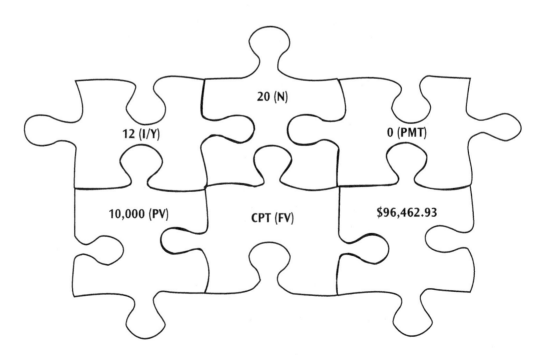

Now we can enter the data into the calculator using the following steps:

We begin by clearing the calculator memory.

◆ Press the "Second" key.

◆ Press the "CLR TVM" key (you have now cleared the memory).

◆ Press the "CE/C" key (just to clear the display).

Enter the $10,000 that Grandma deposited in the beginning.

◆ Press "1", "0", "0", "0", "0" to enter 10,000 onto the display.

◆ Press the "PV" key. The calculator will now display "PV = 10,000.00".

Enter the 12% interest rate that she earned.

◆ Press "1", "2" to enter 12 onto the display.

◆ Press the "I/Y" key. The calculator will now display "I/Y = 12.00".

Enter the 20-year length of time that the money was in the account.

◆ Press "2", "0" to enter 20 onto the display.

◆ Press the "N" key. The calculator will now display "N = 20.00".

Now answer the question, "How much is in the account now?"

◆ Press the "CPT" key.

◆ Press the "FV" key. The calculator will now compute the future value for you. The calculator will display "FV = –96,462.93". The answer is $96,462.93.

*Congratulations!* You have just answered your first time value of money question. Remember, given any three pieces of information, you can answer the question. Let's look at the same account but answer a different question.

Your grandmother deposited some money into an account for you 20 years ago. The money has grown at a 12% interest rate to $96,462.93. How much money did Grandma put into the account in the beginning?

Once again, before we can answer the question using our calculator, we have to determine the three solid pieces of information and fill in our puzzle pieces. We know that Grandma put money in the account 20 years ago. Which puzzle piece does the 20 years represent? We always put the length of time in the (N) puzzle piece. We know that Grandma earned 12% interest. Which puzzle piece does the 12% represent? We always put the interest rate in the (I/Y) puzzle piece. We also know the account now has $96,462.93 in it. This is our ending value. Because the $96,462.93 is the ending value, it goes in our (FV) puzzle piece.

Having filled in three pieces of the puzzle, we have to determine which remaining puzzle piece represents the question and which puzzle piece can be ignored. The only two pieces left are the present value (PV) and payment (PMT) pieces. The question, "How much money did Grandma put into the account in the beginning?" implies a one-time deposit, so we do not want to put it in the (PMT) puzzle piece.

Our question is really asking, "What is the beginning value (PV)?" and we ignore the payment (PMT) puzzle piece.

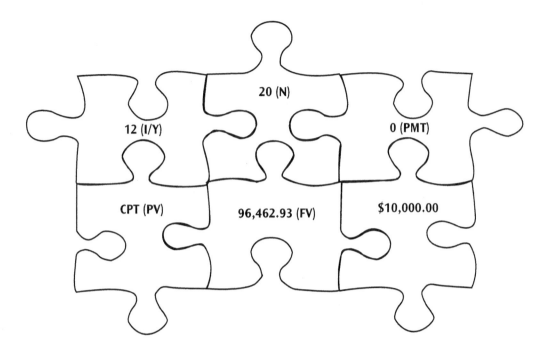

Now we can enter the data into the calculator using the following steps:

We begin by clearing the calculator memory.

- ◆ Press the "Second" key.

- ◆ Press the "CLR TVM" key (you have now cleared the memory).

- ◆ Press the "CE/C" key (just to clear the display).

Enter the 20-year length of time that the money was in the account.

- ◆ Press "2", "0" to enter 20 onto the display.

- ◆ Press the "N" key. The calculator will now display "N = 20.00".

Enter the 12% interest rate that she earned.

- ◆ Press "1", "2" to enter 12 onto the display.

- ◆ Press the "I/Y" key. The calculator will now display "I/Y = 12.00".

Enter the $96,462.93 that is in the account.

- ◆ Press "9", "6", "4", "6", "2", ".", "9", "3" to enter 96,462.93 onto the display.

- ◆ Press the "FV" key. The calculator will now display "FV = 96,462.93".

Now answer the question, "How much money did Grandma put into the account in the beginning?"

- ◆ Press the "CPT" key.

- ◆ Press the "PV" key. The calculator will now compute the present value. The calculator will now display "PV = –10,000.00". The answer is $10,000.

*Double congratulations!* You have just answered your second time value of money question. Just like the first example, we determined three pieces of information and we answered the question. Let's answer yet a different question, but this time with a twist.

Your grandmother left you an account with $96,462.93 in it. She originally put $10,000 in it 20 years ago. What interest rate did Grandma earn?

Just like the previous two examples, before we can answer the question using our calculator we have to determine the three solid pieces of information and fill in our puzzle pieces. We know that the account has $96,462.93 in it. What puzzle piece does this represent? Because the $96,462.93 is the ending value it goes in our (FV) puzzle piece. We know she originally deposited $10,000. Because this is our beginning value, it goes in our (PV) puzzle piece. We put the 20 years in the (N) puzzle piece.

Having filled in three pieces of the puzzle, we have to determine which remaining puzzle piece represents the question and which puzzle piece can be ignored. The question, "What interest rate did Grandma earn?" represents our (I/Y) puzzle piece, and we ignore the payment (PMT) puzzle piece.

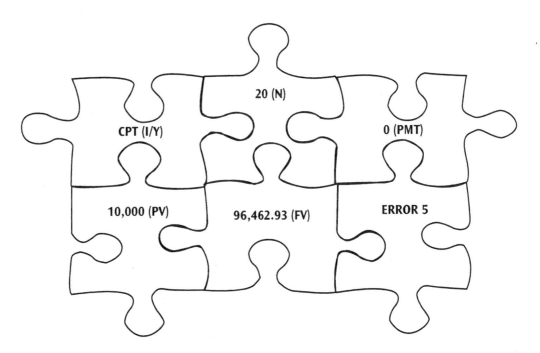

Now we can enter the data into the calculator using the following steps:

We begin by clearing the calculator memory.

◆ Press the "Second" key.

◆ Press the "CLR TVM" key (you have now cleared the memory).

◆ Press the "CE/C" key (just to clear the display).

Enter the $96,462.93 that was in the account.

◆ Press "9", "6", "4", "6", "2", ".", "9", "3" to enter 96,462.93 onto the display.

◆ Press the "FV" key. The calculator will now display "FV = 96,462.93".

Enter the $10,000 that Grandma deposited in the beginning.

◆ Press "1", "0", "0", "0", "0" to enter 10,000 onto the display.

◆ Press the "PV" key. The calculator will now display "PV = 10,000.00".

Enter the 20-year length of time that the money was in the account.

◆ Press "2", "0" to enter 20 onto the display.

◆ Press the "N" key. The calculator will now display "N = 20.00".

Now answer the question, "What interest rate did Grandma earn?"

◆ Press the "CPT" key.

◆ Press the "I/Y" key. The calculator will now compute the Interest Rate for you.

This calculator will display "**ERROR 5**". You may get a similar error in other calculators. Why did we get the error? When you are solving for either the interest rate (I/Y) or the length of time (N), one of the dollar amounts you enter into the calculator must be positive and one must be negative.

Think of it this way, Grandma took $10,000 out of her pocket and put it in the account. Less money means an outflow for Grandma, and we would enter a negative $10,000 as our beginning value (PV) in the calculator. At the end of the 20 years we get to withdraw $96,462.93 from the account and put that money in our pocket. This is an inflow to us, and we would enter a positive $96,462.93 as our ending value (FV) in the calculator. Inflows of money are positive, and outflows of money are negative.

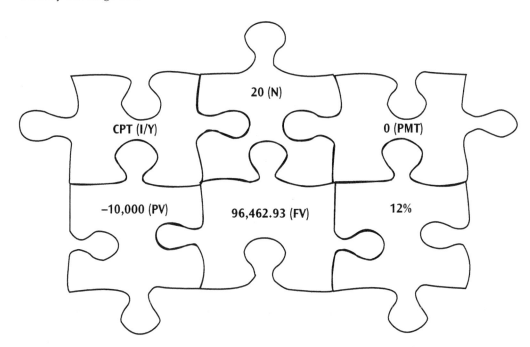

To fix this issue, you need to clear the calculator display to get rid of the error message, but you do not have to clear the memory. We only want to change one number while leaving the others the same in the memory.

Clear the display.

◆ Press the "CE/C" key (just to clear the display).

Enter the $10,000 that Grandma deposited in the beginning.

◆ Press "1", "0", "0", "0", "0" to enter 10,000 onto the display.

◆ Press the "+/–" key. This will change the amount to a negative. The calculator will now display –10,000.

◆ Press the "PV" key. The calculator will now display "PV = –10,000.00".

Now that we fixed the error, we can answer the question, "What interest rate did Grandma earn?"

Press the "CPT" key.

Press the "I/Y" key. The calculator will now compute the Interest Rate for you. The calculator will display "I/Y = 12.00". The answer is 12.00%.

*Triple congratulations!* You not only answered your third time value of money question, but you have also just learned one of the key principles of using a financial calculator; the concept of cash inflow and cash outflow. Let's look at this time value of money example one more time.

Your Grandmother left you an account with $96,462.93 in it. She originally deposited $10,000 at 12% interest. How long did it take for the account to grow this big?

Let's determine the three solid pieces of information and fill in our puzzle pieces. Because the $96,462.93 is the ending value, it goes in our (FV) puzzle piece. Her original deposit of $10,000 goes in our (PV) puzzle piece. We put the 12% interest rate in the (I/Y) puzzle piece.

Having filled in three pieces of our puzzle, we can see that the question, "How long did it take for the account to grow this big?" is our (N) puzzle piece, and we ignore the payment (PMT) puzzle piece.

Now we can enter the data into the calculator using the following steps:

We begin by clearing the calculator memory.

◆ Press the "Second" key.

◆ Press the "CLR TVM" key (you have now cleared the memory).

◆ Press the "CE/C" key (just to clear the display).

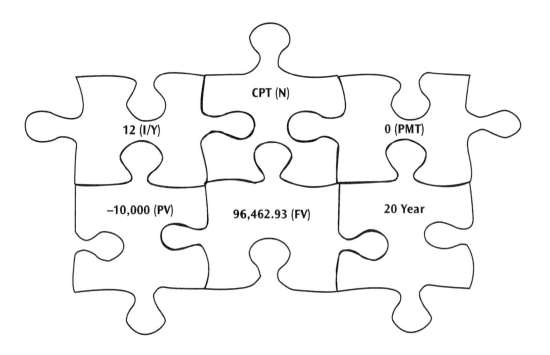

Enter the $96,462.93 that was in the account.

- ◆ Press "96462.93" to enter 96,462.93 onto the display.

- ◆ Press the "FV" key. The calculator will now display "FV = 96,462.93".

Enter the $10,000 that Grandma deposited in the beginning.

- ◆ Press "10000" to enter 10,000 onto the display.

- ◆ Press the "+/−" key. This will change the amount to a negative. The calculator will now display −10,000.

- ◆ Press the "PV" key. The calculator will now display "PV = −10,000.00".

Enter the 12% interest rate that she earned.

- ◆ Press "12" to enter 12 onto the display.

- ◆ Press the "I/Y" key. The calculator will now display "I/Y = 12.00".

Now answer the question, "How long did it take for the account to grow this big?"

- ◆ Press the "CPT" key.

- ◆ Press the "N" key. The calculator will now compute the number of time periods. The calculator will display "N = 20.00". The answer is 20 years.

So far we have solved four of the five puzzle pieces but have ignored the payment (PMT) puzzle piece. What happens if rather than Grandma making a one-time deposit, she made a deposit each year to our account? Remember earlier that we defined an annuity as equal payments at equal time intervals. That means if Grandma makes annual deposits of the same amount into the account, we have an annuity. Any time we have an annuity we will use the payment (PMT) puzzle piece.

Grandma gave Mom a choice 20 years ago. She asked if she should deposit $10,000 into an account when you were born or if she should instead deposit $1,000 a year into that same account every year for 20 years. We know today the account has $96,462.93 in it. Did Mom make the right decision?

This is two separate time value of money questions. We have already answered the first question. We know what Mom chose. She asked Grandma to make a one-time deposit of $10,000 at 12% interest for 20 years, which grew to $96,462.93. The second part of our time value of money question is how much would have been in the account if Mom had made the other choice?

 If Mom had asked Grandma to deposit $1,000 in the account each year for 20 years earning 12%, how much money would be in the account today?

Just like the previous examples, we can answer the question using our calculator after having determined the three solid pieces of information and filling in our puzzle pieces. Our new piece of information here is the $1,000 that Grandma is going to put into the account for us every year. This meets the definition of an annuity and would therefore go into our payment (PMT) puzzle piece. We also know Grandma was going to make 20 payments. This goes in the (N) puzzle piece. Grandma was going to earn 12% interest, and we know this goes in the (I/Y) puzzle piece.

Having filled in three pieces of the puzzle, we have to determine which remaining puzzle piece represents the question and which puzzle piece can be ignored. The question, "How much money would be in the account today?" represents our ending value (FV) puzzle piece, and we ignore the beginning value (PV) puzzle piece. In this case the beginning value was ignored (and is *not* $1,000) because there was not a one-time payment. The first $1,000 payment is accounted for in the payment (PMT) puzzle piece. When we fill in the payment (PMT) puzzle piece, the (N) puzzle piece becomes not just how many years there are but also represents how many payments were made.

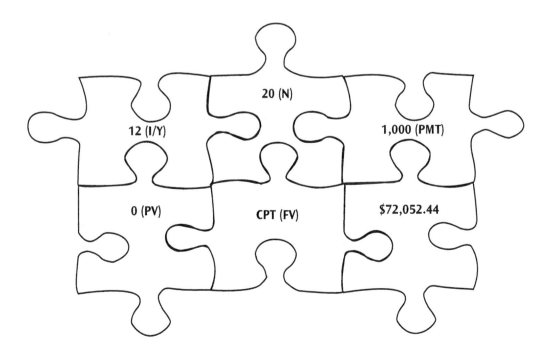

Now we can enter the data into the calculator using the following steps:

We begin by clearing the calculator memory.

- ◆ Press the "Second" key.

- ◆ Press the "CLR TVM" key (you have now cleared the memory).

- ◆ Press the "CE/C" key (just to clear the display).

Enter the $1,000 that Grandma was going to deposit into the account each year.

- ◆ Press "1000" to enter 1,000 onto the display.

- ◆ Press the "PMT" key. The calculator will now display "PMT = 1,000.00".

Enter the 20-year length of time that Grandma will be making deposits.

- ◆ Press "20" to enter 20 onto the display.

- ◆ Press the "N" key. The calculator will now display "N = 20.00".

Enter the 12% interest rate that she earned.

- ◆ Press "12" to enter 12 onto the display.

- ◆ Press the "I/Y" key. The calculator will now display "I/Y = 12.00".

Now answer the question, "How much money would be in the account today?"

- ◆ Press the "CPT" key.

- ◆ Press the "FV" key. The calculator will now compute the future value for you. The calculator will display "FV = –72,052.44". The answer is $72,052.44.

Did Mom make the right decision? Absolutely! We ended up with $96,462.93, which is $24,410.49 more than the $72,052.44 we would have ended with if Grandma had made annual payments instead.

Even though the second option meant Grandma was depositing a total of $20,000 over 20 years, Mom made a smart financial decision because she understood time value of money.

# COMPOUNDING

So far every example we have looked at has expressed time in years. In real life, time is usually expressed in something other than years such as quarters, months, weeks or even days. How do we account for these different time periods? One word: compounding (when your interest earns interest).

Typically you will find the following compounding periods per year:

**Annual** (once per year)          **Monthly** (twelve times per year)

**Semiannual** (twice per year)     **Weekly** (fifty two times per year)

**Quarterly** (four times per year) **Daily** (365 times per year)

This can be represented by the following graph. The only thing that is being changed is the compounding periods per year. As you can see, the more often the interest rate is compounded per year, the more money you have at the end of the year.

*Affect of compounding on $100 at a 12% interest rate with different compounding periods per year.*

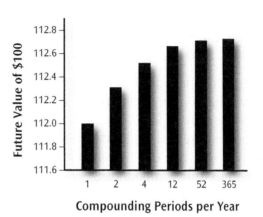

How do we account for compounding when we use the calculator to solve time value of money problems? When you are calculating a time value of money problem using more than one compounding per year, you have to:

Divide the interest rate by the number of compounding periods per year to find the interest rate per period.

**Annual** (divide by 1)          **Monthly** (divide by 12)

**Semiannual** (divide by 2)      **Weekly** (divide by 52)

**Quarterly** (divide by 4)       **Daily** (divide by 365)

And

Multiply the number of years by the number of compounding periods per year to find the total number of compounding periods.

**Annual** (multiply by 1)          **Monthly** (multiply by 12)

**Semiannual** (multiply by 2)      **Weekly** (multiply by 52)

**Quarterly** (multiply by 4)       **Daily** (multiply by 365)

Ultimately, you must have agreement among the time periods, the interest rate, and the payments.

In the real world interest rates are almost always given as annual rates. However, they are almost always calculated as quarterly, monthly, or something other than annual so they agree with our payment and time periods. It is essential that we understand how the interest rates on our credit cards, car loans or student loans are calculated so that we make good financial decisions.

Let's take a look at how this works.

 Remember the account that Grandma left us? She initially deposited $10,000 in it 20 years ago, and it earned a 12% annual interest rate. If the account was compounded *monthly* instead of *annually* how much would be in the account now?

Just like in every example so far, we can answer the question using our calculator after having determined the three solid pieces of information and filling in our puzzle pieces. Our new piece of information here is that the compounding periods per year changed. Because the compounding period is something other than annual, we must have agreement between the time periods and the interest rate per period. How do we do this?

The initial deposit of $10,000 still represents our beginning value and goes in our (PV) puzzle piece. This amount is never adjusted for the compounding periods. It is a one-time deposit. The 20 years is our length of time and goes in our (N) puzzle piece but must be adjusted for the change in the compounding periods per year. In this case this is done by *multiplying* 20 years times 12 months because the example uses monthly compounding. There are 12 months in a year so we get 240 months over 20 years. That means "240" is entered in the (N) puzzle piece.

The 12% interest rate goes in our (I/Y) puzzle piece but must also be adjusted for the change in the compounding periods per year. In this case this is done by *dividing* 12% annual interest rate by 12 months because the example uses monthly compounding. There are 12 months in a year so we get 1% interest rate per month. That means "1" is entered in the (I/Y) puzzle piece.

Having filled in three pieces of the puzzle, we have to determine which remaining puzzle piece represents the question and which puzzle piece can be ignored. The question, "How much money would be in the account now?" represents our ending value (FV) puzzle piece, and we ignore the payment (PMT) puzzle piece.

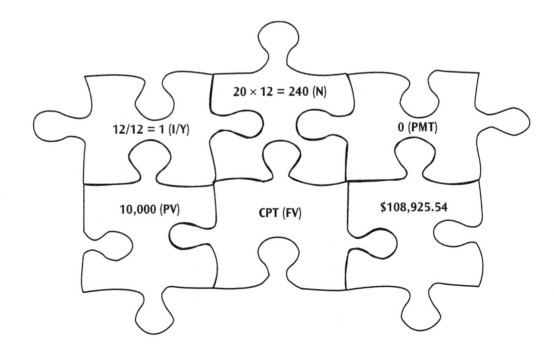

Now we can enter the data into the calculator using the following steps:

We begin by clearing the calculator memory.

◆ Press the "Second" key.

◆ Press the "CLR TVM" key (you have now cleared the memory).

◆ Press the "CE/C" key (just to clear the display).

Enter the $10,000 that Grandma deposited in the beginning.

◆ Press "10000" to enter 10,000 onto the display.

◆ Press the "PV" key. The calculator will now display "PV = 10,000.00".

Enter the length of time that the money was in the account having adjusted for the 12 monthly compounding periods per year.

◆ Press "240" to enter 240 onto the display.

◆ Press the "N" key. The calculator will now display "N = 240.00".

Enter the interest rate Grandma earned having adjusted for the 12 monthly compounding periods per year.

◆ Press "1" to enter 1 onto the display.

◆ Press the "I/Y" key. The calculator will now display "I/Y = 1.00".

Now answer the question, "How much would be in the account now?"

◆ Press the "CPT" key.

◆ Press the "FV" key. The calculator will now compute the future value for you. The calculator will display "FV = –108,925.54". The answer is $108,925.54.

Notice the difference that the change in compounding periods per year made to the ending value (FV) in the account. When Grandma earned *annual* compounding, the ending value (FV) of the account was $96,462.93. When Grandma earned *monthly* compounding, the ending value (FV) was $108,925.54. That's a difference of $12,462.61. Even though the annual interest rate was the same, the account with more compounding periods per year resulted in more money than the account with one compounding period year.

What if Grandma gave Mom another choice 20 years ago? She asked Mom if she should make a one-time deposit of $10,000 into an account that compounded interest annually or if she should instead deposit $100 a month for 20 years into an account with monthly compounding. Did Mom make the right decision?

This is two separate time value of money questions. We have already answered the first question. We know that the $10,000 one-time deposit compounded annually grew to $96,462.93. The second part of our time value of money question is how much would have been in the account if Mom had made the other choice?

 If Mom had asked Grandma to deposit $100 in the account each month for 20 years earning 12% compounded monthly how much money would be in the account today?

Just like the previous examples, we can answer the question using our calculator after having determined the three solid pieces of information and filling in our puzzle pieces. Our new piece of information here is the $100 payment that Grandma is going to put into the account for us every month. This meets the definition of an annuity and therefore goes into our payment (PMT) puzzle piece.

The 20 years is our length of time and goes in our (N) puzzle piece but must be adjusted for the change in the compounding periods per year. In this case this is done by *multiplying* 20 years times 12 months because the example uses monthly compounding. There are 12 months in a year so we get 240 months over 20 years. That means "240" is entered in the (N) puzzle piece.

The 12% interest rate goes in our (I/Y) puzzle piece but must also be adjusted for the change in the compounding periods per year. In this case this is done by *dividing* 12% annual interest rate by 12 months because the example uses monthly compounding. There are 12 months in a year, so we get 1% interest rate per month. That means "1" is entered in the (N) puzzle piece.

Having filled in three pieces of the puzzle, we have to determine which remaining puzzle piece represents the question and which puzzle piece can be ignored. The question, "How much money would be in the account today?" represents our ending value (FV) puzzle piece, and we ignore the beginning value (PV) puzzle piece. In this case the beginning value was ignored (and is *not* $100) because there was not a one-time payment. The first $100 payment is accounted for in the payment (PMT) puzzle piece. When we fill in the payment (PMT) puzzle piece, the (N) puzzle piece becomes not just how many years there are but also represents how many payments were made.

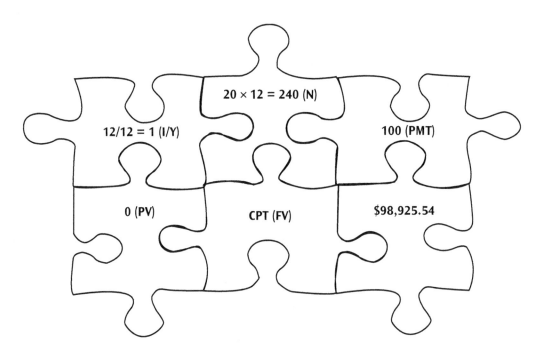

Now we can enter the data into the calculator using the following steps:

We begin by clearing the calculator memory.

- Press the "Second" key.

- Press the "CLR TVM" key (you have now cleared the memory).

- Press the "CE/C" key (just to clear the display).

Enter the $100 that Grandma was going to deposit into the account each month.

- Press "100" to enter 100 onto the display.

- Press the "PMT" key. The calculator will now display "PMT = 100.00".

Enter the length of time that the money was in the account having adjusted for the 12 monthly compounding periods per year.

- Press "240" to enter 240 onto the display.

- Press the "N" key. The calculator will now display "N = 240.00".

Enter the interest rate Grandma earned having adjusted for the 12 monthly compounding periods per year.

- Press "1" to enter 1 onto the display.

- Press the "I/Y" key. The calculator will now display "I/Y = 1.00".

Now answer the question, "How much money would be in the account today?"

- Press the "CPT" key.

- Press the "FV" key. The calculator will now compute the future value for you. The calculator will display "FV = –98,925.54". The answer is $98,925.54.

Did Mom make the right decision? Not this time. We ended up with $96,462.93 which is $2,462.61 *less than* the $98,925.54 we would have ended with if Grandma had made monthly payments instead. Had Mom fully understood time value of money, she would have made a better financial decision.

Let's take a look at one final example. Assume that Grandma did not deposit any money in any account for us. That means we will have to pay for college ourselves. Because we don't have the cash to pay for college, we had to take out student loans.

 After four years of college, we owe $20,000 in student loans. The current annual interest rate is 6% compounded monthly. We are going to take 10 years to repay the loan. How much is our monthly student loan payment?

Just like in every example so far, we can answer the question using our calculator after having determined the three solid pieces of information and filling in our puzzle pieces. Because the compounding period is something other than annual, we must have agreement among the time periods, the interest rate per period, and the payment per period. How do we do this?

The initial loan amount of $20,000 represents our beginning value and goes in our (PV) puzzle piece. In a loan calculation the loan amount is always the beginning value (PV). This amount is never adjusted for the compounding periods. We only borrow the money one-time, and we get it at the beginning.

The 6% interest rate goes in our (I/Y) puzzle piece but must be adjusted for the number of compounding periods per year. In this case this is done by *dividing* 6% annual interest rate by 12 months because the example uses monthly compounding. There are 12 months in a year, so we get 0.5% interest rate per month. That means "0.5" is entered in the (I/Y) puzzle piece.

The 10 years it will take us to pay off our loan is the length of time and goes in our (N) puzzle piece but must also be adjusted for the number of compounding periods per year. In this case this is done by *multiplying* 10 years times 12 months because the example uses monthly compounding. There are 12 months in a year, so we get 120 months over 10 years. That means "120" is entered in the (N) puzzle piece.

Having filled in three pieces of the puzzle, we have to determine which remaining puzzle piece represents the question and which puzzle piece can be ignored. The question, "How much is our monthly student loan payment?" represents our payment (PMT) puzzle piece, and we ignore the ending value (FV) puzzle piece.

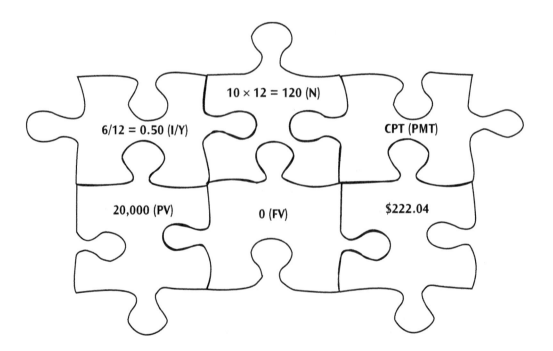

Now we can enter the data into the calculator using the following steps:

We begin by clearing the calculator memory.

◆ Press the "Second" key.

◆ Press the "CLR TVM" key (you have now cleared the memory).

◆ Press the "CE/C" key (just to clear the display).

Enter the $20,000 that we borrowed in student loans.

◆ Press "20000" to enter 20,000 onto the display.

◆ Press the "PV" key. The calculator will now display "PV = 20,000.00".

Enter the interest rate on the student loans.

◆ Press "0.5" to enter 0.5 onto the display.

◆ Press the "I/Y" key. The calculator will now display "I/Y = 0.50".

Enter the length of time that you will be making your student loan payments.

◆ Press "120" to enter 120 onto the display.

◆ Press the "N" key. The calculator will now display "N = 120.00".

Now answer the question, "How much is our monthly student loan payment for the next ten years?"

◆ Press the "CPT" key.

◆ Press the "PMT" key. The calculator will now compute the monthly payment for you. The calculator will display "PMT = –222.04". The answer is $222.04.

A full understanding of time value of money and a simple financial calculator greatly improves your financial literacy. You can easily determine how long it will take to pay off your credit card if you increase your monthly payment, or you can determine how much money you will have to deposit each month to have a down payment for a car. You now have the knowledge and the tools to make the best financial decisions for you.

# THE COST OF  FINANCIAL IGNORANCE

Our student from our first class had waited 10 years before saving for his retirement. He had graduated from college when he was 25 and now at 35 wanted to choose a retirement plan that would allow him and his wife to retire in comfort when they reached 65. He still had 30 years to save for retirement, but waiting just 10 years to get started had cost him a lot of money. In fact, had he started saving just $100 per month when he was 25, he could have stopped now at age 35 and still had more money for retirement than by starting at age 35 and saving $100 per month for the next 30 years.

| | |
|---|---|
| Save $100 per month from age 25 to 35 then withdraw at age 65 | $285,057 |
| OR INSTEAD | |
| Save $100 per month from age 35 to 65 | $183,074 |
| Total Cost of Financial Ignorance | **$101, 983** |

# RULES OF THE ROAD

## Automobiles—The Good, the Bad, the Ugly

A student dropped by our office superexcited. Her grandparents had given her a $5,000 graduation gift that she was using as a down payment on a new car. She spent an entire day shopping, talking with car salespersons, negotiating prices, and arranging financing. She was ready to sign on the dotted line and was particularly proud of the fact that she negotiated the price a whopping $6,500 below the sticker price. In her mind, she was a master negotiator.

However, before she signed all the paperwork she wanted us to confirm that it really was a good deal and that she was not missing any critical pieces. Imagine her disappointment when we told her that she was being ripped off and the dealer was making out like a bandit. How was the dealer taking advantage of her while making her feel good about it at the same time?

# ARE CARS A NECESSITY?

Do you need a car? Is owning a car a necessity or is it a luxury? Do you live in a major city with a reliable public transportation system? Is it simply more convenient to own a car although you really could take public transportation if you had to? Of course owning a car is more convenient than having to wait for public transportation because you can leave exactly when you want to, but have you considered how much you are paying for that luxury? If you live in a rural area or a city with no public transportation, you have little or no choice but to own some type of transportation. Assuming that riding a bicycle everywhere is out of the question, you will likely purchase a car. Now you have to decide what type of car you will purchase. Do you have the cash to purchase a sports car or a luxury car? Maybe you will have room in your budget for a car loan to get something halfway decent. If you are instead going to focus on paying down your college loans and saving to buy a house, you may drive a P.O.S. car instead. (Of course, P.O.S. is short for Piece of Sheet metal. What were you thinking?)

Ask yourself the following question, "How many people do I admire or respect because of the car they drive?" Notice there was no mention of "envy" or "jealousy." The question was how many people you *admire* because of the car they drive. If you are like most people, the answer is going to be zero. People do not admire others because of the car they drive, so there is no reason to expect that anyone will admire you because of the car you drive. Think about it this way. Everyone you are friends with likes you because of who you are; not what you drive. Anyone you do not know who wants to judge you based on the car you drive is too shallow to be worth your time anyway.

When you go to buy a car it is critical that you make a smart financial decision. The dealer will work tirelessly to try to get you to make a decision based purely on your emotions. You will hear phrases such as "Imagine yourself in that car," and "Can't you just see the look on your neighbors' faces when you pull up in that beauty?" Both are examples of little seeds being planted to steer you toward making an emotional decision. Almost any emotion will work in the dealer's favor. You can purchase a car because you are jealous of someone else, or because you are angry about driving your parent's station wagon for the past four years, or maybe you are just excited about graduating. People who make emotional decisions seldom make good financial decisions. Think about the last time you got into an argument with your boyfriend or girlfriend. Now think about some of the things you said (or some of the things that he or she said). Add to that some of the decisions you made immediately after the argument or after a bad breakup. Those same emotions can be used against you when you are making a purchase because you are not thinking rationally.

How many cars over your lifetime do you think you will purchase? Maybe 10 or 15? Do you think at any point in your lifetime that you will become an expert at car buying from purchasing a car about every five years? Now consider that the dealer sells that many cars in a week. Who do you think is better at this game? How much money do you think you will end up spending on cars over your lifetime (just the purchase price, not including maintenance or repairs)? You will easily spend between $200,000 and $250,000 on car purchases throughout your lifetime. The fact is that for most of us, besides our house and our retirement, cars will take more of our money than any other purchase.[22] The auto industry, from the local dealer to the manufacturing facilities, want to take as much of that money from us as they possibly can.

If you add a spouse to the total, you could easily spend more than a half a million dollars on cars over your lifetime as a couple. Now you can begin to understand why so much advertising money is spent trying to convince you that you will feel better about yourself and others will think more highly of you if you drive a particular car.

If we can show you how to save $2,000 to $3,000 for each time you buy a car would you be interested? Would it be worth your time to keep reading? Not only do most people not know the rules, but they do not even realize that there is a game being played. Remember, if you make an emotional decision, the dealer wins.

## A Car by Any Other Name . . .

What is a car? In other words, what are you really buying when you purchase a car? If you guessed transportation, you are partially correct. Let us start with what a car is not. A car is not a status symbol, it is not a fashion statement, and it is not a sign of your masculinity or your femininity. Despite what all the expensive and targeted advertising tries to get you to believe, a car is nothing more than a tool or a machine. A car is, quite simply, a steel box with wheels that contains about 150,000 miles. So, when you buy a car, you are buying a box of miles. If you buy a new car, you will get a box of about 150,000 miles on average. If you buy a used car, you will get 150,000 miles minus the current number of miles already on the car. The question you have to ask yourself is do you want to buy an expensive box, a mid-price box, or an inexpensive box.

### *Total Cost of Ownership*

When you create your cash flow statement and try to determine how much you can afford as a monthly car payment, you need to make sure that you have included a reasonable amount of money for your car maintenance. It is expected that buying a new car will result in minimal maintenance costs, which is generally true. However, keep in mind that all cars have scheduled maintenance that needs to be done, and most of those costs begin after the warranty period expires, but before a five-year car loan is paid off. According to Edmunds.com, the average cost over five years for maintenance and repair of a brand new Honda Civic is almost $1,900, including nearly $800 in year four (based on recommended preventative maintenance), with similar types of cars having similar costs.[23]

In addition, you have to consider how much you will pay for insurance and fuel, as well as any state property taxes and annual title and tag fees. Because state property taxes are based on the value of the car, new cars are going to have higher fees than used cars.

The more expensive your car, the more you can expect to pay in scheduled maintenance and the higher each repair bill will be. A safe bet would be to have 20% of your monthly payment set aside for maintenance and repairs. Understand that for the first couple of years of ownership you may have little or no maintenance or repair expenses, but keeping this money set aside will make it easier when you receive your first major repair bill of several hundred dollars. For example, if you have a $300 car payment, then you should set aside $300 × 20% = $60 per month. Using this same 20% rule for any major purchase will save your budget in the long run.

## Hidden Costs

Assume for a moment that after graduation you land an incredible job that pays an excellent salary. You qualify for a $30,000 car loan for 72 months (six years) at 8%. Using standard time value of money calculations, we can determine that the monthly payment would be $526.58.

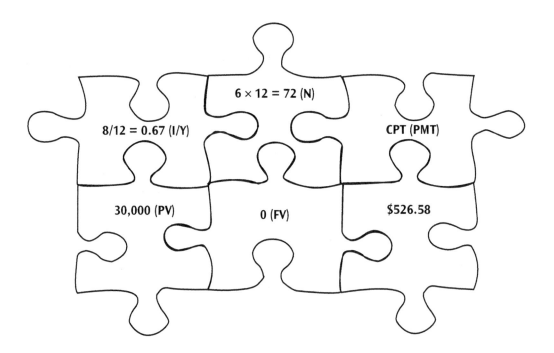

Just because you qualify for the $30,000 car and can afford the very large monthly payments does not mean that you have to spend that much money. There are plenty of nice cars that you could purchase for, say, $20,000. If you would purchase a $20,000 car instead, your payments would only be $351.06.

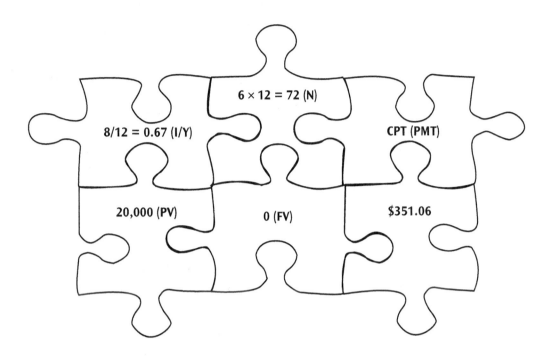

But why would anyone want to settle for a $20,000 car when they could afford a $30,000 car? Because every dollar you spend on a car payment (or anything else that costs more than a few hundred dollars, for that matter) is a dollar you no longer have available for the future. Also, because you committed to a lower payment, when you experience financial difficulties, you can still meet all your monthly obligations and still keep your sanity.

If you take the difference between the two payments, you would have $175.00 extra each month ($526.58 − 351.06 = $175.52). If you invest the $175.52 savings over the next six years (the length of the loan in this example) you would have $16,172.82. Add your investment total to the value of your trade-in, and you will not only be able to pay cash for your next car, but you will actually be able to "move up" and get a slightly nicer car without having to finance anything. If you would do this just one time for your first car, you may never have to borrow money for any future car purchases. There are few sweeter feelings than paying for a car in full with cash.

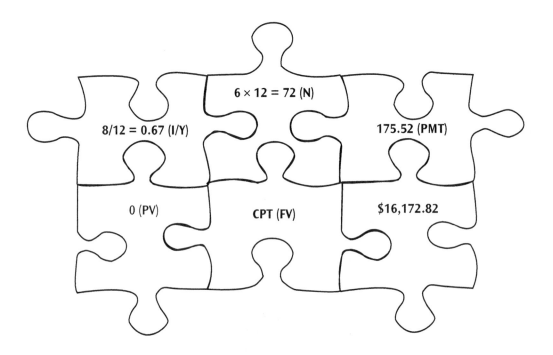

Of course your other option is to pay the full $526.58 toward your $20,000 car, and you will have the loan paid off completely in just 44 months.

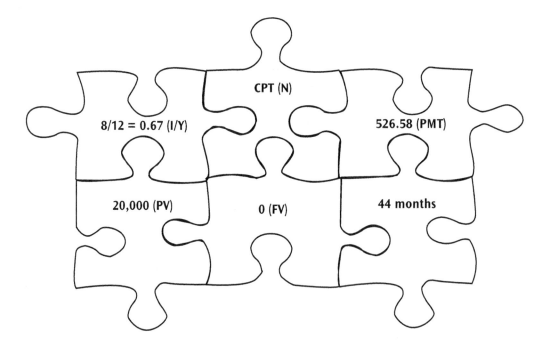

If you continue to invest the $526.58 per month for the remainder of the six-year period, you would also have a very large amount of money available to pay cash for your next car. The key is to figure out the maximum you can afford to pay and then back it down several steps to a less expensive car. Save the difference, and you can pay cash for your next car.

# HOW LONG SHOULD I KEEP MY CAR?

One of the factors used to determine how long to hang on to a car is the depreciation. Because most of the depreciation takes place in the early years of car ownership and slows down as the car gets older, the longer you keep the car, the less you will feel the impact of the depreciation. For instance, if the car depreciates $5,000 the first year but you keep the car for ten years, then that first year of depreciation was only $500 per year. On the other hand, if you only keep the car for five years, then that first year of depreciation is equivalent to $1,000 per year of car ownership.

If you want the luxury of owning a brand new car, then be aware of the extra costs associated with those first few years of depreciation. You will need to keep a new car for a very long time, otherwise the frequency of your car purchases will become a financial burden. You will have an endless cycle of car payments your whole life. Money that you spend on car payments is money that could have been used in other areas of your life such as saving for retirement, paying off credit cards, or saving for your child's education.

Consider the difference between fixed costs and variable costs. Owning a new car or having car payments means that your monthly cash flow statement has fixed costs. You have a constant monthly payment that does not change. You are locked into making your monthly car payment each month. Owning a used car long after you have paid it off means you will not have the fixed costs associated with monthly car payments. You will, however, have more variable costs. Variable costs change according to the need. One month you may have a $500 repair bill. Six months later you may have a $1,200 repair bill, and so forth. A general guide is to keep your car until the repairs exceed the value of the car or until the annual repairs exceed 12 month's worth of monthly payments.

For instance, if you have a repair bill on your used car of about $300 every six months and then you have a large $1,200 repair bill, you will quickly get sick of the car and all its problems. You will probably think it is cheaper to just buy a new car because you are angry at your current P.O.S. The problem is that you are thinking emotionally. If you add the two $300 repair bills to the $1,200 repair bill, that comes out to $1,800 in one year. If you think that you could get a new car cheaper, then you would have to buy a car with payments that are less than $150 per month. Most cars that are that inexpensive are high mileage used cars, which may have both fixed costs (monthly loan payments) and variable costs (repair bills). Deciding how long to keep a car is another emotional decision that may best be made by thinking financially instead of emotionally.

Now that you have determined you need a car, it is time to prepare for what can be one of the most damaging financial decisions you could ever make. You need to be prepared.

# THE CAR BUYING PROCESS

Now we understand that we want to buy financially and not emotionally. We also understand that if we find out how much we can afford and we buy something less expensive, we can save the difference, invest it, and come out much better in the end. How do we go about buying a car? What is the first thing most people do? Do they test drive the car? Look at the price? Look at the gas mileage?

Most people think that the first step is to go to the dealership and start looking at cars. As you can see, going to the dealership is actually the last step in the process. Most people do a poor job of correctly making a car purchase. We can conclude that if most people make poor car buying decisions, then we do not want to do the same thing that most people do. So what should we do first? Where do we start? We start by considering our cash flow statement.

**1. Look at Your Cash Flow Statement**

**2. Determine What You Can Afford**

**3. Decide New vs. Used**

**4. Decide Lease vs. Own**

**5. Research**

- Value of car for purchase
- Value of trade-in
- Financing options (see Credit chapter)
- Insurance cost (see Risk Management chapter)

**6. Now You Can Finally Visit a Dealership and Buy a Car!**

## Look at Your Cash Flow Statement

In the financial planning chapter we created a cash flow statement to determine how much money we have left over every month after accounting for our other bills and debt payments. Now we can determine how much is available for our anticipated car payment. Of course, there is no reason why every last dollar has to be used for a car payment, but at least we know the maximum amount we can spend each month.

We cannot stress this enough. The wrong way to purchase a car is to go onto a car lot first (or even the Internet), make an emotional decision (such as designing "your own car" by selecting all the options and so forth), make our purchase, and then go home and try to figure out how we will ever afford the monthly payments. The smart way to purchase a car is to start with our cash flow statement and determine how much of our remaining surplus we are willing to comfortably spend on our next car purchase.

## Determine What You Can Afford

Decide how much of the remaining budget surplus we are willing to spend on our car purchase. Then look at average financing costs. Why do we need to understand our financing options? Because we need to know how much the bank or finance company is going to charge in interest to calculate how much we can borrow, based on our monthly payment. Using the time value of money calculator again, we can determine how much we can borrow based on the length of the loan and the interest rate.

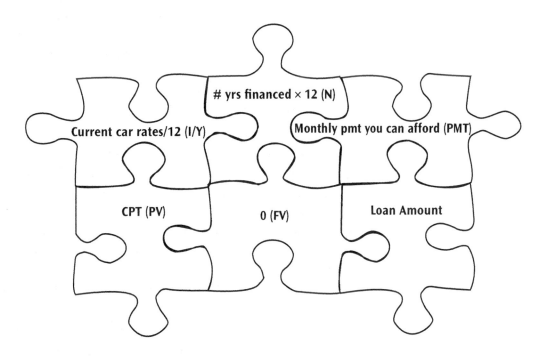

Now take the calculated loan amount and add any down payment and/or any expected trade-in value and we will know the maximum amount that we can pay for our car. Keep in mind, this is the maximum amount that we can pay, including all fees and expenses to drive our car off of the lot. We can always pay less, and then we will have that much more available cash each month to use for other priorities (such as the gas to put into the car).

Like any good late-night infomercial would say, "But wait . . . There's more . . ." We have to look at all the expenses and fees involved in purchasing a car. All costs must be discussed when making our car purchase because the dealer will always want to focus on the smallest dollar amount possible. Because we know exactly how much we can pay for the car based on our previous calculations, the total must include all the extras. Typically we can expect to pay some type of sales or highway tax (for instance, in 2010 the state of North Carolina charged a 3% highway tax). Tags are going to run another $50 to $100, and documentation fees will run as much as $500 or so, depending on the dealer. So what are documentation fees? These are fees that the dealer adds to pay their staff to do the paperwork necessary to complete the sale. In other words, documentation fees are simply additional profit for the dealer.

Be prepared to be offered what are commonly referred to as "rust and dust" fees. Usually these extra fees are only offered after you have already agreed on a purchase price. They are called "rust and dust" fees because they include services such as spraying the underside of your car with an antirust chemical and other similar extras that the dealers use to pad their profits.

## New versus Used

Now that we have determined how much we can afford, it is time to determine if we want to buy new or used. Somebody has to buy new cars for the rest of us to have the opportunity to buy the used ones. Maybe you are the person who will buy new cars. The goal is not to convince you to only buy new or only buy used, but rather to get you to stop and ask yourself "why" you are making the choice to buy new or used. You need to really think so you can determine what is right for you (not what seems right "to" you but what is right "for" you).

Why do most people buy a new car? One of the main reasons is to get that new car smell. Unfortunately, that new car smell will only last about two or three payments. That means that for the remaining 57 or 58 payments, your car will smell used, except you will have the higher payments of a new car. In fact, there really is no such thing as a new car. The moment you drive it off the lot, you become the proud owner of a used car with very low miles. The moment you drive your car off the lot, something else happens as well. Unless you made a huge down payment, you will owe more than the car is worth. This is such a common occurrence that there is even a name for your situation—you are upside down! Well, you are upside down on your car loan. On a five-year loan, you will be upside down for at least three years if you put no money down.

Consider this. When you get insurance coverage for your car, the insurance company only covers the value of the car, not the amount of your loan. So if you borrow $20,000 to buy a car with no money down and you drive it off the lot, it will be worth about $16,000. If you make a left-hand turn into traffic and total the car (hopefully nobody gets hurt), your insurance company will pay you the $16,000 that the car is now worth, but you will still owe the bank $20,000. Of course, there are some less than reputable salespeople that will gladly sell you gap insurance to cover the difference (gap insurance will be discussed later in the insurance section). So after all of this you are probably wondering what if any advantages are there to buying a new car. The major advantage to purchasing a new car is that there is less to worry about if something goes wrong with the car. If anything needs repair you can expect to get at least a three-year, 30,000 mile warranty, or possibly longer.

Because depreciation and finance charges usually represent the largest portion of the cost of owning a car, you will incur more immediate costs when purchasing a new car. Depreciation is much larger for new cars, especially when you consider that the initial depreciation of nearly 20% occurs the day you drive the car home. Used cars depreciate at a much slower rate, partly because the car simply starts out worth less than it did when it was brand new. So the best financial reason to buy a used car is because a majority of the depreciation is already built into the new price. One of the disadvantages is that you may be purchasing someone else's problems. Some of the savings in depreciation while purchasing a used car is offset by higher maintenance costs for used cars.

Generally, if you plan to trade your car in every five years or less, you may very well be better off purchasing lower-mileage used cars. If you are going to keep your car for a long time (several years after you have paid off the loan) then you may benefit from a new car. Essentially, you want to spread the high depreciation from the first few years over several additional years as the car ages and depreciates more slowly. In most cases, a new car will be more expensive to drive than a used one. The car buyer must ultimately decide if the incremental cost of owning a new car is worth the additional excitement from the purchase. Making the decision to buy new or used is more than a financial decision, it is a personal one. At least now you will be able to fully understand the financial implications while making that personal decision well prepared.

## Lease versus Own

Now that you have determined you are going to get a new car, should you purchase the car or lease it? The concept of leasing has always been that you can get more car than you could otherwise afford. Of course, if it is more than you could afford, you should probably not be driving it anyway. Leasing will allow you to drive a car for a lower payment than purchasing it. So, you could get the deluxe or sport edition of a car through leasing when you would only have been able to afford the basic version if you purchased it. You may also be able to step up to an entirely higher class of car.

So if it is cheaper or if you can get "more car" for the money, then why would anyone buy a car when they could lease? To begin with, you will never build any equity if you lease a car. After your three years of payments are complete, you will have to start all over with a new lease. You will not have any down payment available in the form of a trade-in, so whatever you need to put down on your next lease will have to come out of your pocket. In addition, we talked about how most of the depreciation takes place the first three years of a car's life. If you lease a car, you get to pay for the most expensive part of the depreciation, paying for the privilege of using the car during its most expensive period.

There are other disadvantages as well. Leases have mileage restrictions. If you drive more miles than the lease allows, you will have to pay a penalty for every mile you go over as determined by your contract. Similar to how cell phone plans with limited minutes charge exorbitant fees for every minute you go over, leases can result in the same type of penalty. Nothing says freedom like not being able to drive your own car the last few months of the lease, while still making the lease payment because you cannot afford the expensive per mile overage fee.

What exactly is a lease? Well, if you lease an apartment it means that you can use someone else's house or apartment for a period of time based on certain restrictions. You have to pay a fee to the owner and pay for any damages outside the normal wear and tear. The same thing applies to a car lease. You are essentially paying to borrow someone else's car. Again, keep in mind that you are responsible for any damage. Sometimes you may disagree with the dealer about what is considered normal wear and tear, so be prepared to plead your case.

In essence, with a lease you pay for the most expensive part of the depreciation period of the car, you have no equity, you have a limited number of miles you can drive without penalty, you have to continue the cycle because you have to give the car back at the end of the lease and get a new car, you are still responsible for the wear and tear on the car, and if your state charges property taxes, you are responsible for those as well, even though you do not own the car. The only real reason to lease a car may be if you own your own business and your car is designated for business purposes only. There are tax implications that may make sense for businesses to lease.

Owning a car on the other hand means that the car is yours, and it comes with all the benefits and all the problems. You do not have to worry about the mileage because the decision is up to you, without penalty. You will only have to deal with oil changes and basic maintenance for newer cars, whereas some major repairs may be necessary on older and higher-mileage used cars. You will also have some equity when you trade your car in for the next purchase, assuming you have paid off the loan.

Regardless of whether you are going to lease or buy, you still start with your budget. Determine how much you can afford for the payment first and then choose your vehicle. Once you have picked out the car you want, you are still not ready to visit the dealer. Now it is time to begin your research.

# Research

Now that we know how much we can afford and what kind of car we like, we want to make sure we determine fair value. In every step of the car-buying process, the seller, regardless of whether it's a dealer or individual, is interested in getting the most money for the car he or she is selling. If you do not want to pay the seller's price, then you better do your research.

## *Determine the Value of a New Car*

Now that you have established the amount you are willing to pay for a car, you can begin to look for cars in that price range. Everybody starts with the MSRP (Manufacturer Suggested Retail Price) or sticker price. The problem is that the MSRP has no real relationship to the value or the price you should pay for the car. It is simply a number that is set artificially high to get you to start your negotiation and work your way down.

By getting you to focus on the MSRP, you start with an extraordinarily large number, and you are excited when they start taking thousands of dollars off the sticker price. You feel like you got a really good deal. You are a master negotiator. You just bought your new car at 10 percent below sticker. Never mind that you still overpaid for the car.

We cannot stress this strongly enough. The sticker price is worthless.

---

**STANDARD EQUIPMENT**

*Functional*
- 4.2 EFI V-6 w/ 100K Miles
- Fail-safe cooling system
- 16" polished alum wheels
- Power windows/locks/mirrors
- Remote keyless entry
- Power steering
- 25 gal fuel tank

*Exterior*
- 4 doors
- Color keyed door handles
- Locking trailer tow wiring

Total MSRP  $37,500

*Interior*
- 40/60 reclining split bench
- Color keyed carpet
- Carpeted floor mats
- Leather wrapped steering wheel
- AM/FM stereo w/ single CD
- Visor vanity mirrors
- Dual cup holders

City MPG
15

Highway MPG
19

---

The real trick is not to start with the sticker price and work your way down, but to start with the price the dealer paid the manufacturer and work your way up. Notice that we did not say the invoice price. There is a difference between what the manufacturer "bills" the dealer for the car and the "price" the dealer actually pays for the car. So how do we get started?

First we want to know how much the dealer really paid for the car. Dealers love to show customers the invoice. They will tell you that you are buying the car at or below invoice price; that they will make their money on servicing the car. But how can a dealer sell you a car below what they paid for it? They can't. Not if they are going to stay in business. And you want the dealer to stay in business; otherwise there would be no one to service your car and nowhere to buy your next one. So you want to pay a price that is fair for you and fair for the dealer. You want the dealer to make a little profit off the car that you buy, but you do not want the dealer to spend a week in Tahiti with the profits from selling you that new SUV.

The problem is that the invoice price is padded to help line the dealer's pockets. Incentives and holdbacks are invisible to you, while inflating the dealer's profit. Incentives are "cash back" from the manufacturer to the dealer if the dealer sells you a car. Incentives can be just a few hundred to several thousand dollars. Holdbacks help the dealer finance the inventory he or she keeps on the lot. Typically holdbacks boost the invoice price by a small percentage. The dealer pays the "invoice" price to the manufacturer. At the end of each quarter, the manufacturer sends the dealer the holdback percentage for each car sold during that quarter. Even if you pay invoice price for the car, the dealer is still profiting from the sale.

Let us go back to the student mentioned at the beginning of the chapter. She was using a $5,000 graduation gift from her grandparents as a down payment on a new car. The car she wanted had an MSRP or sticker price of $37,500. The dealer showed her an invoice price of $30,900. The salesperson asked her what she thought a fair profit should be. Feeling very empowered she fervently answered, "No more than $100!" After the salesperson checked with the sales manager, they agreed to a price of $31,000 for the car. The salesperson actually told her that they would make it up on servicing the car for her. She gets the car for $6,500 off sticker. What a deal! The problem is she would have just overpaid for the car.

After looking up the car on both the Edmunds[24] and Consumer Reports[25] Web sites, we learned that the dealer would receive a $2,500 incentive and a 2% or $618 hold-back when the car sold. So the dealer originally paid the manufacturer the $30,900 invoice price for the car, but the manufacturer will turn around and send the dealer $3,118 as soon as the car sells.

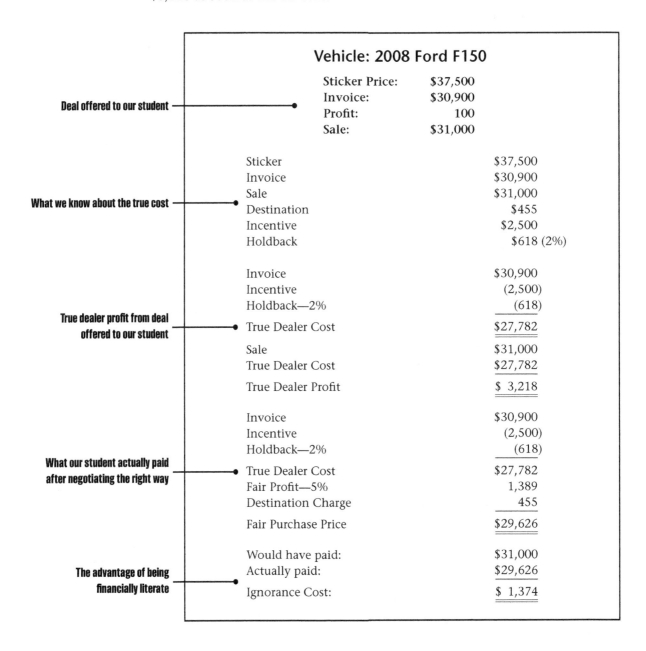

**Vehicle: 2008 Ford F150**

| | | |
|---|---|---|
| Deal offered to our student | Sticker Price: | $37,500 |
| | Invoice: | $30,900 |
| | Profit: | 100 |
| | Sale: | $31,000 |

| | | |
|---|---|---|
| What we know about the true cost | Sticker | $37,500 |
| | Invoice | $30,900 |
| | Sale | $31,000 |
| | Destination | $455 |
| | Incentive | $2,500 |
| | Holdback | $618 (2%) |

| | | |
|---|---|---|
| | Invoice | $30,900 |
| | Incentive | (2,500) |
| | Holdback—2% | (618) |
| True dealer profit from deal offered to our student | True Dealer Cost | $27,782 |
| | Sale | $31,000 |
| | True Dealer Cost | $27,782 |
| | True Dealer Profit | $ 3,218 |

| | | |
|---|---|---|
| | Invoice | $30,900 |
| | Incentive | (2,500) |
| | Holdback—2% | (618) |
| What our student actually paid after negotiating the right way | True Dealer Cost | $27,782 |
| | Fair Profit—5% | 1,389 |
| | Destination Charge | 455 |
| | Fair Purchase Price | $29,626 |

| | | |
|---|---|---|
| | Would have paid: | $31,000 |
| The advantage of being financially literate | Actually paid: | $29,626 |
| | Ignorance Cost: | $ 1,374 |

In our student's case that means the dealer profited $3,218, not the $100 our student was lead to believe. The dealer's true cost of the car was $27,782. That is the invoice price of $30,900 minus the incentive of $2,500 and minus the holdback of $618. Our student was ready to pay $31,000 for the car. A sales price of $31,000 minus the true dealer cost of $27,782 leaves a hefty profit of $3,218 for the dealership.

We suggested to our student that she begin with the true dealer cost of $27,782 and add 5% as a fair profit for the dealer. It is unreasonable to expect the dealer not to make any money off the sale of the car. However, you want the dealer's profit to be fair to both the dealer and to you. Five percent is a good place to start. If you get a car at less than 5% profit then so much the better for you. If you pay more than 5% profit then so much the better for the dealer. In this case let's take the $27,782 and add $1,389 (5%) to get $29,171. To this we need to add the destination charge of $455. This is a legitimate charge the dealer had to pay to get the car shipped to the dealer's lot. You also can find average destination charges on any of the previously mentioned Web sites. This gives us a fair purchase price of $29,626 for the car.

So our student would have paid $31,000 for the car. After doing her research she paid $29,626 for the car. Her financial ignorance almost cost her $1,374 ($31,000 minus $29,626).

## Determine the Value of a Used Car

Unlike determining the value of a new car, where we can see exactly what the dealer paid, determining the value of a used car is not an exact science. Because you will never know exactly what the dealer paid for the used car, the best you can do is to make sure you do not pay more than fair market value. Some of the best Web sites to use to determine a fair price for a used car are

- www.edmunds.com
- www.nada.com
- www.consumerreports.org
- www.cars.com

Each Web site will give you a slightly different value for the same car depending on its condition. By researching the various Web sites you can take the average of each individual Web site's value to estimate a fair price. Do not try to start at the dealer's listed price and work your way down. Instead, use the average you just determined as the basis of your offer to the dealer.

If you have a car that you will be trading in to the dealer, you can use this same approach to determine its fair trade-in price. Look at the trade-in value of your car, based on its condition on the various Web sites, recognizing this will always be significantly less than what you could sell it for yourself.

## Stepping onto the Lot—Buying a New Car

There are hundreds of potholes on the way to buying a car, and getting you to make an emotional decision is just one of them. Dealers want to tap into your emotions the same way that pet rescue groups like to put the smallest kittens and puppies in front of you. Car dealers want you to fall in love with the car. If they can get you to make a decision while you are in love with the car, or they can appeal to your sense of excitement or self-worth, they know they have you.

There are many people who depend on you buying a car: the salesperson, the dealer, the car manufacturer, the parts manufacturer that supplies the car companies, the advertisers, the finance people, and even the truck driver who delivers the cars. If you do not buy a car, then they do not get paid. With so many people having a vested interest in your purchasing a car, particularly a new car, what chance do you have of coming out on top without being properly prepared? You are now armed with knowledge of how the industry works. More important, you, rather than someone else, have determined what fits your needs.

The real danger in the car-buying experience is that it is a very convoluted process. By mixing all the stuff together, financing, price, and trade-in, it is hard to tell how much you will actually pay for the car. That is why it is critical to look at each piece individually. Ultimately, you want the best price on the car, the most money for your trade-in and the best rate for the financing.

We have already used the budget to determine how much we can pay for the car, so we are starting the process correctly. The key is to not allow the salesperson to talk you into a more expensive car than you can afford. Once you do your research based on a car of a certain price, the salesperson will start the payment creep approach. Once they know how much you are willing to pay, they start to look for other cars that are just $25 to $50 more per month. After all, what's another $50 if it means a sexier or sportier car? Besides the fact that you already determined your maximum price, you are now looking at cars that you did not research because they are in the higher price range.

## *Negotiate the Price*

The key is that you already did your homework. You checked the various car-related Web sites and determined the fair value. If you have a subscription to *Consumer Reports,* make sure you check out their Web site or look at their car-buying issue. The point is that you are finally ready to step on the lot and begin negotiations.

One of the easiest ways to take advantage of a consumer is to make sure they are thoroughly confused. Combining the value of the trade-in and the financing with the car purchase price definitely muddies the water. However, it is critical to look at each piece individually. Your first goal is to negotiate the purchase price of the car. At this point you should have established an amount that you can afford and the amount you are willing to pay for the car (a fair price). How did we do that? After properly researching and determining the fair compensation for the price of the car, we went to the dealership and told them that we were not going to need financing and we were not going to trade in our previous car.

Why is it so important to establish that you will not be financing nor will you have a trade-in? Because you want to get a fair price on the new car you are purchasing. You will eventually want to get a fair price on the car you trade in, if you decide to do so. Then you want to make sure that you get the fairest price for financing.

If you go in and combine all three, then it will be very difficult, if not impossible, to determine if you are getting a deal on one aspect, such as purchase price, while getting taken on another aspect, such as trade-in value or financing.

Dealers understand that everyone has a weakness or an emotional trigger. If your emotional trigger is the value of your trade-in, a dealer can offer you more money for your trade-in but will keep the price of the new car or the interest rates on the loan higher. Because your emotional trigger was the car you were trading in, you are just so happy to get that much out of the trade-in that you don't really care what the new car costs. In fact, you will spend the next two or three years bragging to your friends about how much you got for your trade-in. Who cares if you spent $3,000 extra on the new car, they gave you $2,500 for your old clunker, which you think was only worth about $50.

On the other hand, maybe your emotional trigger is on financing. Many car dealers offer 0% financing to people who do not want to pay interest. After all, what can be better than free money? Who cares if you had to give up $4,000 cash back if it means you paid zero percent financing. After all, being the master negotiator that you are, you borrowed money for free. It feels like you do not have any debt at all if the interest is free. Now you can brag to your friends that you are paying zero percent financing, but you are forgetting about the $4,000 you gave up to get the "0%" financing.

Some individuals absolutely must get the best price possible on their new car purchase and will do as much research as it takes to get the absolute best price. They may get a great deal on the purchase, but may pay a higher interest rate on their loan and get less than fair market value on their trade-in. Yet, they will be able to brag to their friends about the great deal they got on their new car. ("They only wanted to take $2,000 off the MSRP but I negotiated to the point that the poor salesperson was in tears. I got them to take $5,000 off the MSRP.")

Hopefully, it is now clear that the best way to negotiate the best price is to look at each piece individually. Do your research to determine a fair price for the car, then a fair price for your trade-in, and finally a fair price for the financing. Now you are armed with the ability to get a fair deal without wasting any of your hard-earned dollars during the whole process.

## *How Low Will They Go?*

Be prepared to be wooed by the salesperson. Now we are at the point where the tricks and the games begin. You will make an offer, and the salesperson will say, "We have never sold a car that low before." After a few more moments he or she will say, "I don't have the authority to approve a price that low. Let me call my manager." As you can imagine the manager is not available, so the salesperson will have to go "track down" the manager.

Now you are left at the salesperson's desk, with your spouse or parents, to discuss the car, how much you are really willing to pay, how much you really like the car, and so forth. For all you know, the salesperson could have put the phone on speaker and is sitting in their manager's office listening to your entire conversation.

If you are "daddy's little girl" and you make it clear how much you really, really, really want the car, then your poor dad has no chance of negotiating a fair price. If you and your spouse are talking about how much better the current offer is than you thought, then you are finished negotiating because they know they have you at the current price.

The key is to have your discussions in private. Walk outside and discuss any issues, prices, etc. You do not want to take the chance that a salesperson will hear anything that you have to say. You are not being rude nor are you inconveniencing the salesperson by stepping outside for a private conversation. In fact, if you think about it, the whole process is designed to wear you down so that you make an emotional decision rather than a financial decision.

Remember, your goal is to make your decisions financially, not emotionally. If you think your car is unique, you are about to be surprised. You may not have seen a single other car like it before, but once you buy one, you will see it everywhere. There are hundreds more like it in your city alone. There are thousands across your state and across the country. It is silly to become emotionally attached to a box of miles.

Timing is important. You want to negotiate at the right times. Dealers are more likely to negotiate better prices for you toward the end of the month because they either know they are getting some of their sales incentives at that point or they are close to their next sales goal. It is also a good idea to buy new cars toward the end of the model year. Dealers need to clear out their inventory so they can get the new model year cars onto their lot.

Now we need to say a word about financing. We know that the dealer will try to play a game with the price of the new car you are considering. We also know that they will play a game with the price they are willing to pay for your trade-in. Guess what? They also play a game with financing. Once you have established your fair price and fair trade-in value, you can discuss financing options. The dealer will call a finance company they have a business relationship with and find out, based on your credit score, what the lowest rate is that they can offer you. Then they will come to you and tell you that the best rate they can offer is . . . get this . . . about ½% to 1% higher than what the finance company quoted.

Why would they want to do this? In many instances, the finance company will split the difference with the dealer if you finance at a rate higher than the minimum. For instance, if the finance company says they can lend money to you at 6.5%, the salesperson may tell you that they can get you into that car for as little as 7.5%. Because you have already done your research with several lending institutions; local and national banks, credit unions, and membership clubs such as Sam's and COSTCO, you know that you can get financing for less. Once you tell the salesperson that you can get a better rate and you will have to go to your bank tonight and return tomorrow to purchase the car, they will suddenly find a way to get you into the car at 6.5% (probably after "discussing it with their manager".)

So why would the dealer suddenly want to offer the lower interest rate, even if it means that they do not get any extra commission? All good salespeople understand that purchases are emotional decisions, and they are trying to get you to make an emotional decision. Once you walk off the lot and have some time to think about the purchase and any other options you may have, there is a good chance that you could end up talking yourself out of purchasing the car. You may decide the price does not fit your budget, or you may look at other cars. Because the whole process is designed to wear you down and play off your emotions, they know that *now* is the time to get you to make that purchase, otherwise they may lose the sale forever.

## Buying a Used Car

When you choose to purchase a used car, you have several options. You may buy a used car from a dealer or car lot or buy from a private individual. Either way, you will need to do your research. It is impossible to determine what a dealer or anyone else paid for the used car he or she is trying to sell to you. And more important, it doesn't matter. Who cares what the person selling the car to you paid for it. What you care about is what is the fair market value of the used car you are interested in buying.

One step that you can take to protect yourself when purchasing a used car is to ask the dealer to show you the CarFax.[26] Of course you can also purchase your own CarFax, but most reputable dealers will pay the fee for you. Any time you are thinking of purchasing a car from an individual, you will want to take a look at the CarFax. CarFax is a vehicle history report that will show the number of owners, what state the car has been registered in and during what time period, and if any major body work has been performed on the car due to an accident.

After major floods and natural disasters, such as Hurricane Katrina, some people will take cars that have been in a flood zone, clean them up (cosmetically), and sell them to wholesalers. Knowing if a car was registered in a disaster area during the disaster may help you avoid purchasing a car with problems that are not detectible by the naked eye.

Another step to protect you from purchasing a problem car is to take the used car to a trusted mechanic. Most reputable mechanics can do a basic inspection of a car for about $100. Any reputable dealer will allow you to have the car inspected by a mechanic of your choosing. If the dealer hesitates or tries to talk you out of it, then at the very least you do not want to purchase that car. You may not want to do business with that dealer at all. Do not let them justify not allowing you to take the car off the lot. They may say, "I can't really afford to let the car off the lot because we do not have very many to sell." This is poor logic because you already agreed on the price and already agreed to buy the car. The only thing that would stop you from making the purchase is if something is wrong with it. Part of the reason dealers have such a large markup between the trade-in value and the retail value is to allow them to make any necessary adjustments or repairs to the car before selling it to you.

## Negotiate the Price from a Dealer

While negotiating the price of a used car, you still have the ability to walk away. Do not let yourself get so emotionally attached to a specific car that you end up paying much more than you should because you are afraid to let "someone else buy *your* car." There is no such thing as a once in a lifetime deal. If it were a once in a lifetime deal, what are the chances that *you* are the one person able to get it? If everyone in America has the chance for a once in a lifetime deal, then that means there are more than 300 million "one-time" deals out there to be had.

Because we know that used cars are either out of the manufacturer warranty period or they are well into the warranty, we can expect some higher repair bills over time. For this reason, you need to consider any warranties that come with the car from the dealer. Legally, there are two types of warranties, express and implied.

An express warranty is simply one that is expressed or documented. For instance, a used car dealer may offer a 60-day or 90-day express warranty. They may also offer a full year warranty. If you purchase a preowned certified car from any of the major car companies, you will basically have an extended warranty attached that may take the car to six years or 100,000 miles from the original date of purchase.

An implied warranty is one that is required of dealers by the Federal Trade Commission (FTC). An implied warranty simply means that it is implied that if you drive the car off the lot and the transmission drops out as you make your first left-hand turn, then the dealer must fix the problem or refund your money. Essentially an implied warranty means that if you are sold a car to be driven (as opposed to a purchase for spare parts), then you should be able to drive the car home.

If a car is sold "as-is" then there may not even be an implied warranty. You are basically buying the car exactly as it is. Any major defects, flaws, or problems are now yours to deal with because you bought the car "as-is." In a handful of states it is illegal for dealers to sell their cars "as-is," but most states still allow them. For your purposes, there is no reason to buy a car from a dealer "as-is." One of the reasons to buy a car from a dealer is because there is some form of accountability behind an established business. In theory, they paid someone for the trade-in and then they had their mechanic fix any major issues before cleaning the car, putting it on their lot, and marking up the price. If you are going to pay any markup to a dealer, then you should at least get a 30-day warranty.

You may be offered an extended warranty from the dealer. They will tell you that even the most basic repairs will cost upwards of $500, with a new transmission costing more than $2,000. You may be able to get a 3-year extended warranty for $350 to $750. In most cases, the extended warranty is a bad purchase because of the high price-to-benefit ratio. In all cases, extended warranties are marked up with a lot of profit built in. If you are a very risk-averse person and feel the need to purchase a warranty for your own "peace of mind" then you need to research warranties the same way you researched your car and make sure you get the best deal. In no case should you pay anywhere near the asking price for the warranty. You should arrive at the dealership armed with printouts of third-party warranty offers and negotiate from there. You will probably pay around 50% to 70% of the original asking price for the warranty. Also consider that low-mileage used cars may still have some of the factory warranty remaining.

## *Negotiate the Price from a Private Individual*

If you purchase a used car from a private individual, you are most certainly getting the car "as-is." A private individual has no obligation to warranty the car he or she is selling. Purchasing a used car from an individual is no different than shopping at a person's yard sale. It is in your best interest to test drive any car before you purchase it, but especially a used car, and definitely a used car purchased from an individual. You should also take the car to a trustworthy mechanic and pay the $100 to have the car looked over to identify any major mechanical problems. It is difficult for most of us to detect something like a blown head gasket because the symptoms can be masked by changing the coolant. Not having your mechanic look at the car before buying it could result in a $750 mistake, or more.

When you are purchasing a car from a private individual, you should still research the price the same way you would for a used car from a dealer's lot. The difference is that you should not even look at the retail price because it is not a retail transaction. You want to look at one of the lower prices for trade-in value. If the seller is considering trading the car in to a dealer, then you may be able to offer them the same or a little bit more than the fair trade-in value. If there is no indication that they are trading in the car, then you should be able to offer a little less than trade-in value. In any case, once you determine what you think is a fair price for the car, be prepared to walk away if the seller will not meet your price. You can always check back a few days later or even a week or two. If the car has not yet sold, the person may be more willing to bargain.

Of course there are Web sites that allow you to search for a used car anywhere in the country. You can even bid on a used car on eBay! There are plenty of used cars within driving distance of your city. If you purchase a car, sight unseen, and you trust just the description and picture you see on a Web site, then you are taking unnecessary risk. At the very least, you will need to look at a CarFax on the particular vehicle, but you should really find a way to have a mechanic look at the car. If that is not possible, then you should reconsider whether the deal you are about to get is really a great deal, or one of your first major financial mistakes.

Car buying is a very convoluted process. By mixing all the negotiable parts together; financing, price, and trade-in, it is hard to tell how much you will actually pay for the car. That is why it is critical to look at each piece individually. You want the best price on the car, the most money for your trade-in, and the best interest rate for the financing.

# THE COST OF  FINANCIAL IGNORANCE

It is easy to see how we overpay for a car given how the industry is structured to confuse us. Our student at the beginning of the chapter was ready to overpay by $1,374 for her new car. Now multiply that by the number of cars she expects to purchase over her lifetime. If she buys a car just once every six years, she will purchase eight new cars by the time she retires. Overpaying on each of those cars adds up quickly.

| | |
|---|---|
| Amount overpaid on each car | $ 1,374 |
| Number of car purchases before retirement | × 8 |
| **Total Cost of Financial Ignorance** | **$10,992** |

# THE HOUSING DECISION

## Factors and Finances

Two of our students were graduating with advanced degrees in accounting in the same semester. They both landed great jobs with a large accounting firm in the same city. They were getting married soon after graduation and had started to look for their first home. This was a very exciting time in their lives. Their future was so bright they had to wear shades. Not wanting to make a mistake with their first big decision and knowing that we teach personal finance, they stopped by our offices for a little advice. These were smart students. They had undergraduate and graduate degrees in business and both recently passed the CPA exam. They had researched the housing market. They found a good real estate agent. They had a plan. They thought they were doing everything right. Yet, they were getting ready to make one of the biggest financial mistakes of their lives. Why?

# YOUR FIRST HOME

So far so good, right? They did exactly what they were supposed to do. They were on their way to achieving the American dream. They were about to be married, move to a city where they would each have a great job, and had found a real estate agent to help them buy their first home. So what did they do wrong? Just about everything.

First, they simply did what everyone else does. That in and of itself should send up warning signals because most people lack financial literacy. Second, they decided to buy a home right away in a new city. Third, they decided to buy a home immediately after getting married and starting their careers. In addition, they were seeking a house much larger than they needed as their first home. Finally, they let the real estate agent tell them how much house they could afford.

When you begin to seek advice about buying your first home, everyone seems to have an opinion about where you should live, what type of house you should buy, and in what neighborhood. What most people fail to warn you about is that a home can become a money pit. Unfortunately, once you become emotionally attached to a specific home, you are simply putting yourself in a position to become house rich and cash poor, a position very familiar to way too many Americans.

Our young couple found their dream home in a very nice neighborhood. It had three bedrooms plus a finished room over the garage. He was already shopping for a huge plasma television. She was picking out a new living room suite. The house had upgraded hardwood floors and granite countertops. The kitchen was equipped with all stainless steel appliances. The baths were all tile. There was even a dedicated office. It was everything that they wanted, and best of all, they qualified for the mortgage.

The danger is that everyone is interested in you buying the biggest, most expensive house for which you qualify. The reality is that you almost always qualify for much more than you can afford. Everyone from the real estate agent to the mortgage lender to the landscaper makes no money unless you buy a house. And the more house you buy, the more money they make. The outcome is that you are house rich and cash poor. You end up purchasing a home that is more expensive than you can really afford. Although you are able to buy a home and make the payments, you have no money left over for vacations, eating out, home improvement projects or even basic home maintenance.

At this point, particularly with our newlyweds, arguments are likely to be about the lack of money. Both individuals are working very hard in their new careers, and they both feel they "deserve" to spend some money on themselves, but there is very little left over in the budget. He gets mad when she buys shoes, and she gets mad when he buys a new part for his car or truck. This can be avoided by buying a home that fits your budget.

So what big mistake was our young couple with their fresh graduate degrees about to make? They did not consider their lifestyle. Did they really need such a large home? They are not going to spend much time at home anyway because they should be focusing on their new careers. Did they need to be in the suburbs? The house in the suburbs means they would spend more of their valuable time commuting, and that nice big yard would mean more Saturdays mowing the lawn. In fact, should our young couple even buy a house?

The decision about where to live does not begin with choosing which house to buy, but begins with deciding whether to buy or rent. Every major purchase decision begins with your cash flow statement, except buying a house. Here we must consult our net worth statement first. Our net worth statement tells us if we have sufficient funds to cover the cost of obtaining a loan and the down payment. The decision to buy or rent may be made right here. Ultimately, there will be three possibilities when it comes to choosing a home: You can choose to buy, and you have the financial resources to do so; you choose to buy, and you do not have the financial resources to do so and must rent; or you choose to rent.

Regardless of whether you buy or rent, the first thing you must consider is what you can afford. Your cash flow statement will allow you to determine the most you are comfortable spending on a monthly basis, whether it is a mortgage payment or a rent payment. Now you can narrow your search for houses or apartments you can afford. The important point is you are the one determining what you can afford and not letting a real estate agent or landlord talk you into something you cannot afford.

In the case of our young couple, they wanted to focus on their careers. This means remaining flexible enough to take advantage of opportunities that will come along in the first couple of years. That big promotion may only be available in another city or another state. Owning a home limits that flexibility. Just because you have the money to buy a house does not mean that you should. As homeowners, our young couple would have to put their home on the market and endure the home-selling process. In the meantime, they may have to rent in their new city and pay rent at their new place while paying the mortgage on the house they are trying to sell. They may even have to turn down a promotion in another city because they are saddled with their home mortgage. In almost every case, recent graduates are better off renting rather than buying.

# Renting

There are several advantages to renting. Renting offers more mobility. When your lease is up, you can leave. If you want to leave before your lease has ended, you at least know that you are only obligated for a fixed amount of commitment (the number of months remaining on your lease times the monthly payment). In many cases, with a huge exception for apartments that are near college campuses, you may be able to go month-to-month with your lease after your initial one-year contract has ended. This option offers you even more mobility.

Renting also means that you have virtually no maintenance. You will not have to spend any time, money, or energy maintaining your rental. With the exception of anything that you may damage or destroy by accident (or on purpose), the landlord is responsible for any major repairs—anything from roof repairs to those small inconveniences such as leaking pipes.

Not only will you have virtually no expenses related to maintaining your rental, but you will also have low initial costs. Unlike the 5% to 10% you may need to have up front to purchase a home, most apartments only require one month's rent plus a security deposit that may be equal to another month's rent.

Of course there are several disadvantages to renting as well. The foremost disadvantage is that you will not have the opportunity to gain any equity. Similar to a car lease, you are renting someone else's property for a period of time for a set fee, and then you have to give it back (or turn the keys in) at the end of the lease term. You have certain restrictions as well, such as limitations on how loud you can play your music or how late at night you can do your laundry. There are various legal concerns with the lease because it is a legal document and you agree to abide by all of the terms and restrictions. Also, if you do move frequently, each time you may have to pay the setup fees for your cable and other utilities.

## *The Search*

At this point, the assumption is that you have decided to rent, based on your budget and your lifestyle. Now you have to begin your search for the perfect apartment: the one that fits your budget, permitting you to save toward your goal of homeownership (if that is one of your goals), and also suits your lifestyle. You will need to consider the location of apartments relative to where you will work. Maybe you can live within walking distance of work. Perhaps you will only need one car for two people, which means less money spent on gas, insurance, maintenance, and other fees. Remember to account for the wear and tear on your car, which takes into account oil changes, the amount of miles a typical car will last, and so forth.

Another option may be public transportation. If you are located close to public transportation, you may be able to survive without a car, or let your car last longer. Be sure to account for the cost of public transportation and weigh that against any convenience factor. Of course, with public transportation, you may be able to avoid the high fees to park your car. For example, in Washington, DC, it will cost about $15 per day just to park your car. New York City and several other large cities cost even more.

Do not discount any time that you will have to spend behind the wheel, based on where you live compared to where you work. The time you spend driving could be better spent doing something else, such as going to the gym or relaxing at home. Perhaps you prefer to have a little time to prepare for your workday or to decompress after a long day. If you do end up with a longer commute, make sure you find a way to use that time to improve your life or your career.

Many apartments tout all their amenities as a way to justify higher costs. Make sure you fully compare the costs versus the amenities. Do not pay for a place with a gym and a pool if you are not going to use them. A portion of the cost to operate or offer those amenities is built into your monthly payment, even if they charge an additional fee to join. If you are going to use those services and the price is reasonable, then perhaps it is a better deal. Just be honest with yourself. If you are going to be too tired to use the gym and too busy to use the pool, then you may be able to find a better-priced apartment that does not offer these amenities.

Do not overlook one of the most obvious ways to evaluate an apartment or a community. Most people love to talk and give their opinion. Think about the last time you hung out with friends or attended a party. There are some people that will not shut up. All you have to do is ask a couple of the residents what they think about the apartment, how it compares to any others they considered or used to rent, and any other relevant questions, such as how safe they feel in the area.

## Before Signing the Lease

Keep in mind that a lease is a legally binding contract. That means that whenever you sign a lease, you are agreeing to all the terms in that lease, and you can be held accountable for everything written in the document. That means that there should be no open blanks on the lease. If something does not apply, such as a pet deposit, then you should fill in the space with "N/A" which means "not applicable." If you simply leave it blank, a dishonest landlord could fill it in after the fact and try to hold you responsible. Of course, your best recourse in that instance would be to produce your copy of the lease on the day you signed it that shows the line was blank, but your strongest defense is to not leave it blank in the first place.

Make sure that all the relevant information is clearly represented on the lease (such as costs, dates, penalties). Talk to a lawyer about any aspects of the lease that are unclear. It may cost about $100 to have an attorney review the lease for you, but it could end up saving you thousands of dollars if there is something you misunderstood or you have to break the lease for whatever reason.

Before you move into the apartment, you should have a walk-through with the landlord or his or her representative. The condition of the unit should be noted in writing either on the lease or an addendum (extra sheet of paper) attached to the lease. Include in the notes anything of significance such as a large stain that already exists in the carpet or a door that looks chewed up by the previous renter's dog. A dishonest landlord may have already charged the prior renter for the damage but chose not to fix it and may try to charge you for the same damage as well. Without documentation, you cannot prove that the damage already existed. You should open every door, run the hot water, flush each of the toilets, make sure the dishwasher turns on, etc. You may even want to take a video camera with you to record the state in which you found the apartment when you moved in.

*The lease should include certain legal details such as:*

- ◆ Description and address of the property
- ◆ Name and address of the landlord (or property management company)
- ◆ Name of tenant(s)
- ◆ Effective date and length of the lease (technically it is your apartment at 12:01 AM the first day until 11:59 PM the last day of the lease)
- ◆ The dollar amount of the rent, date and time the rent is due, and any late penalties
- ◆ Location where rent is due (this should be a physical location, not a P.O. box)
- ◆ List of all appliances and utilities that are included with the house
- ◆ Any restrictions such as the number of parking spaces, pets, guests, etc.

It is critical that the details of the lease be in writing. You do not want to get into a verbal argument about whether the dishwasher was included as part of your lease, or how much the penalty will be if you are one day late on the rent. Legally, the landlord would have the upper hand based on whatever is written on the lease, even if you had agreed verbally that there would be no penalty if you were only a couple of days late.

If you are going to rent an apartment unit at a large apartment complex, it is critical to see the actual unit that you will be renting. Do not make the mistake of viewing a "similar model." Although the layout may be similar, the location can be completely different. The model unit may be the most pristine one in the complex, but your unit could be the one with the worst view, next to the laundry room, or near the water pipes. Make sure you see exactly where you will be renting or ask to see multiple units if the one you will rent is unavailable for viewing.

Do you know one of the biggest mistakes that renters make? They assume that if they have one or more roommates they are only responsible for their own portion of the rent. If you sign a lease agreement with other people, then any one of you can be held responsible for every one of you. In other words, if you have a roommate and he or she decides to stop paying his or her half of the rent payment, the landlord will not accept your half and then go after your roommate. The landlord has every right to come back to you and demand the other half of the rent. It is your responsibility to get your roommate to pay you back. In many instances utilities work the same way. Worse yet, if you put the utility bill in just your name and your roommate skips town or stops paying, not only are you responsible for the full bill, but you have no recourse against your roommate. It is important that you understand your rights and responsibilities before you sign any lease.

## Know Your Rights

The Fair Housing Act makes discrimination illegal. A landlord cannot discriminate and refuse to rent to you because of race, religion, ethnicity, and so forth. Refusing to rent to you because you have a bad credit score or you have no income is not considered discrimination, it is smart business sense. Normally, if you are moving to a new area and are just starting a new job, the landlord will require a copy of the offer letter you received from your employer, or they may ask for a letter directly from the employer indicating your starting date and salary. They simply want to verify that you will have an income that is sufficient to pay the rent. If you already have a job, you may be required to provide a copy of your last couple of pay stubs. Again, the landlord wants to verify not only that you are employed, but also that you earn enough to make the rent payments. Most apartments run by a property management company require a certain level of income to "qualify" to rent an apartment.

Neither the landlord nor the repairperson can legally enter your apartment without advance notice and consent, except in the case of an emergency. For instance, if you live on the third floor and the landlord receives a call from the person living on the floor directly below you stating water is pouring in through the ceiling, then the landlord has the right to enter your apartment. To save the apartment from suffering additional damage and to spare the other residents, this would be classified as an emergency. Your landlord should still knock on the door first to give you a chance to answer or open it yourself before he or she enters with the master key.

The residential unit must be habitable. The unit must provide access to heat in the winter, have running water, etc. Of course, if you do not pay your electric bill, that is not the fault of the landlord. You have a functional heating unit in your apartment; you have simply not paid to use it. Also, if the property is not sanitary or has large rodents running throughout your apartment, you have some legal recourse. Unfortunately, you may only be able to break the lease and find a new apartment.

Repairs and maintenance must be made in a timely manner. What happens if your toilet stops working on a Friday night? Will the landlord have to pay weekend rates and get the plumber to your apartment right away or can the landlord wait until Monday to save a little bit of money? It depends on how many bathrooms your apartment has. If you rent an apartment with two or more toilets and one stops working, then the apartment is still habitable. If you only have one toilet and it stops working, then the apartment is not habitable, so the landlord must fix the problem right away. If a tree limb falls through the wall, then the landlord is responsible for getting the damage fixed, but having the tree removed and the wall repaired all in one day is not reasonable given the severity of the damage. The landlord's insurance may provide a temporary place for you to stay, or you will have to consider your other options, including any legal claims you have against the landlord for costs incurred due to relocation or temporary housing (a great reason why you should always have renter's insurance).

The landlord cannot seize your property for nonpayment. If you are behind in your rent, your landlord cannot just take your stuff as compensation or penalty for missing rent payments. Your landlord can evict you, which will require certain legal steps that he or she must take first. If you abandon the property, as opposed to simply failing to pay your rent, then your landlord has different rights and may be able to seize your property. In either case, the landlord may still come after you for the remaining rent balance or will likely turn your account over to collections.

## Moving Out

So, now it is time to move out. Just as you did your homework before moving in, you need to do your homework before moving out. Ultimately you want your departure to be as pleasant an experience as your arrival.

Your goal is to receive your entire security deposit. You have been a good tenant so far. You made every payment on time, you never threw loud parties (at least none that your neighbors complained about), and you did not cause any damage to the unit. So why would the landlord not give you back your full deposit? You have to clean and leave the unit in the same condition as when you first moved in. You should vacuum, wipe the floors, clean the refrigerator and the oven, and so forth. Essentially, you become a maid for the day. Otherwise, the landlord may use part of your security deposit for cleaning fees.

For your own financial protection, you should do a walk-through with the landlord before you turn in the key. Just like the walk-through you did when you moved in, you should do the same thing when you are moving out. This time it is up to the landlord to make sure everything still works. Your goal is to get the landlord to sign off that the apartment is still in good condition with no damage and you have no further responsibility. If any damage is found and it was already there when you moved in, you can point that out in the lease or the addendum that you signed when you first moved into the apartment. Just as you did when you moved in, it is a good idea to video the apartment when you move out.

Any deductions that the landlord does take from your deposit should be documented by line item. Do not let the landlord withhold $250 of your security deposit and say "cleaning fees." Make sure everything is listed, such as $50 to clean the oven, $100 to steam clean the carpet, and so forth. By requiring the line-item deduction you can now argue fairly and reasonably. If your landlord wants to charge you $250 to clean the oven, you have a good legal argument that the fee is excessive.

Now that you are parting ways, it is essential to give your landlord a forwarding address. Although your mail should automatically be forwarded, any packages that arrive from UPS or FedEx will not. Perhaps most important, your landlord will need your address to mail your security deposit refund. Overall you want to try to move out in good standing. You may need to list the landlord as a reference for the next place you rent or on other applications such as for a mortgage or even a job. Making payments on time and taking care of your apartment could mean the difference between getting a mortgage and having to continue to rent. For most of us we reach a point where home ownership makes the most financial sense.

## ADVANTAGES OF OWNING A HOME

Home ownership is part of the American dream. The concept of actually owning your own place and having a piece of land that you can call your own are part of the work ethic of our society. Although renting serves its purpose for some people, or is used as a temporary adjustment period for many others, the vast majority of Americans ultimately want to own their own home.

There are many advantages to owning your own home. Homeowners have a sense of pride or a pride of ownership. In communities with more homeowners than renters, the buildings and properties tend to be in better shape and crime rates are generally lower. When you own the place you live in, you are more likely to take better care of the property.

Owning a home is also a hedge against inflation. As costs rise, apartment rental rates rise as well, so having a home that is paid for or one with a fixed-rate mortgage will mean that your payments remain the same. When you sell your home in the future, the price should have increased at least with the rate of inflation (over a long period of time). Your increase in home equity will help offset price inflation in other areas such as college costs, car prices, and so on.

Owning a home will help you build equity over time. As you pay down your loan balance, you own more and more of your home, giving you increasing equity in your home, which will help increase your net worth. At the same time, your home may also increase in value. Although housing bubbles cause temporary price deflation or lowering of housing prices, over the long run, your home value should increase at least at the rate of inflation. So not only do you owe less and less on your mortgage each year, but the value of your home increases as well. The increasing home value combined with your decreasing loan balance can result in a huge boost to your overall net worth, especially after several years.

Another advantage to owning a home, particularly if you have a mortgage, is that you can reduce your income taxes. The federal government encourages home ownership through the tax code. Because the government wants taxpayers to own homes, the tax code offers a break to taxpayers by allowing homeowners to deduct a portion of their mortgage payment from their taxable income, which has the effect of lowering the cost of home ownership.

Another advantage that comes to you indirectly through home ownership is an increased credit rating or credit score. Your credit score will increase as you continue to make your steady mortgage payment, month after month. In addition, home owners are considered more stable than renters because a renter can simply move out as soon as their lease ends. A home owner cannot simply move without selling their home, which can be a long process. On most applications for loans and credit cards, two important questions are "How long you have been at your current residence?" and "Do you rent or own?"

Although home ownership should provide a hedge to inflation and help to build equity, your house should not be viewed as an investment. Real estate can be a good investment, but relying on your home as your main source of net worth or planning to use the equity in your home to fund your retirement may not be the best financial decision. Housing values can and do fall. In a worst-case scenario, you could end up owing more on your home than it is worth.

## Disadvantages of Owning a Home

One of the disadvantages of owning a home is financial uncertainty. Although everyone likes to think of homes as assets that go up in value, home values can also go down. Even the lenders and investors throughout the late 1990s and early 2000s forgot that home values could decrease. Home ownership is one of the few "investments" that can actually cause you to lose more money than you paid. For instance, if you invest in a share of stock that costs $10, the most you can lose is $10, even if the company goes completely out of business. On the other hand, if you buy a house for $100,000 and only invest $10,000 but borrow the other $90,000 and the house drops in value to $70,000, you will owe $20,000 more than you already spent! In other words your $10,000 investment could cost you $30,000.

Another disadvantage of home ownership is limited mobility. Early in your career you may want to remain mobile so you can move to where the jobs are or where your next promotion opportunity may be. In a normal economy it can take three to six months to sell a home. During economic recessions, it could take even longer, and you may have to sell your home for a loss. Unlike an apartment, where you could leave at the end of the lease, or simply take the hit and pay the last couple of months of the lease to leave your current city, you do not have the same options with a house. Losing out on a great job offer simply because you cannot sell your house in time could not only hurt your career, but will also be financially frustrating.

Owning a home also comes with higher living costs. Unlike a rented apartment, when the pipes leak, the toilet overflows, or a tree comes through the ceiling, you are responsible for the maintenance and repairs. Although you know exactly what your expenses will be every month if you are a renter, you can only estimate what your added expenses will be when you own a home. In addition, you will want to make improvements to your home, such as upgrading the appliances, adding a back patio, planting trees and shrubs, and making other improvements to both the inside and the outside of the home.

As just discussed, there are many good reasons why you should not buy a home right after graduation. However, there will be a lot of pressure from family, friends, and others for you buy your first home as early as you possibly can. The worst part is that they will use convincing arguments that sound good but in reality have no basis in fact. When should you never buy a house?

# THE THREE WORST REASONS TO BUY A HOUSE

**#1** If you think that buying a house is always a good investment, think again. You will be told over and over that buying a house is one of the best investments you can make.

Historically, the stock market has much higher returns than the housing market. Of course, there are small pockets of time when the stock market went down while housing prices went up, but overall, stocks have been a much better investment than houses. Although everyone understands that the stock market goes up and down, most people tend to forget that housing prices can also go down. The recent financial crisis may have reminded many people of this fact, but this is not the only time houses have dropped in value. A house should not be treated as an investment the same way that stocks are. Of course, real estate is a valid investment vehicle within a person's overall investment portfolio, but the home you live in should be treated differently than a real estate investment.

**#2** You constantly hear that renting is throwing your money away.

Why do you think you are throwing money away on rent? You have to live somewhere, so you are spending money to have a place to live. Keep in mind all the disadvantages to owning a home. Renters have a much more mobile lifestyle. Renters also do not have all the hidden and added expenses that come with owning a home. You should buy a home when you are ready, not because you think you are throwing money away. You do not build equity while renting, but you also do not have to worry about losing money either. Although many people point out that they can buy a home cheaper than they are renting, usually what they mean is that they have a found homes whose mortgage payment would be less than what they are spending on their current apartment. It is likely that there are many other places to rent that are much cheaper.

**#3** You can take a tax write-off. A house gives you a tax deduction.

The tax deduction on a mortgage is only part of the overall equation. Keep in mind that deducting something from your taxes does not mean that you will get all your money back. Instead you only get a portion and usually only a small portion at that. Once you start to consider the standard deductions and tax brackets, you will be better equipped to understand that your deduction for your mortgage is much less than you might think. In addition, as you pay down your mortgage, your deduction gets smaller as well. Because nobody wants to pay more in interest than they have to, it is obvious that our goal should not simply be to get a deduction.

The goal here is not to talk you out of buying a home, but to make sure that when you are ready to buy your home, you are doing so for the right reasons. You want to purchase your first home with your eyes wide open.

## So You Want to Buy a House?

Now that you have had a chance to weigh the advantages and disadvantages of owning a home, you have decided you are ready to make a purchase. Before we begin discussing the home-buying process, there are still some things you need to consider.

Even though the timing is right for you to buy, if you are moving to a new city it still might be better to rent before buying. If you only have a weekend to choose a place to live, then do not buy a house. Sign at least a 6- or 12-month lease. Use that time to drive around, ask questions, and explore the new area. You want to figure out the traffic patterns. In some major cities, you can spend over one hour in the car traveling just 10 miles during rush hour traffic. In some instances, simply living in the other direction (such as east of the city instead of west of the city) can cut your commute time in half. What if your home is just a few trees away from a hog farm? Nothing flavors your morning coffee more than the fresh smell of hog waste with every sip. You also have to consider what school district your new home will be in. You may be thinking, "I am not even thinking about having kids any time soon." It does not matter, because you always need to buy a home with resale value in mind. If you are located in a better school district and the next person that comes along to buy your house has children, then your home will appeal to them more.

Any good real estate agent will tell you that the three most important things to consider when buying a house are (1) location, (2) location, and (3) location. Think about it this way. There is a ton of land available in the world. You can drive through the Midwest and drive past hundreds of thousands of acres of land. Are there any jobs there? Are there any beaches? There is only so much land near major cities and around lakes and at the beach. It is not about how much land but rather where the land is located. Where is the house built? Is it near schools? Which schools? Is it near the noisy train tracks or in a quiet part of town? The main feature that matters is location. You can improve a house by making it bigger, painting it, adding a garage or a porch, etc. What you cannot do is improve its location. All these factors will affect the value of your home.

Keep in mind, if you are able to get a great bargain because of a simple flaw, such as it is the only house without a garage, or a noisy airport is nearby, you will end up having to give the same great bargain when you sell the house. In other words, whatever causes the house to be a bargain now will cause you to have to sell at a bargain later, unless it is something that you can fix.

## The Home-Buying Process

All major purchases are done after consulting your cash flow statement . . . except for housing. The first step in the home-buying process is to consult your net worth statement. Your rent or buy decision may be made right here. You can expect to pay between 5% and 10% as a down payment. On average, you can also expect to pay an additional 3% to 5% in loan fees, which are generally referred to as closing costs. The money you will pay in closing costs will go to the appraiser, lender, home inspector, closing attorney, title insurance company, property appraiser, and many more individuals and companies. The point is that your net worth statement lets you know if you have the financial resources to purchase a home.

### Look At Your Net Worth Statement

If your net worth statement indicates that you have enough in assets to use for a down payment, or after you have saved long enough to reach that point, then you are ready to consult your cash flow statement. When you create your cash flow statement, it is important to be realistic, not idealistic.

### Look At Your Cash Flow Statement

The next step in the home-buying process is to look at your cash flow statement. Remember, you need to determine how much you are willing to spend on your house. The bank does not look at your cash flow statement, so your loan officer will not consider how many times you like to eat out per week or the types of vacations you like to take or even what type of car you plan to buy next. The loan officer simply runs numbers based on some maximum limits and determines the most they are willing to lend.

Although the bank will certainly tell you how much they are willing to lend you, that will usually be a much higher number than what you can actually afford. From the lender's point of view, you can be approved for up to 28% of your gross monthly income for the entire principle, interest, taxes and insurance (PITI), which is your total monthly house payment. As much as 36% of your gross monthly income can go toward your total debt payments (this includes the PITI as well as car payments, student loan payments, credit card payments, and any other loan payments). This figure does not include any utilities such as gas, electric, cable, or cell phone. A rough figure, which changes during periods of high interest rates, is that you can borrow roughly 2.5 times your annual income. This is how a bank may be willing to approve you for a house that you cannot afford. It is especially true that you can easily be prequalified for a house that you definitely cannot afford, especially if you carry a large amount of debt.

Assume for a moment that you make $36,000 per year. How much house could you afford, including taxes and insurance? Because the bank looks at your gross monthly income (which is before taxes are taken out) you can take your annual income and divide by 12:

$$\$36,000 \ / \ 12 = \$3,000$$

Because they will lend up to 28%, you can multiply your monthly amount by 28%:

$$\$36,000 \ / \ 12 = \$3,000 \times 0.28 = \$840.00 \ (\text{PITI})$$

If you make an allowance for taxes and insurance of about 20% of the principle and interest you would take:

$$(1.2) \times ? = \$840 \ \Rightarrow \ \$840 \ / \ 1.2 = \$700 \ (\text{PI}) \ \Rightarrow \ \$840 - \$700 = \$140 \ (\text{TI})$$

From our calculation, we were able to determine that the principle and interest portion was $700 and the taxes and insurance were $140.

We can now use time value of money to calculate how much house we can afford once we determine what the current mortgage interest rates are. We will assume 6% for our example.

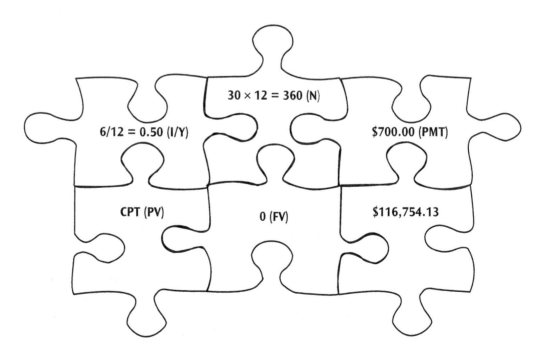

We were able to calculate that to stay within our budget, we could borrow $117,000. We can then add our down payment to that amount to come up with a total we can afford to pay. Assuming we have $13,000 for a down payment, then we can spend $130,000:

$$\$117,000 + \$13,000 = \$130,000$$

At this point we know exactly what we can spend, so there is no point in looking at homes that are outside this price range. Otherwise you can become emotionally attached to the more expensive homes, or some of their features, and you and your spouse could end up arguing and turning the exciting home-buying experience into something miserable.

One of the features of the 30-year mortgage that most people do not understand is how the loan is actually paid off. During the first 15 years, significantly less than half of the mortgage is paid off. It is only in the last 10 years that the amount you owe really starts to decrease quickly. Let us take a look at an example (for simplicity we will round our answers):

### 30-Year Mortgage

Sale price of $167,000 with a 10% down payment
Loan amount is $150,000, interest rate is 6% = P&I of $899
After seven years the loan balance is $134,000

Assume you have made your payment for seven years and you decide to sell. You have only paid off a total of $16,000. If your home increased in value 3% per year during those seven years, it would now be worth about $205,000. The real estate commissions that you will pay to sell a $200,000 house will run about $16,000. In other words, during your first seven years, you have only paid enough of the mortgage off to pay the real estate agent's commission when you sell!

Assuming a 7% commission rate on $205,000, you would actually pay about $14,300.

| | |
|---|---|
| Sale price: | $205,000 |
| Less Loan Balance: | $134,000 |
| Less Sales Commission: | $14,300 |
| You net: | $56,600 |

Now, let us compare that to a 15-year mortgage instead.

### 15-Year Mortgage

Sale price of $167,000 with a 10% down payment
Loan amount is $150,000, interest rate is 5.5% = P&I of $1,225
After seven years the loan balance is $95,000

After seven years of payments, your loan balance will be reduced by $55,000 instead of just $16,000 with the 30-year mortgage. Notice also that the interest rate was about ½ of a percent cheaper for the 15-year mortgage because shorter mortgages are less expensive. Also notice that although the length of the mortgage was cut in half, the monthly payments did not double.

Assuming a 7% commission rate on $205,000, you would actually pay about $14,300

| | |
|---|---|
| Sale price | $205,000 |
| Less Loan Balance: | $95,000 |
| Less Sales Commission: | $14,300 |
| You net: | $95,700 compared to only $56,600 with a 30-year mortgage |

By choosing a 15-year mortgage instead, you will have a very large down payment for your next home, which could mean even smaller monthly payments or a larger or more expensive home. Of course, if you cannot afford the higher monthly payments for the 15-year mortgage, then you could simply calculate a smaller mortgage for yourself using the Time Value of Money, but make it 15 years instead of 30.

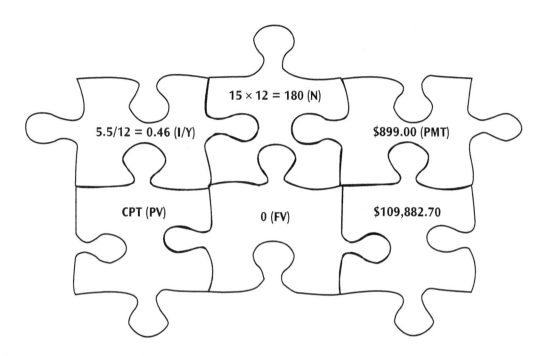

Take your new amount, plus the $17,000 down payment, and now you know how much house you can afford if you get a 15-year mortgage instead. Of course, you are sacrificing a little for your first house to have more money for your next home, and each one after that. You can choose to live a little better today or a lot better the rest of your life.

### DETERMINE YOUR HOME OWNERSHIP NEEDS

Your next step is to determine what you need from your house. Do you need two bedrooms? Do you need an office? Do you need to be close to public transportation or close to your work? Do you need a large backyard for horses or a small backyard for grilling and entertainment, but not too much that you need a riding lawnmower? If you are making this purchase with a spouse, then sit down with him or her and start talking about what you really need in your first home. Start thinking about practical matters as well, not just wishes. For instance, everyone loves a jetted Jacuzzi tub in the master bathroom, but nobody ever actually uses it. Do you really need a large room or basement for your exercise equipment? Will you really work out at home? Take a look at Craigslist and you will see home gyms and weight sets for sale or for free all the time because nobody ever actually uses them, even though they are good in concept.

### OBTAIN FINANCING (THE MORTGAGE MYSTERY REVEALED)

As if buying a home was not confusing enough, buying a mortgage has its own set of complications. Now that you know what you can afford, what you are willing to spend, and what you are looking for, it is time to obtain your financing. You would not simply buy the first house or the first car you ever saw, so you should not necessarily buy the first mortgage you see either. Shop around for mortgage companies that have the best rates and the service that you like. You can start by searching the Internet for rates with various lenders and then begin talking to your local lenders. Mortgage brokers may be able to shop around and help you obtain the best rates, whereas individual mortgage companies, such as Wells Fargo, can only offer you their products and rates. This does not mean that you should avoid the large mortgage companies; it just means that you need to shop around. If you complete the three steps first, you will feel much more relaxed and confident. There is nothing worse than finding the house you absolutely love first, and then going through the three steps only to discover you cannot obtain the loan.

You know you want a house and you know that you will need a loan to purchase it, but did you know that there were so many options available to you? There is more to a mortgage than just the interest rate. To begin, there are three types of mortgages; fixed-rate, adjustable-rate, and hybrid. The fixed-rate and adjustable-rate mortgages may come in 15-year, 20-year, or 30-year maturities. The hybrid loans will also come in these same maturities, but they will have a little twist to them, which will be covered shortly. Another subset, most commonly available with the fixed-rate mortgages, is conventional and government-guaranteed programs. Conventional mortgages are those where the first mortgage is no more than 80% of the home's value. The government-guaranteed programs include an FHA mortgage or a VA mortgage. The FHA mortgage is part of the Federal Housing Authority (FHA) and is designed to assist first-time home buyers, low-income families, or others who qualify for a mortgage, but do not have enough cash for a 20% down payment. A VA loan is from the Veteran's Administration (VA) and is designed to help veterans and other qualifying military members purchase a home with little or no money down.

A fixed-rate mortgage is exactly what the name implies. The mortgage rate is fixed for the entire length of the loan. If you secure a 30-year fixed-rate mortgage at 6%, then you will pay 6% on the outstanding principle (the amount you still owe) for the next 30 years. The principle and interest portion of the mortgage will remain the same for the next 30 years, just like a car purchase where your monthly payment is the same every month until the loan is paid off. Fixed-rate loans are recommended for those who are risk-averse, or who plan to spend many years in their new home. The advantage of a fixed-rate mortgage is that you have the security of knowing what your monthly payments will be. The only real disadvantage of a fixed-rate mortgage is that they tend to be higher than those of a variable-rate or hybrid mortgage. Of course, if you can afford the higher payments, a 15-year fixed rate mortgage has a lower interest rate, usually around ½ of a percent, than a 30-year mortgage. Banks reward the shorter-length mortgage because they are taking less risk because you will only borrow the money for 15 years instead of 30.

The only amount of your monthly payment that could change is the taxes and insurance portion. Most mortgage payments include an escrow amount, which simply means that an amount of money is set aside each month in escrow or on hold. When your annual or semiannual home owner's insurance premiums are due, the payment will come out of the escrow balance. Also, when your annual real estate taxes are due, including county and city taxes, these payments will also come out of your escrow balance. Essentially, you pay what is called PITI, which stands for principle, interest, taxes, and insurance. When you calculate your mortgage payment with an online or financial calculator, you are only calculating the PI, the principle and the interest. Your actual monthly payment will usually include the TI, taxes and insurance, portion as well. Because tax rates can change and because home values tend to increase over time, it stands to reason that your taxes and insurance will increase over time as well. This portion of your monthly payment will increase even if you have a conventional fixed-rate mortgage. It is your principle and interest that will not change.

A variable-rate mortgage has an interest rate that is tied to a certain index, which varies or changes. Different lenders use different indices, but they are always tied to a major financial index that is widely reported and monitored. Similar to credit cards, they charge a certain percentage above the index. For instance, your mortgage rate may be 2% above a certain index. If the index is currently 3.5%, then your mortgage interest rate is 5.5% (3.5% + 2%). Of course, if the index rate jumps to 7%, then your interest rate can jump to 9% (7% + 2%). To prevent major swings in your mortgage rate, most variable-rate mortgages do have annual caps on them. In other words, your rate may be 2% above the index, but it can only increase by a total of 2% per year or a maximum of 8% over the life of the loan. That means if the index jumps from 3.5% to 7% in one year, your rate can only go up by 2% based on the cap, even though the index rose by 3.5%. Of course, if the index does not come down, then your rate can increase again the following year until you are once again paying 2% above the index. Because the bank is taking less risk with a variable-rate mortgage, your initial rate will be less than that of a fixed-rate loan. Basically, you are taking more risk, so the bank is willing to give you a discount for that risk.

A hybrid mortgage is a combination of a fixed-rate and an adjustable-rate mortgage. A hybrid consists of a fixed time period, such as 5, 7, or 10 years, and will then become adjustable from that point forward. A hybrid will usually have a slightly lower rate than a fixed-rate mortgage, but a slightly higher rate than an adjustable-rate mortgage. The advantage of the hybrid is that you will have several years to determine if you are going to stay in your house or refinance your mortgage before the rates become adjustable. In many instances, if you are only planning to own your home for a period of seven years or less, then the hybrid mortgage may make the most sense. Keep in mind that plans can change, and the option to refinance may not exist when you want to. Make sure you choose the length of the loan and the type of mortgage carefully.

Purchasing a home is one of the biggest financial decisions we will ever make. Almost no one can afford to pay cash for the full purchase price, so we need to borrow the money. However, the lender is going to want us to have some "skin in the game." That means we need to pay part of the purchase price ourselves. This is called making a down payment, a percentage of the purchase price. This is usually a minimum of 5% but can go as high as 20%. Assuming that you are unable to come up with a full 20% down payment, but you still want to purchase a home, you still may be able to do so utilizing one of many special programs offered by lenders.

Of course, any time you put less than 20% down and borrow more than 80% on your first mortgage, the first mortgage lender will require you to purchase private mortgage insurance (PMI). PMI is an insurance that protects the lender in case you default on the loan. On a $200,000 FHA loan, with excellent credit, it would run about $95 per month, in addition to some upfront premiums that you will pay during closing.

The concept of PMI is that the lender is taking a greater risk by lending you money because you only put a small amount of money down, relative to the cost of the home. It makes sense when you think about it. If you put $40,000 down on your $200,000 home and you begin to have financial difficulties, you would likely do everything in your power to continue making payments on your house so you would not lose it to the bank. After all, you sank a large amount of money into the transaction already. On the other hand, if you only put $10,000 down (a 5% down payment) on that same $200,000 home, then perhaps you may decide if the payments get to be too much that you would rather consider it a loss and walk away from the mortgage and let the bank take over. Such action would result in a huge expense and hassle for the bank. The really bad news is that if you stop paying for your house, the PMI does protect the bank, but you would still lose your house and destroy your credit rating, even though the bank does not really lose money. One of the key disadvantages of PMI is that now, even if home values increase rapidly, or you accelerate your payments so that you quickly own more than 20% of your home's equity, you are still obligated to pay the premiums for PMI for a minimum of five years. At $100 per month, that means you are guaranteed to have to pay about $6,000 in PMI premiums.

Because PMI is expensive and most people do not have 20% to put down on their first home, one would expect that most everyone is paying PMI. On the contrary, there are ways to avoid paying PMI. Obviously if you are currently in college this information may not be immediately relevant to you, but tuck this away and in a few years it could save you a lot of money. If you put 10% down on your house and borrow 80% on your first mortgage, then your first mortgage lender would not require PMI because the loan is for 80%. Of course, that leaves 10% not yet accounted for, otherwise it would not add up to 100%. You can get a second mortgage, also referred to as a home equity line of credit (HELOC) for the remaining 10%. In other words, with a $200,000 house, you can put $20,000 down, borrow $160,000 as your first mortgage and then get a second mortgage for the remaining $20,000. A $20,000 HELOC would have a monthly payment of about $160. After tax considerations, you could end up paying the same or less than you would in PMI premiums, with your entire money going toward reducing your overall loan amount instead of paying an insurance premium that does you no good directly.

If you are not able to get a conventional mortgage and you choose a government-sponsored program, you will need to understand some of the restrictions and details. For VA loans, only certain military veterans are eligible. If you are eligible or interested in an FHA loan, you will need to be aware of the disadvantages. When considering an FHA loan with less than 20% down, you will still be required to purchase the PMI. One of the advantages of an FHA loan is that you may still be eligible to put just 5% down on your house if you meet all the criteria for an FHA loan in your area. You should also be aware of any first-time home buyer programs available in your state and sometimes locally. In addition, for certain professions such as teachers, firefighters, and police officers, certain communities have home purchase incentives as well. Be sure to research all your options so that you can get the best deal possible for your situation.

Evaluating your mortgage alternatives is very complicated. There are some basic do's and don'ts of which you need to be aware. You should properly prepare your finances long before you actually get your mortgage. It seems that everyone has an opinion on what you should do to prepare. In fact, entire books are written about the mortgage and home-buying process. We have narrowed the list down to the top five recommendations.

# THE 5 DO'S FROM THE MORTGAGE EXPERTS

### #1 Make your loan and debt payments on time.

Your credit score is the golden key to getting approved for your mortgage. One of the key components to keep your credit score high or to improve your score is going to be making the payments on any loans or credit cards on time. The longer your history of on-time payments, the higher your credit score. A higher credit score could mean the difference between getting a mortgage and getting denied. It could also mean the difference between getting a great mortgage rate and paying a much higher rate which could result in hundreds of dollars more per month in interest.

### #2 Prioritize your bills if you do have to skip some payments.

In the world of credit scores, not all bills are created equal. Your debt and loan payments are more important. Do not skip your rent or car payment. Most people choose to skip these larger payments because they figure that skipping one car payment could save them $300 per month or one rent payment would save them $600 per month; whereas they would have to skip multiple other bills, such as the cable, utilities, and cell phone to come up with the same $300 to $600. In this instance, more is less. You would be better off skipping the cable or utility bills first. The reason is because late debt payments and rent payments get reported to the credit bureaus first.

Most cable and utility bills do not report late payments to the credit bureau until they reach at least 90 days late. If you are in a temporary bind one month, choose to pay one of these other bills late and then try to catch up within the next couple of months. Keep in mind this advice is only useful for temporary setbacks, such as a computer glitch at work that delays your paycheck, or a car accident with a deductible that you could not otherwise meet. For long-term financial issues, your rent and electricity would take priority, as you do not want to be evicted or have your power shut off. Of course, if you are facing a long-term financial setback, now is not the time to be purchasing a house anyway.

#### #3 Consider paying off more debt and have a lower down payment.

Assuming that you are saving for or already have your down payment, you will have to decide how much you want to put down on the house and how much other debt you are willing or able to carry forward. If your current debt level is preventing you from purchasing the house you want based on the bank's calculations, perhaps you could take some of what you put away for your down payment to reduce or eliminate one of your debts, such as a car loan or a credit card. For example, if you have saved enough for a 10% down payment, perhaps you could use half of that money to pay off one or several loans and put just 5% down on the house.

Eliminating a loan payment or credit card, or reducing the balance on a credit card, could result in more cash flow each month. For example, if you still owe $5,000 on your car loan, which has payments of $300 per month, you could pay off the car loan right away with cash you have saved for the down payment, and now suddenly you will have an extra $300 per month to spend or put toward your mortgage payment. In addition, the bank may see that you have $5,000 less in debt and $300 more per month in cash flow, which could help you qualify for the mortgage. Of course, you will still have to anticipate that at some point in the future, you may end up with a new car loan.

#### #4 Get the mortgage first.

You have two options when you start house hunting. You can get prequalified or preapproved. Prequalification is easy. Any real estate agent can pre-qualify you, as well as a mortgage company. Prequalification simply means that a professional has asked you what your income is and what your debt payments are, and then they use a basic formula to determine the absolute most you could afford to spend on a house, based on current estimated interest rates.

Getting preapproved is a much more involved process. To get preapproved, you must go through a mortgage company (or a bank that sells mortgages). You will be required to show proof of income, including several pay stubs, and possibly last year's tax return. You will also have to list all your debt payments and allow the mortgage company to pull your credit report. For pre-approval you will have to pay a minimal fee because there is more work involved.

Preapproval means that you are telling the seller that you are serious when you make an offer on a house. You have more negotiating power with the seller. If two people put an offer on a home and one is prequalified and the other is preapproved, the seller is more likely to accept the one from the buyer who is preapproved. Otherwise, the seller will have to wait to see if the other buyer even gets approved by the mortgage company. Once the seller accepts a contract, the status changes from "for sale" to "contract pending." A house that is under contract tends to stay off the market for four to six weeks. That means other potential buyers do not get to see the house during this period of time. What if the seller accepts a contract from someone who is only prequalified and they end up not getting approved? Now the seller has to relist the house, losing precious time, and making yet another mortgage payment. That is a lot of unnecessary risk for the seller. A seller cannot accept any other offers, even if they are for more money, while their house is under contract.

### #5 Increase the size of the down payment.

Although this suggestion may seem counterintuitive to suggestion #3 mentioned earlier, keep in mind that personal finance must reflect the person's finances. In some instances cash flow may be the impeding factor. In other instances the size of the down payment may be the one thing keeping you from getting a mortgage. You have to look at the factors involved and see what makes the most sense for your situation. If you want a $200,000 house with $10,000 down and the mortgage company will only lend you $180,000, then you will need to come up with an additional $10,000. In this instance, it may not be your monthly debt payments keeping you from your home, but your down payment. Of course, if you need this much money, you may not be able to get it right away, but you may be able to save up in a short period of time or get assistance from your family.

As you may have suspected, because we compiled our favorite top five "Do's" from mortgage experts, we have also compiled our favorite top five "Don'ts" as well.

# THE 5 DON'TS FROM THE MORTGAGE EXPERTS

### #1 Do not make any large purchases, especially on credit.

Do not buy a car 90 days before purchasing your home. Although you budget your money wisely, a mortgage broker is concerned that you may not fully understand the impact of the new debt on your budget. You will not have had enough time to get used to your new monthly car payment, which means your budget may be much tighter than you realize. In addition, by taking on more debt, not only will your credit score be slightly lower but you may also not be able to qualify for as much mortgage or at least not at the best rate.

### #2 Do not try to shoot for that six-bedroom house right away.

Do not buy more house than you need right now. There is a reason why they call it a starter home. You may be planning to have six kids, but you do not need to start out with a six-bedroom house to accommodate all of them, unless you are already pregnant with sextuplets. The average family stays in their home for less than seven years. Think about how many more opportunities you will have over the next seven years. How long were you planning to wait until you start a family? How long before your sixth child? Make your first home purchase one that is low maintenance, close to everything you will need, and well within your budget.

### #3 Do not just get prequalified, but get preapproved.

Because preapproval means the bank has already agreed they will lend you a certain amount of money (with certain restrictions of course), you will look more serious as a buyer and you will be in a stronger position to negotiate. In addition, you will not be looking at homes that end up out of your price range if the bank will not agree to lend enough money to make the purchase. Of course, you should also take the preapproval amount with a grain of salt, so-to-speak, because the bank may be willing to lend you more than you can afford for your lifestyle. Remember, the bank does not care if you want to save for retirement, take vacations, or eat out every night. They assume you are willing to give all those things up if they lend you the maximum amount.

### #4 Do not forget your money personality.

Following along with the preapproval, you need to keep in mind what your goals are and how you like to spend money. Perhaps the house is most important to you and you are willing to give up vacations for the next five years, and you do not like to shop nor do you expect to buy a new car for several years. On the other hand, what if you were looking forward to more free time on your new boat, or you like to shop on the weekends or go snorkeling or diving. Do not let yourself become house rich and cash poor. A couple in this situation may have a nice house, especially for their age and income bracket, but they have no money left over for anything else, including entertainment, maintenance, repairs, and upgrades.

### #5 Do not forget that home ownership comes with burdens, expenses, and repairs.

Most people understand that cars come with some basic maintenance and some unexpected repairs as well. We also expect that at some point the repairs become too expensive so we buy a new car. Houses also have repairs and maintenance, but in many cases you are dealing with a house worth a few hundred thousand dollars, not a car worth ten or twenty thousand dollars. That means that the maintenance and repairs may also be more expensive. For instance, a new heat pump may run several thousand dollars, and a new roof may cost $5,000 to $10,000. You should be able to set some money aside to make these repairs when the time comes. In addition, you will want to make improvements to your home over time. Perhaps you would like granite countertops or hardwood floors. Maybe you want to finish your basement or put in a nice closet system. Owning a home involves more than simply paying your mortgage so you have a place to sleep.

### EVALUATE PROPERTIES

With the knowledge of how much you are willing and able to spend, you can begin to evaluate properties. Keep in mind that part of the property evaluation process includes knowing the different communities and locations throughout the city and/or county where you are looking to purchase. At this stage you should consider selecting a real estate agent. A good real estate agent will be able to explain the various communities, school districts, crime rates, and so forth. In addition, he or she should be showing you homes that are within your price range and meet as many of your specifications as possible. Keep in mind that you have the right to "fire" your real estate agent if you are not receiving the kind of service you desire. You are essentially interviewing real estate agents to determine who you want to work with. Visit open houses, check the homes listed in the local newspaper, and use the

Internet for your research as well, such as www.realtor.com.[27] The more knowledge you have about the local housing market, the better positioned you will be to get the best deal on your house purchase.

A good real estate agent will show you properties in your price range. They can also help you arrange the home inspection and appraisal. It is nearly impossible to avoid a real estate agent given that you are making a large transaction requiring a professional with ample real estate knowledge. Considering that real estate agents must complete an extensive training program and pass a state-mandated exam, they are much better equipped to handle all of the legal aspects of a real estate transaction. In addition, although you are likely to purchase between three and five homes in your lifetime, most real estate agents handle that many transactions each year or possibly each month.

You want to learn as much about the area as you can before making your buying decision. Be aware of the zoning laws, not only on the property you are looking to purchase but also on the surrounding property. It is not uncommon to buy a home that has a beautiful view of a forest or of a peaceful farm landscape only to find out within a few years that it was zoned commercial, and you are now staring into a grocery store parking lot or a 500-unit apartment complex. A good rule of thumb is that you can only control what you own. That means any empty fields around you can be converted into almost anything within its zoning laws. You can even Google Earth[28] the property. This will give you an aerial perspective of the land. Perhaps a large industrial plant or a hog farm is just on the other side of some nearby trees. If the trees are removed or the wind shifts slightly, you could be in for a big surprise. An even bigger surprise might be learning who your real estate agent really represents.

# Who Is Working for You?

We are going to change directions for just a moment to make sure you understand how real estate agents are compensated and that you understand who is working for whom. There is nothing wrong with asking an agent how they are being compensated. In fact, it would be irresponsible not to ask. You want to make sure that you do not have to pay your buyer's agent because they will receive a portion of the sales commission. Make sure that you understand the difference between the buyer's agent and the seller's agent.

A huge warning is that real estate agents are compensated by the seller. In fact, if you are talking to the agent who listed the home for sale, they must work in the seller's best interest. It is recommended that you avoid dual agency, which could be a large pothole. An agent really cannot serve both interests. The seller wants the biggest price, and the buyer wants to pay the lowest price. A listing agent will represent the seller's interest. For example, if you tell the agent that you would actually be willing to pay much more for the house, then the listing agent is obligated to tell the seller this information. For this reason, you need to choose your own buyer's agent. You want to have someone who represents your best interest so they can better negotiate a fair price. Some experts recommend that you should not even choose a buyer's agent that is with the same firm as the seller's agent. The choice is up to you.

Real estate commissions generally run between 5% and 8%, with most falling in the 6% to 7% range. Normally, the buyer's agent and the seller's agent end up splitting the commission, so each will receive half. On a 7% commission rate, a $200,000 house would result in $14,000 total commissions compared to $10,500 on a $150,000 home. If you were the person receiving the commission, which house would you try to persuade someone to buy?

The commission levels are one of the many reasons real estate agents will allow price creep with home prices. You will start with looking at a $150,000 house, and then you will be shown a $170,000 house that has a larger backyard and an extra bonus room. Next you will be shown an $180,000 house that has a large dining room with crown molding and 9-ft ceilings. Pretty soon you are looking at homes that are much more than you can afford. And because the bank may approve you for a loan for that amount, it makes the original $150,000 house that much smaller and less desirable. It is important that once you have determined your budget, you must make a point to have your real estate agent stay within your desired price range.

Although the buyer has little control over the commission rates, at some point in the future you will likely be the seller instead. As a seller you have the power to negotiate the real estate agent's commission rate. Of course, most people believe that asking for a lower commission will result in less service from the agent, but that is not entirely true. According to a *Consumer Reports* National Research Center's Annual Questionnaire, agents provided the same amount of guidance and attracted good buyers at almost the same rate, no matter what their commission levels were. In fact, slightly more homes sold in less than a month from those agents whose commission rates were 3% or less as compared to those who were compensated 6% or more.[29]

Even if you are purchasing directly from a builder who has a model home and a representative on site, you want to have your own agent with you to represent your interests. Many people just work with the builder's sales agent, but they are simply a seller's agent, working in the best interest of the builder.

## PRICE THE PROPERTY

Once you have selected the properties that you are most interested in, you will need to choose your favorite and make an offer. This is the part where you will need to negotiate. In a very hot seller's market, which means that there are more buyers than homes, you may have to make an offer that is more than the asking price or add an escalation clause in your offer that says you are willing to spend $1,000 more than the highest offer, up to a certain maximum (similar to how you can bid on eBay). In a buyer's market you have much more power to negotiate by asking for a lower price, asking the seller to pay some or all the closing costs, or in the case of a brand-new home, you may ask the builder to add a fence, or back porch, or any other number of upgrades. Even in a normal housing market, you still may have some wiggle room with the price and closing costs. You will want to work with your real estate agent to make that determination.

When you are ready to make an offer on a home, keep in mind that you are negotiating, so you should be prepared to walk away. Of course your real estate agent, along with your own personal research, should help you understand the market. With rare exception, the seller needs to sell their home, which is why they have it listed in the first place. They can only wait so long because they are either moving or have already moved to another home and are paying two mortgages during that time. You should make an offer and be prepared to wait. The longer it sits, the more willing they are to come down in price.

Keep in mind that during a buyer's market, everything shifts in the buyer's favor. Generally, there are more homes for sale than there are buyers, so each seller is competing against the others to get you to buy their house. During the buyer's market you have more room to negotiate in terms of price as well as other conditions such as the closing date, the amount the seller will pay toward closing, and so forth. On the flip side, during a seller's market, prices are generally creeping upward due to a high demand for housing with few homes available for sale. In this type of market, the buyer has little room for negotiation and may actually have to offer more than the listing price of the house.

Part of the overall pricing of the property is the actual binding offer that you make or the accepted contract. On nearly all real estate contracts there are contingency clauses. For instance, if you are also trying to sell your home, you may have a home-to-sell contingency. That would mean that if your house does not sell, you could get out of the contract. You may also have a contingency based on the home inspection or even the mortgage interest rates because they can change daily. There are countless numbers of contingency possibilities, so you will need to discuss these with your real estate agent and consider any contingencies that the seller puts into the contract as well to make sure you are comfortable with them.

## Close the Deal

After all the negotiations are complete, it is time to close the transaction. Unfortunately, an accepted agreement between the buyer and the seller is just one early step in a long process. Most real estate transactions, after the agreement has taken place, will last approximately three to six weeks. The mortgage company will require an appraisal of the property to make sure that the amount they are lending is in line with the actual value of the house. There is also other paperwork involved, much of which takes place behind the scenes. A real estate settlement company or an attorney will be involved in the process as well; making sure everything is as it should be. The good news is that you will have time to pack your existing belongings and be better prepared to make the move when the day of settlement does arrive.

When it is time to close the loan, you will spend several hours signing documents. This is an arduous process that although significant, does not require both spouses to be present. You may both choose to attend the closing but if you both have limited vacation time it may make more sense to have one spouse give the other one "Power of Attorney" to sign in their place. Your real estate agent can even sign the paperwork for both, if you so choose. It is here at the closing where you write your check, and everyone involved in the home buying process gets paid.

# WHERE DID ALL THE MONEY GO?

Of course, there are more players involved in a real estate transaction than just the real estate agent. Do not forget about the mortgage lender. In most instances, a mortgage lender is also paid a commission. That means that the more you borrow, the more they get paid. An attorney or settlement company also gets involved. Sometimes they are paid a fixed fee, and other times their fee varies based on the price of the house.

The list continues to grow. You have to buy home owner's insurance. Nobody will lend money against an asset unless that asset is insured. You will also have to pay title insurance. Title insurance is a one-time fee that will protect both you and the lender in the event that someone else comes along later and claims that they have true title to that property or the land it sits on.

The mortgage company will require an appraisal of the property, which you will have to pay for. The appraisal is to ensure that they are lending you an amount of money that is in step with the true value of the home. In many cases you will also be required to have an inspection of the property, or you may choose to have an inspection done regardless. Whereas the appraiser looks at the value by comparing your home to similar homes, the inspector actually looks at the electrical wiring, the plumbing, the condition of the roof or the foundation. The inspector makes sure that everything still looks up to code and identifies any major issues such as rotting wood or cracks in the foundation that may need repair.

Part of any home purchase will include real estate taxes and some fees that are paid up front. Most people will at least have to pay county taxes and in most instances, there will be city taxes as well.

Now you can see where all the money goes from your original check. But you are still not done. As you are unpacking and trying to settle into your new home, several more expenses will come your way.

You will likely pay a hookup fee for your cable and Internet service. You may also have to hire movers or at least rent a moving truck. Once you move into your new home, you will be solicited by several businesses for other services and products you may want or need. After all, once you purchase a house, the purchase becomes part of the public record, allowing businesses to identify new home owners. The termite or pest control company will stop by your house or send you something in the mail. Lawn care service companies will send flyers in the hopes that you simply do not have enough time to care for your lawn on your own, which includes not only cutting the grass but also properly fertilizing the lawn and spraying for ticks, fleas, and even grubs. You may decide you want a fence for some privacy or to keep your dog from running through the neighborhood. You will find that there are more alarm companies than you can count, and each one will want you to buy their monitored service. Of course, a monitored alarm service will require a home phone line as well.

Do not forget that you now have a new home but no furniture, or you may still have your old furniture. That means that you will likely be shopping at furniture and mattress stores soon. In addition, because you want to make your home your own, you will want to plant some flowers and paint the walls, requiring a visit to home improvement stores as well.

Keep in mind that when you purchase a house, and all these transactions take place and all these business and service providers have their hand out for some money, the only person who wrote a check in this scenario is you, the home buyer. Even though the commissions on the sale of the house were paid by the seller, the fees really came out of the money that you paid; it just filtered through the real estate agents' hands. Notice also that the more you spend on the house, the more money all these people make. A larger yard means more fencing and more lawn care. A larger house means more furniture and a larger insurance and tax bill. More rooms mean more hookup fees for cable. The list continues. The point is that everybody but you is hoping that you spend the most money possible on the largest and most expensive home you can find because it is in their best interest. Nobody is going to stop and think about what is in your best interest except you.

# THE COST OF FINANCIAL IGNORANCE

Our young couple almost bought a house that was much more than they needed and would have stretched their cash flow to its very limits. It would also have tied them to a particular location very early in their careers. As it turned out, after just her first year with the firm she was offered a big promotion. However, it was in another part of the country. Not being saddled with a house allowed them to easily pick up and move so she could take advantage of a wonderful job opportunity.

Had they bought the house and then sold it the following year it would have cost them lots of money. The house would not have appreciated enough nor could they have built enough equity in the house by paying down the mortgage to even cover the real estate commission, much less all the other costs associated with moving.

Assume they paid $250,000 for a house. Even if the house appreciated 5.4%[30] and they could sell it for full price, the young couple would lose on just the real estate commission alone if they had to sell it so soon after buying it.

| | |
|---|---|
| Appreciated value after one year | $263,500 |
| Sales commission at 6% | 15,810 |
| Net proceeds from sale | $247,690 |
| | |
| Original purchase price | $250,000 |
| Net proceeds from sale | 247,690 |
| The Cost of Financial Ignorance | −$  2,310 |

# TAXES

## A Dollar Saved Is a $1.30 Earned

Two students were lined up after class to ask us a couple of questions. The first student proudly boasted that he had just received his tax refund of more than $2,200. Excited does not even begin to describe how this student felt about his recent windfall. He started listing off all the things he was going to do with his money. The second student overheard the first and made a comment that she too received a refund but it was only $80. She wished she had received such a large refund as her fellow student and congratulated him on his good fortune. She asked us what she could change so she could get a larger refund next year.

Imagine both of their surprises when we congratulated her for being a far superior tax planner and chided him on receiving such a large refund. What did he do wrong?

# WHO PAYS THE TAXES?

Let us start with the basics. How much do you plan to make when you graduate? Hopefully you have researched your career field and at least have some idea of the average starting salary for your job in whatever city you will live. If you have no idea, then you should refer to the careers chapter of this book.

Although starting salaries vary greatly depending on the career field and the city in which you will live, it is not uncommon to expect upwards of $30,000 to start. Teachers and social workers may earn less in many cities, whereas accountants and engineers may earn more. Of course, these are only starting salaries. You may find that early in your career your salary will rise rapidly. For instance, you may start out making $30,000 and could find yourself earning $40,000 to $45,000 within a few years of graduation.

Keep in mind that people generally marry within the same socioeconomic class. Because you are going to be a college graduate, you are likely to marry a person who will also be a college graduate, or at the very least a high-paying skill-related trade. You can expect that your spouse will make about the same amount of money that you will earn. That means if you are each earning $45,000 within a few years after graduation, and you are married, then your household income will be $90,000. Throw in a couple of bonuses, and you may very well be making a six-figure income as a couple. This means you are now going to have a significant tax liability.

To understand the U.S. federal tax system, it is important to know who actually pays the taxes. Although there are many different levels of taxation and several tax brackets, one way to break down the tax burden is to divide taxpayers into three categories: rich, middle class, and lower class. But how do you define rich? What is the cutoff for middle class? How poor do you have to be in order to be considered poor by definition? Maybe a better way to divide taxpayers is by where they rank in terms of income compared to everyone else.

How much money do you think someone has to earn to be in the top 1% of wage earners, meaning they make more money than 99% of everyone else? How much would someone have to earn just to be in the top 10% of all wage earners in our country?

We asked a group of students to take their best guess. The students guessed that the top 1% must be really, really rich, just like you see on the MTV show Cribs. Perhaps the Bill Gateses and the Warren Buffets of our country represent the top 1%. The top 10% must be the top company CEOs and the most elite that Hollywood has to offer. The students also guessed that the top 1% of all taxpayers must pay a very small portion of the overall taxes, even though they are rich, because they only represent 1% of all taxpayers.

Now take a look at the actual numbers from tax year 2008:

| AGI PERCENTILE | AGI THRESHOLD | % OF TAXES PAID |
|---|---|---|
| Top 1% | $380,354 | 38.0% |
| Top 10% | $113,799 | 69.9% |
| Top 25% | $67,280 | 86.3% |
| Top 50% | $33,048 | 97.3% |
| Bottom 50% | < $33,048 | 2.7% |

\* AGI: Adjusted Gross Income.
*Source:* http://www.ntu.org/tax-basics/who-pays-income-taxes.html.

NOTE: Keep in mind that the top 10% includes the top 1% as well, and the top 25% include the top 10%, so the percentages keep increasing as you move down the table except for the bottom 50%.

There are a couple of things you really need to pay attention to with the tax numbers. First, the top 10% of wage earners carry almost 70% of the entire tax burden. That would be like a group of 10 people splitting $40 worth of pizza for lunch and one person has to pay $28 by himself or herself and the other nine people get to split the remaining $12. The other significant piece of information that you should notice is that you, as a college graduate, will be that one person who pays the $28 for the pizza in the group. Your income, combined with your spouse's income, will put you close to, if not over, the $113,799 mark, which means you will be among the top 10% of all wage earners in the country. You will be among the rich.

So how does it feel to be rich? You may not believe that you will be among the rich because in movies and on television we only hear about the very rich. We hear about people who earn millions of dollars per year, but there are so few of them that to be in the top 1% of all wage earners, the multimillionaires along with many doctors and small business owners are all grouped together.

It may seem strange to think that a college degree can launch you and your spouse into the top 10% of wage earners, but you have to consider the fact that fewer people finish college than you may expect. To begin with, not everyone graduates from high school. For various reasons, some students simply do not complete their high school education, and they tend to be the lowest wage earners. Then, just over half of all high school graduates attend college. High school graduates simply do not earn as much money as college graduates. Of the students who choose to attend college, not all of them make it through to graduation. So just making it all the way through college, particularly if you get an undergraduate degree, puts you into an elite group. If you go on and get an advanced degree you are even more likely to earn a high salary and become part of the top 10% or even top 1% of wage earners in this country. According to the IRS definition, you are going to be "rich." Because Uncle Sam takes a portion of what you earn, the key is to think about the tax effect on your decision making. You cannot ignore taxes even when making normal, everyday decisions about your life.

## 2010 Schedule X—Single

| TAXABLE INCOME IS OVER: | BUT NOT OVER: | THE TAX IS: | OF THE AMOUNT OVER: |
|---|---|---|---|
| $0 | $8,375 | $0 + 10% | $0 |
| 8,375 | 34,000 | 837.50 + 15% | 8,375 |
| 34,000 | 82,400 | 4,681.25 + 25% | 34,000 |
| 82,400 | 171,850 | 16,781.25 + 28% | 82,400 |
| 171,850 | 373,650 | 41,827.25 + 33% | 171,850 |
| 373,650 | — | 108,421.25 + 35% | 373,650 |

## 2010 Schedule Y-1—Married Filing Jointly or Qualifying Widow(er)

| TAXABLE INCOME IS OVER: | BUT NOT OVER: | THE TAX IS: | OF THE AMOUNT OVER: |
|---|---|---|---|
| $0 | $16,750 | $0 + 10% | $0 |
| 16,750 | 68,000 | 1,675.00 + 15% | 16,750 |
| 68,000 | 137,300 | 9,362.50 + 25% | 68,000 |
| 137,300 | 209,250 | 26,687.50 + 28% | 137,300 |
| 209,250 | 373,650 | 46,833.50 + 33% | 209,250 |
| 373,650 | — | 101,085.50 + 35% | 373,650 |

## 2010 Schedule Y-2—Married Filing Separately

| TAXABLE INCOME IS OVER: | BUT NOT OVER: | THE TAX IS: | OF THE AMOUNT OVER: |
|---|---|---|---|
| $0 | $8,375 | $0 + 10% | $0 |
| 8,375 | 34,000 | 837.50 + 15% | 8,375 |
| 34,000 | 68,650 | 4,681.25 + 25% | 34,000 |
| 68,650 | 104,625 | 13,343.75 + 28% | 68,650 |
| 104,625 | 186,825 | 23,416.75 + 33% | 104,625 |
| 186,825 | — | 50,542.75 + 35% | 186,825 |

## 2010 Schedule Z—Head of Household[31]

| TAXABLE INCOME IS OVER: | BUT NOT OVER: | THE TAX IS: | OF THE AMOUNT OVER: |
|---|---|---|---|
| $0 | $11,950 | $0 + 10% | $0 |
| 11,950 | 45,550 | 1,195.00 + 15% | 11,950 |
| 45,550 | 117,650 | 6,235.00 + 25% | 45,550 |
| 117,650 | 190,550 | 24,260.00 + 28% | 117,650 |
| 190,550 | 373,650 | 44,672.00 + 33% | 190,550 |
| 373,650 | — | 105,095.00 + 35% | 373,650 |

# TAX EFFECT

If your income places you in the 25% federal marginal tax bracket, then you only get to keep 75 cents of every dollar you earn. In other words, you get to keep 75%, and the federal government gets the other 25%. To have a full dollar of spending money left over after taxes, you have to earn much more than $1.00. In fact, you have to earn $1.33 to have $1.00 left over after taxes. The result is that you have to work 33% harder because of a 25% tax rate.

So how did we determine that it takes $1.33 before taxes to have $1.00 left after taxes? We use some basic math. We know that we want to end up with $1.00 after taxes, and we know that taxes represent 25%. Because taxes are 25%, then that means we get to keep 75%. The algebra question is 75% of what amount of money equals $1.00?

| ? (.75) = $1.00 | What times .75 (which is 75% written in decimal form) equals $1.00? |
| --- | --- |
| ? = $1.00/.75 | Divide both sides of the equation by .75 to keep the "?" by itself on the left |
| ? = $1.33 | $1.00 divided by .75 = $1.33 |

We were able to determine that it takes $1.33 before taxes in the 25% tax bracket to have $1.00 left over after taxes. You can now double-check your answer by multiplying the answer of $1.33 by the tax rate of 25%.

| $1.33 (.25) = $0.33 | We have determined that the amount of taxes on $1.33 = 33 cents |
| --- | --- |
| $1.33 – $0.33 = $1.00 | When we subtract the 33 cents tax expense from the $1.33 we get $1.00 |

A few years ago, a student came to us and said they had an "Aha!" moment. We work in a pretax world. Yet we live and play in a posttax world. In other words, when you are told by your employer how much they are going to pay you, they are referring to your pretax dollars. So in your mind you are earning a certain amount of money that you can spend. However, when you go to make purchases you cannot think in terms of pretax dollars anymore because you do not get to keep your whole paycheck. You only have posttax dollars that you can spend, which means you actually have less money to use for living and playing than what you think you have.

For instance, assume you make $30,000 per year. Your hourly earnings (assuming a 40-hour workweek) are about $15 per hour. When you buy a $30 video game, you may think you worked for two hours to make that purchase. That is because you are paid in the pretax world. Because the "tax man" always gets "his" piece first, you need to realize that you are making your purchase in the posttax world. You may find that you really only get to keep about $10 per hour after all taxes are deducted, which means you really have to work three hours to buy the video game instead of two.

Let's take a look at another example. Assume that your toilet needs repair because it is leaking at the base. With a little bit of effort on the Internet, you can easily determine that the issue is with the O-ring that seals the base of the toilet to the floor. Your brief Internet research should have also revealed that the purchase of a new O-ring would cost around $2.00, and a DIY Web site can easily show you how to do it yourself in about 30 minutes. If you call a plumber, you may get a quote of around $150.

Now that you understand the difference between a pretax and posttax world, you want to determine what your true pretax cost is. In other words, how much money do you have to earn at work to have $150 left over after taxes to pay the plumber? Assuming that you are in the 25% federal marginal tax bracket, you would use the following calculation:

| ? (.75) = $150 | What times .75 (which is 75% written in decimal form) equals $150? |
|---|---|
| ? = $150 / .75 | Divide both sides of the equation by .75 to keep the "?" by itself on the left |
| ? = $200 | $150 divided by .75 = $200 |

The $150 fee charged by the plumber is after-tax dollars. The $200 calculated number is the pretax dollars. You will have to earn $200 at work to have $150 left over after taxes to pay the plumber. Assuming you make $20 per hour, you have to decide if it is worth 10 hours of work to pay the plumber instead of spending a few dollars and 30 minutes of your time to do it yourself.

Now that you can see the difference between making decisions in a posttax world instead of a pretax world, we have more bad news to share with you. At this point we have only used the 25% federal marginal tax bracket. Now we need to add state taxes as well. Plus a little something called FICA, which stands for the Federal Income Contribution Act. Say what? FICA is the combination of Social Security and Medicare taxes. State taxes vary depending on your state and your income. In fact, your state taxes may include some local taxation as well, so it really depends on which city or county you live in within any particular state. Seven states currently do not charge a state income tax (Alaska, Florida, Nevada, South Dakota, Texas, Washington, and Wyoming), with the remaining 43 states, plus Washington, D.C., charging some form of income tax. Although the average tax rate for all states is difficult to determine, we will use 4.35% to keep the math simple.

| | |
|---|---|
| Federal marginal tax rate | 25.00% |
| State marginal tax rate | 4.35% |
| FICA | 7.65% |
| Total marginal tax rate | 37.00% |

When you add payroll taxes (FICA), to your marginal federal tax rate and your marginal state tax rate, you could easily be paying 37% of your marginal income in taxes. That means that more than one-third of what you earn will be "lost" to taxes, so making smart financial decisions with what you have remaining becomes even more important.

Let us take a look at how much an iPod really costs. If you walk into a store such as Best Buy and see an iPod on sale for $199, you may think that is a pretty good deal. If you are thinking in terms of dollars spent or the hours you will have to work to make the purchase, you may decide that the purchase is no big deal because it is less than $200. Now that we have explained the concept of the posttax world, you can calculate how much you will have to earn in pretax dollars to make the purchase. Keep in mind that we now know our total marginal tax rate is 37%. That means the government gets 37% of our money and we get to keep 63%.

$$? (.63) = \$199$$

$$? = \$199/.63$$

$$? = \$315.87$$

To purchase a $199 iPod, you will have to earn around $316. You may still decide you want to purchase the iPod, and there may be nothing wrong with the purchase. The point is that you are now making the purchase fully aware of the true cost to you. There are limited options when it comes to saving money on products, except looking for sales, coupons, or purchasing used items. For instance, you cannot make your own iPod. However, we can save money on services. Everything that we can do ourselves can help us save money. You should never pay people to do those things you are capable of doing yourself. The key word here is "capable," as we don't always have the skills to do everything, and knowing those limitations can save you money in the long run.

The average oil change costs around $35. Five quarts of oil costs around $18. That means we spend an average of $17 on labor. Using our math, we can calculate that we have to earn more than $27 to pay for the labor portion of our oil change. If you are making $30,000 per year, then you have to work two full hours to pay for a 20-minute oil change. You can apply the same math to anything that you pay someone else to do for you. You can also apply the same math when you spend money to eat out. The point is to keep yourself aware of what everything really costs so you can make a much more informed decision with your money.

# AFTER TAX MULTIPLIER

To make the math even easier, we can use a tool called the After Tax Multiplier (ATM). Now don't get this confused with the little machine that spits out cash to you. The ATM is versatile because it can be used to determine both the after-tax dollars as well as the after tax rate. The ATM can be defined as:

$$ATM = 1 - \text{Tax Rate}$$

It really is the simplest math. You can multiply the ATM times the pretax dollars or you can multiply it times the pretax interest rate. For instance, if you know that you are going to make $100, and your tax rate is 35%, then you can take the ATM and multiply it by the $100 you will earn to determine how much money you will have left over:

*NOTE: Keep in mind that when you are converting a percentage to a decimal, you simply move the decimal two digits to the left. So 35% would be .35, and 5% would be .05.

$$ATM = 1 - .35$$

$$\text{After Tax Earnings} = \$100(1 - .35)$$

$$\text{After Tax Earnings} = \$100(0.65)$$

$$\text{After Tax Earnings} = \$65$$

After having made $100, you have just $65 left to spend!

The ATM tool is used the same way you would calculate a sale when you go shopping. For instance, assume you walk into a store and find a great pair of shoes that is regularly $75, but is now on sale for 40% off. How can you determine the sale price?

$$\text{Sale Multiplier} = 1 - .40$$

$$\text{Sale price} = \$75(1 - .40)$$

$$\text{Sale price} = \$75(.60)$$

$$\text{Sale price} = \$45$$

The formula simply indicates that if the sale is 40% off, then you are still paying the remaining 60%. The same logic applies to taxes. If you pay 35% in taxes, then you keep the other 65%.

The formula also applies to pretax interest rates. For instance, if you are in the 25% marginal tax bracket and you can earn 10% interest on your investment, you want to take into account the tax consequences. Because you earn 10%, but have to pay 35% of your earnings in taxes, you want to see what your true effective rate will be.

$$ATM = 1 - .25$$

$$\text{After-Tax Interest} = 10\% \text{ times } (1 - .25)$$

$$\text{After-Tax Interest} = (.10)(1 - .25)$$

$$\text{After-Tax Interest} = (.10)(.75)$$

$$\text{After-Tax Interest} = .075 \text{ or } 7.5\%$$

Essentially, because of your tax bracket, you are effectively earning 7.5% on your investment. Another way to look at that is to say your 10% investment with tax consequences is the same as a 7.5% investment that is tax free.

You can also use the ATM to determine the pretax amount if all you have is the after-tax amount and the tax rate. For instance, if you were to eat at a restaurant and spend $21.26 for your meal, and you were in the 35% tax bracket, then you can easily determine how much you had to earn, before taxes, to have $21.26 left over to pay for the meal. This time, you have to divide by the ATM, instead of multiply.

$$ATM = 1 - .35$$

$$\text{Pretax Earnings} = \$21.26 / (1 - .35)$$

$$\text{Pretax Earnings} = \$21.26 / (0.65)$$

$$\text{Pretax Earnings} = \$32.71$$

Essentially, you had to earn $32.71 to pay for your $21.26 meal. The same principle applies to sales as well. If you see a shirt on the sale rack marked down $45 and the sale is supposed to be 40% off, then you can see what the regular price was or you can make sure the store took enough off the regular price so they are not ripping you off:

$$\text{Sale Multiplier} = 1 - .40$$

$$\text{Regular price} = \$45 / (1 - .40)$$

$$\text{Regular price} = \$45 / .60$$

$$\text{Regular price} = \$75$$

### TRY THIS

You are employed as a surfboard wax technician for $65,000 annual salary. You own a house with an accompanying 30-year, 6.9% APR (annual percentage rate) mortgage. You currently have an extra $100 a month to save or spend, and you are trying to decide what to do. You may pay the extra $100 on your mortgage, buy U.S. government bonds that pay 6% interest (U.S. government bonds are tax free), or buy shares of a mutual fund that pays 6.5% (your capital gains tax rate is 10%). You found the following table in the instructions with this year's tax return.

| INCOME RANGE | | BASE | MARGINAL TAX RATE |
|---|---|---|---|
| $0 | $7,550 | 0 | 10% |
| $7,550 | $30,650 | $755 | 15% |
| $30,650 | $74,200 | $4,220 | 25% |
| $74,200 | $154,800 | $15,107 | 28% |
| $154,800 | $336,550 | $37,675 | 33% |
| $336,550 | no limit | $97,653 | 35% |

# WHAT SHOULD YOU DO? WHY?

Because you have made the wise financial decision to do something with your money to positively affect your net worth, you have identified three opportunities. Which of the three makes the most financial sense?

With an annual income of $65,000, your marginal tax rate is 25%. Marginal tax rate is simply the tax rate on the next dollar you spend. You know that the government bond is tax free, but it only pays 6%. The mutual fund pays 6.5%, but it has a 10% capital gains tax (which replaces the marginal income tax; it is not added to it). Finally, the 30-year mortgage is currently costing you 6.9%, although you get to deduct the interest from your income for tax purposes.

To make the best financial decision we must first understand the true value of each option after accounting for the taxes we must pay. In the end we want to choose the option that results in the most extra money in our pocket.

On the surface it would seem that paying off the mortgage would make the most sense. If we invest in the bond we get an extra $6.00 in our pocket. We buy a $100 bond that pays us 6% interest. At the end of the year the bond company will send us $6.00 in interest earned. If we buy the mutual fund shares, we get $6.50 extra in our pocket. The $100 in mutual fund shares pays us 6.5% interest or $6.50 interest earned at the end of the year. If we pay the $100 on our mortgage, it will save us some interest the mortgage company is charging us to borrow that $100. For every $100 dollars we borrow on our mortgage, the mortgage company charges us 6.9%, or $6.90. So for every $100 we do not borrow, or pay off, we save $6.90. Paying $100 to the mortgage company means we have an extra $6.90 in our pocket. That's our best choice. Or is it?

Before we send our extra $100 to the mortgage company let's account for the taxes in our decision making. The bond is tax free. We get to keep all of the $6.00 the bond company sends us. The $6.00 in interest earned is our pretax interest and our aftertax interest. The interest earned on the bond is tax free. However, the mutual fund is not tax free. Yes, the mutual fund company will send us $6.50 in interest earned, but that is not how much we get to keep. We must pay 10%, or $0.65, in taxes. That means we keep only $5.85. Our pretax interest earned is $6.50, but our aftertax interest earned is $5.85. Even though the stated interest rate on the mutual fund is 6.5%, which is higher than the stated interest rate on bond of 6.0%, the bond is a better choice than the mutual fund because we end up with more money in our pocket after we account for the taxes we must pay.

A shortcut to getting to our after-tax interest earned or our aftertax rate is to multiply our pretax interest earned or pretax interest rate by one minus the tax rate (1 – tax rate). Multiplying by one minus the tax rate (1 – tax rate) simply gives us how much we have left over after we pay taxes. For the mutual fund we would do the following:

|  | PRETAX |  | AFTERTAX MULTIPLIER |  | AFTERTAX |
| --- | --- | --- | --- | --- | --- |
| Interest earned ($) | $6.50 | × | (1 – .10) | = | $5.85 |
| Interest rate (%) | 6.5% | × | (1 – .10) | = | 5.85% |

We must also account for taxes when looking at our mortgage. That is because interest paid on a home mortgage is tax deductible when it comes time to file our income tax return with Uncle Sam. In our case we pay the mortgage company $6.90 or 6.9% in interest expense on every $100 that we borrow. However, we get to deduct that interest expense from our taxable income. So the interest expense we pay on our mortgage saves us some amount on our income taxes. This is true only for interest expense we pay on our home mortgages. Interest we pay on credit cards, car loans, or other consumer debt is not tax deductible.

How much does the interest we pay on our mortgage save us on our income taxes? Because we make $64,000 in salary, we are in the 25% income tax bracket. For every extra dollar we make, we have to pay $0.25 or 25% in income tax. However, Uncle Sam lets us deduct our mortgage interest expense from our income first before we multiply it by our 25% tax rate to determine our tax expense. This means the interest expense paid on our mortgage reduces our taxable income and therefore reduces our tax expense. Let's compare our taxable income and tax expense if we did not have a mortgage to our taxable income and tax expense if we do have a mortgage.

| | | WITHOUT MORTGAGE | WITH MORTGAGE |
|---|---|---|---|
| Salary | | $64,000 | $64,000 |
| Mortgage tax expense | – | 0 | 100 |
| Taxable Income | = | 64,000 | 63,900 |
| Income tax rate | × | 0.25 | 0.25 |
| Income tax expense | = | 16,000 | 15,975 |

The difference in income tax expense is $25 (16,000 – 15,975). The $100 in mortgage interest expense saved us $25 in income taxes that we would have otherwise had to pay. The pretax mortgage interest expense is $100, but because it saved us $25 dollars in income tax expense, the aftertax mortage interest expense is $75.

Rather than doing all the math as above, we can multiply our pretax mortgage interest expense or interest rate by one minus the tax rate to find the true after-tax cost of the mortgage.

| | PRETAX | | AFTERTAX MULTIPLIER | | AFTERTAX |
|---|---|---|---|---|---|
| Interest rate (%) | 6.9% | × | (1 – .25) | = | 5.18% |

What originally looked like the best decision is actually the worst decision once we account for taxes. We first thought that taking the extra $100 and paying on the mortgage would save us $6.90. Once we account for taxes, we now see that it really saves us only $5.18.

Taking our extra $100 and buying the bond that pays us 6% interest results in the most money in our pocket.

| | PRETAX | | AFTERTAX MULTIPLIER | | AFTERTAX |
|---|---|---|---|---|---|
| Bond | 6.0% | × | (1 – .00) | = | 6.00% |
| Mutual Fund | 6.5% | × | (1 – .10) | = | 5.85% |
| Mortgage | 6.9% | × | (1 – .25) | = | 5.18% |

| | INVESTMENT | | AFTERTAX RATE | | EXTRA MONEY IN OUR POCKET |
|---|---|---|---|---|---|
| Bond | $100 | × | 6.00% | = | $6.00 |
| Mutual Fund | $100 | × | 5.85% | = | $5.85 |
| Mortgage | $100 | × | 5.18% | = | $5.18 |

# FOUR TYPES OF TAXES

Trying to understand income taxes is very difficult because there are so many variables that must be considered. Income taxes are only one part of the overall tax burden. On the whole, there are really four types of taxes. We pay taxes on purchases, property, income, and wealth. The U.S. tax code is so complicated not only because it is a source of revenue for the government, but also because the government uses it to influence our behavior. For instance, the government promotes home ownership by allowing you to deduct your mortgage interest expense from your taxes. So it is important that we understand the impact not only of income taxes but also of all taxes on our decision-making processes.

## Taxes on Earnings

We have already spent most of the chapter discussing taxes on earnings, which includes income taxes (federal, state, and city) as well as other payroll deductions such as FICA (Social Security and Medicare). Essentially, a portion of all that you earn will be collected by various government entities. The amount you pay depends on a multitude of variables, including how much you make, where you live, what deductions and credits you are eligible to claim, and so forth.

Sometimes people are not clear on the definitions of earnings. For instance, Don Cruz won the HGTV Dream Home in 2005.[32] The home was a 6,000-square-foot mansion located in Tyler, Texas, valued at more than $2 million. The tax bill for winning the home was $672,000. Mr. Cruz had to put the home up for sale because he could not afford to keep the house due to the taxes on his winnings. The 2010 HGTV home giveaway included $500,000 in cash as well, which may help the winner keep his or her dream home. Of course, the winner will also have to pay taxes of almost $200,000 on the $500,000 cash![33]

## Taxes on Purchases

Taxes on purchases include sales taxes and excise taxes. Most of us are familiar with sales tax because 45 states, plus the District of Columbia, have some type of sales tax on purchases. The average state sales tax is just over 5.5%, with some local taxes added on top. For instance, in Pitt County, North Carolina in 2010, the state sales tax was 5.5%, and the county sales tax was 2.5%, for a total of 8.0%.

Excise taxes are very similar to sales taxes but are designated for certain products or industries. For instance, there is an excise tax on gasoline. You do not pay a separate sales tax for every gallon of gasoline because you are already paying an excise tax. Each state has its own gasoline tax rate per gallon, in addition to the federal gasoline tax. In 2007, the national average state gasoline tax was 24.8 cents per gallon, in addition to the federal tax of 18.4 cents per gallon for an effective total average tax of 43.2 cents per gallon.

## Taxes on Property

Property taxes can affect home owners (real estate taxes) as well as automobile owners (personal property taxes). Although renters may believe that they can escape real estate taxes, the truth is that the landowner pays the property tax, but then builds that expense into the cost of the rent. In other words, like many other taxes that are paid by businesses and corporations, the taxes get passed down to consumers. One of the weaknesses of most online financial calculators that help consumers determine their monthly mortgage payment is the calculator only looks at principal and interest, but ignores property taxes, which can be a significant portion of a true monthly house payment. For instance, a $200,000 home purchased in Greenville, North Carolina, in 2010 results in the following taxes:

| | |
|---|---|
| Excise Transfer Tax | $ 400 |
| Pitt County Property Tax | 1,300 |
| Greenville City Property Tax | 1,040 |
| Total Property Tax | $2,740 |

That means when you purchase a $200,000 home, you will pay $2,740 in taxes just to purchase the home. In addition, you will continue to pay the city and county taxes of $2,340 per year. Put another way, you will pay almost $200 per month in property taxes.

Personal property tax is paid on the value of the things you own. This is our cars, trucks, boats, and even pets in some states. Personal property tax is a recurring tax paid every year on the significant assets you own. It is usually levied by counties to pay for schools, sheriff's offices, and other county services. You must account for the additional expense of property tax when making large purchase decisions such as whether to buy a brand new $30,000 truck or a previously owned truck at $15,000.

## Taxes on Wealth

Generally, wealth can be taxed at the state level through a state inheritance tax. The state inheritance tax, for those states that have this tax, requires that an estate pay a certain percentage of all wealth that is transferred as part of an inheritance. For example, if your parents leave their $1 million investment portfolio to you, then you may not actually receive the full $1 million dollars, but rather a portion of that amount after state inheritance taxes are withheld. Of course, paying taxes on cash that is inherited may not be fun, but is certainly affordable. On the other hand, you may inherit a business from your parents, which has a certain value. You may be required to pay taxes on the value of the business. This becomes more problematic if you do not have the cash available to pay the taxes.

The federal government also has an estate tax. An estate is simply the entire collection of one's wealth including their home, investments, other property, etc. The concept is the same as a state inheritance tax, but at different rates. The good news is that the first $3.5 million is excluded, meaning that an estate that is worth $3.5 million or less will not have to pay any federal inheritance tax. Everything over the $3.5 million in value is taxable.

In addition, the federal government taxes gifts. Of course small gifts, such as the $20 your grandmother gives you for your birthday is not taxable, but larger gifts, those over $13,000 per year, are subject to taxation. That means if your grandmother slipped a $20,000 check into your birthday card instead (thanks grandma!), she would have to pay a gift tax. Notice that the person giving the money has to pay the taxes, not the person receiving it, so make sure grandma understands this when she cuts you that big graduation check. Of course, you may want to point out to grandma that she can give you $13,000 and your grandfather can also give you $13,000, and there would be no tax consequences because each person gave within the federal limit. Later in life, when you start to accumulate wealth, this law may affect you as you look to transfer your wealth to family members.

# PLANNING YOUR TAX STRATEGY

About one-third of each marginal dollar you earn will go toward taxes. Because your tax burden may actually be your largest annual household expense, an effective tax strategy is vital for successful financial planning. Your goal, as an informed and responsible consumer and taxpayer, is to legally minimize your tax liability. One of the ways to accurately file your taxes and prepare yourself for future tax years is to use computer software to prepare taxes on your own. The advantage of using a tax software program is that you do not have to understand a tax return form to use the software. Most tax software for personal taxes are designed to simply ask you questions that you answer, such as "Do you own a home?" Based on your answer to the question, the software continues to direct you until it indicates what documents you will need and what information you should input into the computer.

Another advantage of computer software is that you will not have to fill out all the information each year because it has most of your data in memory. A third advantage, and perhaps the most important, is that you can estimate next year's taxes by going through the return again and using what you think you will earn next year instead of what you actually earned this year to estimate how much you will have to pay in taxes.

Finally, computer tax software is relatively inexpensive. For instance, you can use TurboTax Free Edition if your income is below a certain level and you have a minimal amount of deductions and credits. Basic editions of tax software usually cost around $30 to $35 for the federal edition, with an additional cost for your state. More advanced versions usually sell for $50 to $70 and can be purchased at office supply stores and big-box chain stores.

You can also choose to hire a tax preparer from the various locations that pop up around January of each year or you can hire an accountant. An accountant should be the most skilled of all tax professionals, but will also be the most expensive. The other tax preparation firms that open seasonally also use trained individuals, but with less formal training. Those firms use software similar to what you can purchase, but they hire someone to actually walk you through the process. If you choose this option, you may be able to deduct the expense of your tax preparation on the following year's taxes. The choice is yours, but make sure you keep in mind that any money you spend is yours first, and you get to decide where you are willing to spend it.

## Tax Lingo

It is critical to understand a few key tax terms, what they mean, and what the consequence is to you if you ever come face-to-face with situations involving these key terms. Taxes can be difficult and confusing enough just because there are so many different types and so many rules involved with each. In fact, taxes can be so difficult that you may even make a mistake on your taxes that the IRS may discover. If the IRS were to take you to court and you are found guilty of tax evasion, you may face stiff fines and penalties. Tax evasion means you are guilty of not paying all taxes you owe, such as not reporting all income or making false claims for credits or deductions that you are not eligible to use. On the other hand, your goal should be tax avoidance, which is utilizing legitimate methods to reduce your tax obligation to your fair share.

Tax evasion would be similar to shoplifting, whereas tax avoidance would be like going shopping and using coupons and rebates to get the lowest price possible.

To practice the most effective tax avoidance methods, you also have to understand the difference between tax credits and tax deductions. For instance, if you are in the 25% marginal tax bracket, would you prefer a $100 tax credit or a $200 tax deduction? Your understanding of the two tax definitions will determine your ability to minimize your tax expense. A tax credit reduces your taxes by the same amount as the credit. A tax deduction reduces your income by a percentage of the deduction equal to your marginal tax rate. In other words, for this example, a $100 tax credit reduces your tax burden by $100. The $200 tax deduction only reduces your taxes by 25% of $200, which is $50 (25% $\times$ $200 = $50). That means if you are in the 25% marginal tax bracket, a tax deduction of $400 equals a $100 tax credit. Anything less than $400, and you would be better off with the $100 tax credit.

Another way to think about this is to consider the following two tax scenerios:

Tax Credit—Your tax liability is $5,000, and your marginal tax rate is 25%. You receive a $100 tax credit. You now owe $4,900.

Tax Deduction—Your tax liability is $5,000, and your marginal tax rate is 25%. You receive a $100 tax deduction. That means you save $100 × 25% = $25. You now owe $4,975.

## Tax Planning Strategies

Any time a major life event occurs, you need to review your tax situation to avoid the "April 15th Surprise." A major life event may include a marriage, a divorce, having a baby, adopting a child, receiving an inheritance, changing jobs, or significantly reducing or increasing your income. An "April Surprise" could mean filing your taxes only to discover that you owe a large amount of money because you did not have enough taxes deducted from your paycheck during the year. It could also mean that you find out you will receive a large tax refund, which means you had too much tax money deducted from your paycheck during the year.

At first, it may appear counterintuitive to be upset about receiving a large tax refund, but large refunds as well as large tax bills are signs of improper tax management. A large tax bill could obviously be very damaging to your budget. If you do not have enough money in a savings account to cover your large bill, you may have to go into debt to pay your taxes, or worse yet, you may not be able to pay all that you owe, which the IRS frowns on. A huge refund, on the other hand, represents an interest-free loan to the government.

Some people argue that a huge tax refund is like having a built-in savings plan. They are excited that they get a lot of money at one time to use for vacations or something else. What they do not realize is they are building in a delayed-spending plan because all they are doing is using it to spend on something else. Others use the excuse that banks pay such low interest rates that they are not really losing much by getting a large refund, but they fail to consider other debt such as credit cards. If you have a credit card balance, you should pay down the debt and save the interest expense rather than give the government an interest-free loan.

Your goal is to come as close as possible to paying exactly what you owe to the government during the year. This allows you to use your money more efficiently. The advantage of using tax software is that you can estimate your next year's tax liability by running estimated numbers through the software to see what the results might be. You can divide your annual liability by the number of paychecks you receive each year to determine how much should be withheld each pay period.

# THE COST OF  FINANCIAL IGNORANCE

Our student that received the large tax refund of $2,200 essentially gave a tax-free loan to Uncle Sam. That $2,200 is income tax withheld from his paycheck throughout the year that is above and beyond his total tax expense. In addition, he deprived himself the use of his $2,200 for the past year. He could have saved the money and earned interest, or paid down his credit card, or this is $2,200 he would not have had to borrow in student loans.

| | |
|---|---|
| Total tax withheld from his paycheck | $4,600 |
| Total tax expense | $2,400 |
| Total tax refund (borrowed in student loans) | $2,200 |
| Interest expense on $2,200 in student loans[34] | **$  838** |

# RISK MANAGEMENT

## Covering Your Assets

One of our students stopped us after class to ask about where she might get her car repaired. She had backed into a telephone pole and dented the rear bumper of her car. We walked out to take a look at the damage. It was minor damage and barely worth repairing. However, even though the car wasn't brand new, it was her baby. It was a bright red convertible. She washed it every week and waxed it twice a month. No way was she going to ignore a scratch on her baby.

About a week later she came by our office almost in tears. The repair was going to cost over $750, and her insurance would not cover it. How could that be? She paid her car insurance bill every month. Her insurance agent came highly recommended by her roommate. She didn't understand. What was insurance for anyway? How could she have done everything right and still not be protected?

# RISK

What our student failed to realize is that it is not about insurance. It is about risk. Risk determines our actions, influences our decision making, and determines our costs. So what do we mean by risk? Is it possible to live your life free of risk? Because this chapter is about risk management and not total risk prevention, you may have figured out that there must be at least some risk that is unavoidable. Risk is part of our everyday lives. You cannot avoid all risk at all times. If you hide in a corner in your house to avoid all risk, you run the risk of alienating yourself, getting fired from your job, being evicted from your house, and so forth. The point is you cannot live without risk, but you can minimize and manage risk throughout your lifetime.

Risk is one of those things that will not go away just because you choose to ignore it. If you walk across campus listening to your iPod while texting on your cell phone and fail to see the manhole cover missing from the sewer access, the risk of you stepping into that hole and being injured still exists. Even if you do not see the hole, you still run the risk of getting hurt. In fact, failure to recognize risk is a de facto acceptance of that risk. But how do we define risk?

In general, risk is the probability or likelihood of an unfavorable event occurring. To manage the likelihood of such an event, we need to distinguish between the two main types of risk: Pure risk and speculative risk.

## Types of Risk

Pure risk is accidental or unintentional. However, the very nature of the risk can be predicted. In fact, the amount of likely financial loss can be predicted as well. Pure risk can include risk to a person (physical or emotional risk), risk to property (damage or destruction), and liability (your responsibility for the loss). For example, pure risk may include the risk that a tree may fall onto your car or someone may fall while they are walking on your property. If the unfavorable event associated with the risk occurs, the only possible result is some type of loss. If a tree lands on your car, then you lose your car or lose money to pay for the repair of your car. If someone falls while on your property, then they may be injured (which is a form of loss) or you may lose money because you have to pay for their medical bills. The two key points are that pure risk is insurable and pure risk is loss only.

Speculative risk is more complex. With speculative risk there is a chance of loss, but there is also a chance of significant gain. Think about what happens when you play the lottery or participate in any other form of gambling. There is a chance that you will lose because your numbers were not called or your cards were not good enough to beat the house or the other players. The point is that you lost the amount of money you were using to gamble. On the other hand, there is also a chance that your numbers will be called or your cards will be better than those held by the house or the other players, in which case you actually win money. The same holds true for starting a new business. There is a chance that you can lose all the money you put into the business, or you could even lose more than you invested. On the other hand, your business may become very successful, and you could earn a lot of money. The key is that speculative risk is not insurable, and it may result not only in a loss but also in a gain.

Think about the concept of trying to insure speculative risk. If you start a new business and use $100,000 of your own money, or money you borrowed that has to be repaid, then you are likely going to work harder to make sure your business does not fail. Despite the amount of hard work, you will not want to just quit and lose all your money. On the other hand, if you could also buy insurance that would pay back the $100,000 investment in the event that the business failed, what incentive is left for you to work really hard? You may decide it is just too much work to run your own company, so you could just shut the business down and collect your $100,000 in business failure insurance money. If you can influence the outcome then it is not pure risk. The risks that we want to pay attention to are pure risks because we can choose not to engage in speculative risk.

# Risks We Face

Now that we understand that pure risk is the one we need to be concerned with, what are the specific types of pure risk that we face? To lower your chances of losing money, we need to further distinguish between a peril and a hazard. A peril is the cause of the possible loss. For instance a fire, a robbery, a windstorm, or even a disease may all be forms of perils. The peril may not be completely avoidable, as it may be caused by nature or by someone else. A hazard is something that increases the likelihood of a loss occurring. For instance driving while under the influence of alcohol increases the likelihood that a crash may occur, which could lead to property damage, as well as injury or loss of life for yourself or others. Smoking also increases the likelihood of developing lung cancer or emphysema and could also increase the likelihood of starting a fire. Even something as simple as a wet floor may increase the likelihood that someone may fall and be injured. So what are some of the perils or risks that we face?

- Disability
- Illness
- Death
- Retirement
- Financial loss
- Property loss
- Liability

## *Disability*

We run the risk of becoming disabled in one way or another. The cause could be medical, such as a progressive muscular disease or a neurological disease that causes us to become incapacitated. Perhaps a fall or a car accident could lead to some type of disability. There are many different events that could lead to a disability, and there are also many types of disabilities. Most people think of disability as a permanent disability such as the loss of the use of your arms or legs, the loss of your eyesight, your hearing, or even your voice. A piano player who loses a couple of fingers or a surgeon who develops a tremor in their hands is certainly permanently disabled. But sometimes people may be disabled for a temporary period of time.

For instance, during the six months it takes you to recover from your skiing accident you are disabled. A pregnant woman confined to bed rest due to a high-risk pregnancy is considered temporarily disabled. The point is a disability can be any period of time where you medically are not permitted to work.

## Illness

What happens if you get a sinus infection or the flu? Keep in mind that illness is a risk, even if you do not have to go to a hospital or visit a doctor. The very fact that the illness could prevent you from doing something else such as go on vacation or go to work makes it a risk. At the very least, the fact that it causes you to suffer makes it a risk. Illness also includes more serious conditions such as having cancer or having a heart attack.

## Death

Although death is inevitable, in that it will happen to each of us, it is still a risk. You have probably heard the phrase, "risk your life." For instance, someone may say, "I would not be willing to risk my life just to make more money." In other words, you are putting your life at risk, but the resulting loss equates to death. How can death be a risk if it is going to happen to everyone at some point in time? The timing of your death becomes a risk, as well as your ability to be prepared for the death of others, or their ability to be prepared for your death. Your own death may result in not only emotional suffering but financial suffering as well for your family and friends and business partners.

## Retirement

When you reach the age of retirement, you risk the inability to maintain a certain lifestyle. We are not entitled to retire at a specific age and still spend the same way when we were working. Although your employer may require or offer for you to retire at a specific age, it is your responsibility to have planned your finances and your future the right way. You also risk living longer than your money will last. In this case, maybe you were able to maintain your lifestyle for several years, but at the end of your money you are still alive.

## Financial Loss

Any time you make a purchase you risk financial loss. If you do not understand the value of what you are purchasing, you could end up overpaying or buying inferior products. For instance, when you purchase a car, you could pay more than the car is actually worth. Or you may spend less money buying a television on an auction site, but the product may not work properly or only last a few months. Even your investments could result in a financial loss. If you do not understand how to evaluate risk, you could lose money in bad investments.

## *Property Loss*

In the event of a tree falling on your car or a fire starting in your home, you are likely to suffer some type of property loss. Even a small fire can result in significant smoke and water damage. Smoke can quickly flow through your home with soot, and the odors can get into your clothes, carpet, walls, and so forth. In addition, when the fire department arrives, their main goal is to put the fire out. It may take a lot of water to ensure that the fire is completely out, including all the hot ashes and smoldering debris. In fact, the fire may have caused very little damage because the fire department put it out quickly. However, the water may have caused even more damage.

## *Liability*

Liability simply means that you are responsible for the loss. For instance, if you back your car into someone else's car, then you are liable, or responsible, for the accident. There are different types of liability. For instance, if you walk into a department store after they have mopped their floors, and you fall and become injured, they are most likely liable for your injury. If they did not place signs in the recently mopped area to warn you that the floor was wet and slippery, then they may be considered negligent. Negligence occurs when you are not properly warned about a condition or the condition is outside what a reasonable person would expect. If the staircase at your own home is falling apart and the pizza delivery person falls off the porch as your hand railing breaks apart, you can be held negligent, which could result in a larger lawsuit against you as well as possible fines.

In addition, you need to understand vicarious liability. If your child causes damage to someone else's property, you may be responsible. For instance, many children like to play baseball in their backyard, but sometimes, if they hit the ball too hard or in the wrong direction, it may break the neighbor's window. Can your actions result in liability for your parents? There are many variables, such as your age, but if you are on your parent's auto insurance policy and you cause an accident, they most likely will be held responsible. While most college students do not have children, you have to also consider pets. If your dog bites someone, you are vicariously liable, even though you did not physically bite the person. The dog belonged to you, and therefore you are liable.

# Four Ways to Manage Risk

To manage risk, we first have to understand what it means to do so. Risk management is a long-range, organized, systematic, planned strategy to protect your assets, your family, and yourself. There are four ways in which you can choose to manage the risk that you will face: *avoidance, assumption, reduction,* and *shifting.* You can use any of the four ways, depending on the amount of risk and the circumstances. In some instances you may choose to use a combination of all four.

## Avoidance

Avoidance of risk is the cheapest and easiest way to manage risk. You can choose to avoid certain types of risks altogether by adjusting your lifestyle, making different decisions, or removing yourself from certain situations. For instance, you may choose to stay on the ground while your friends go skydiving. You are avoiding the risks associated with skydiving. Not getting in a car with a drunk driver is avoiding risk.

## Assumption

You may choose to take on the risk or assume the risk. For instance, if you decide to walk home by yourself late at night, you are assuming a certain level of risk. This approach may not always be the smartest way to manage risk but there are plenty of times when it makes sense. For instance, if you purchase a $100 camera and the store clerk asks if you want the three-year extended warranty for $35, you may decide to simply assume the risk that the camera will function for the three years after the manufacturer warranty expires rather than spending an addition $35.

## Reduction

In many instances, there are steps you can take to reduce your risk. For instance, you can drive the proper speed limit, wear your seatbelt, and remove distractions such as your cell phone (or any annoying passengers). Making these choices will help you reduce your risk of being in an accident. You cannot completely avoid the risk of being in an accident while you are driving because you cannot control the other drivers on the road.

## Shifting

You can transfer or shift the financial exposure of your risks to another individual or entity. In essence, that is what insurance companies are designed to do; shift the financial exposure of the risk from you to them. Notice that we said you can transfer the financial risk only. You cannot pay someone else to sustain your injuries in a car accident. You can, however, pay someone else to keep you from suffering a financial loss from the accident. The insurance company may pay for your hospital bills and the repairs to your car. If the accident was your fault, they may also pay to repair the other person's car and the hospital bills for any injuries you may have caused, along with some other liabilities resulting from a lawsuit.

# INSURANCE

Because the first three strategies for risk management—avoidance, assumption, and reduction—are based on basic decisions you can make, we will spend the rest of the chapter focusing on shifting risk. The primary way to shift risk is to purchase insurance. You can purchase insurance for so many different scenarios, but we will focus on insurance for your personal property, health, ability to earn a living, and to protect your family. Before we get into the details of specific types of insurance coverage, there are some insurance fundamentals we need to discuss first.

Insurance is protection against possible financial loss. An insurance company, or insurer, is a risk-sharing firm that assumes financial responsibility for losses from the insured in exchange for a fee. People purchase a policy from the firm, and the firm then assumes the risk for a fee, called a premium, which the insured policyholder periodically pays. In other words, if you are willing to pay an insurance company a certain amount of money, they will guarantee to pay you a certain amount of money in the event that a specific situation arises. The purpose is to help you avoid or offset any major financial loss as a result of some type of event that would otherwise lead to a large financial loss.

Purchasing insurance is both like and unlike purchasing any other product. Similar to other purchases, you need to do your due diligence to determine the best product for you. Different from any other purchase, you are buying something that you hope you never have to use. This leads most of us to make poor decisions when buying insurance.

## Three Costly Myths

Insurance is a mystery to most people. It is so complex we rarely understand what we are buying. Although we all need insurance, we cannot turn to our friends or relatives for advice, yet that is what we do. Very few people have the knowledge or skills with which to evaluate the various insurance products available. Because of the confusion around insurance, most people fall victim to one or more of the three costly myths about insurance:

### #1 Your benefits should roughly equal the premiums you have paid.

If your benefits (meaning what the insurance company pays you) should be the same as what you have paid for the insurance, then why would you need to purchase insurance in the first place? In other words, if you pay $1,000 for insurance and expect to receive $1,000 back from the insurance company in claims, then why would you need to use them at all? You could have just set the $1,000 aside yourself and used it when the financial loss occurred without the need for the insurance company. The point of insurance is to protect us in those times when the financial loss is more than we can handle.

### #2 Insurance should cover disasters that are likely to happen.

If disasters are likely to happen, then you should focus on the other three risk management strategies instead, preferably avoidance or reduction. If a flood is likely to occur in a certain area, then why not practice avoidance and move to an area that does not flood? If that is not a practical solution, then look for ways to reduce the risk, such as landscaping your yard in a way that redirects the water around your property, or install flood walls around the foundation of your house. If the scenario is likely to happen and the insurance company knows that it is likely, they will either refuse to insure you against that risk, or they will charge a very high premium to insure you. The point of insurance is to protect us from those disasters that we are unable to predict.

### #3 Insurance is a rip-off. You should only buy the minimum required.

Buying only the minimum required is absolutely the wrong way to look at insurance. Would you rather have enough insurance to pay for some of the damage, most of the damage, or nearly all the damage? In other words, if you are responsible for a car accident, do you want the insurance company to pay for some of the costs, leaving you to pay the rest on your own, or would you prefer that the insurance company pay for all the costs? The point of insurance is to protect you against those financial losses that you cannot cover with your own money.

## How Insurance Companies Work

With an understanding of how insurance companies make their money, the concepts of insurance become clearer. Most people believe that insurance companies make their money by collecting more than they pay out in benefits, by ripping people off with confusing policies, or by denying claims. In reality, insurance companies make their money through investments. Their goal is simply to collect as much in premiums as they pay out in benefits. If they think they will pay out $1 million in benefits, their goal is to collect $1 million in premiums from their customers.

Why do insurance companies not just charge more than they plan to pay out to increase profits? It is a matter of basic economics. There are several insurance companies competing for your dollars, so if one company increases its rates to cushion their profits, another insurance company can come along and price their policies cheaper, which would drive the more expensive companies out of business. Basic competition keeps insurance costs within a certain price range.

So how can insurance companies be profitable if they only collect as much as they pay out? Think about it this way. You are unlikely to get in a vehicle accident the very day that you pay your insurance policy. If you were to get in an accident this coming year, your insurance company will have had your money from the time you made your payment until the time of the accident. During that time they have been able to invest your money and earn some type of interest. Now if you start to think about millions of dollars collected through thousands of customers with many not having an accident or a claim for several years, the insurance company has made money off the investment on these dollars during this entire time period.

To continue our understanding of insurance basics, the next question to ask is, "Why do people buy insurance?" After all, to win (to collect money from the insurance company), you have to lose (you have to have suffered a financial loss)! We buy insurance because we are *risk averse*. We prefer the known cost of the premium rather than the possibility of a huge financial loss. In other words, we prefer to know that we have to pay a certain amount each month even though it is a guaranteed loss, than to take the chance of having to pay a large amount of money in the event of a possible large loss, such as our house burning down, or an auto accident.

For example, would you rather pay $100 per month for your car insurance, or would you rather take your chances and hope you never have an accident? Keep in mind if you do have an accident that causes damage to your car as well as that of the other driver, assuming nobody gets injured, then you could be looking at anywhere from $2,000 to $20,000 in damage. Of course if someone gets injured, you could be looking at a lawsuit of more than a million dollars.

Think about it this way. We buy insurance in the hopes that we never have to use it. How does that make sense? The concept is not as foreign as you may think. Does your car have an airbag? Do you hope that someday you will get to use that airbag? Do you have a fire extinguisher in your apartment or your house? Are you hoping for a fire so you can use it? Of course, you do not want to use your airbag or your fire extinguisher, but you pay for them anyway. Sometimes we pay for products or services as a safety net just in case something catastrophic happens to us. We buy insurance for the same reason.

With insurance, there is a risk/return relationship. The greater the risk that the event will actually take place, the more the insurance will cost. For instance, insurance to protect against wind damage will cost more money for a beachfront wooden cottage than it will for a brick home 150 miles from the beach. If you are a bad driver, with the dents and scratches in your vehicle to prove it, the insurance company will charge you more for your auto insurance policy because you are more of a risk to them. You are more likely to get into yet another accident than the average driver.

You also have to avoid the psychology of buying insurance. You do not want to "get your money's worth" from your insurance policy. You do not want to ever have to use the policy if you can help it. What you are buying from the insurance company is protection. The ability to shift the risk in case something does happen is the actual product. You are using your insurance policy every day. If you have auto insurance, then you are using the policy every time you drive, or maybe even while your car is sitting in the parking lot. Your renter's insurance is protecting you while you are in class, or studying in the library, or even when you are out late at night. The fact that you do not have to worry about paying to replace everything you own in the event of a disaster means that your insurance is doing exactly what it is supposed to do.

## How to Buy Insurance

We now know that insurance is just one piece of a larger, more encompassing risk management plan. However, we're still not ready to go out and purchase insurance. There are a bazillion insurance products out there. How do we know what kind of insurance to buy? How much should it cost? Should I buy from an agent or online? How do I best protect my family and me?

Before answering questions about specific types of insurance, we need to understand a few basics applicable to buying all types of insurance. Significant savings and better protection can be had if we pay attention to three simple rules. It doesn't matter if you're buying car insurance or health insurance, you will be better protected and pay less money doing it if you follow the following guidelines.

## *Insure for the Big Stuff*

Your goal when you purchase insurance is to protect your most valuable assets and to protect against large expenses. You want to avoid the little policies including extended warranties, repair plans, and package insurance. If you can pay for it without much heartburn, then you should not insure it. Do you really need to buy a separate protection plan for your television? If you can afford to replace it then you do not need to protect it. On the other hand, can you afford to replace your house or your car with cash? Because you most likely cannot pay for these large items, then you need to insure them against losses. Can you pay for a hospital stay or surgery? Most people cannot afford to pay such large expenses, so you should consider health insurance.

Almost anywhere you go to shop and for almost anything that you purchase, retailers try to sell us some type of extended warranty. What is an extended warranty? An extended warranty is basically just an insurance policy. You are trying to shift the risk of the loss of the item (or the money you would have to spend to replace or repair the item) to a third party (the extended warranty company). Policies for individual items, such as an iPod or a refrigerator are expensive compared to what you are actually insuring, resulting in huge profits for the retailers for something you are very unlikely to use. Statistics show if there is going to be a problem with a major purchase, it will happen during the manufacturer's warranty period. Purchasing extended warranties could easily result in adding 10% or more to your purchase. For example, to insure a $200 cell phone with a two-year contract, you will pay around $7 per month for a total of $168 over the two-year period. In addition, most extended warranties require a deductible or copay. After adding the $50 deductible required by your policy, you end up paying more than the replacement cost of the phone. Everyone else who buys a policy is paying $168 to provide extra profit to the cell phone company.

If you make a purchase and you have enough in your emergency fund, savings account, etc., then you will not need to purchase a policy to cover the item. In fact, if you are in a situation where you feel that you absolutely must purchase the extended warranty, then you probably cannot really afford the item in the first place. Once again, the more money you have (such as cash in an emergency fund), the less you need to spend on insurance (you do not need to buy an extended warranty), which helps you accumulate even more money. You can save the money you would have spent on an extended warranty and add it to your emergency fund.

Of course, what you can afford to replace depends on your income level and where you are in your life. Most likely, your professor can afford to replace more items than you can at this point. Although you may be able to replace your television or your computer or your clothes, you may not be able to replace all of them at the same time in the event of a fire or burglary. Although none of us likes to be inconvenienced or have unexpected expenses, insurance should not be used to smooth out the bumps of everyday life. Your goal with insurance is to insure against financial catastrophe. You should not be using your homeowner's insurance to replace your carpet because you spilled a glass of wine. The small stuff that happens is called "life." Deal with it. If you insure for every little inconvenience that could happen to you, you will go broke from insurance payments.

The best way to save money while insuring for only the big items is to buy insurance with the biggest deductible you can afford. What is a deductible? The deductible is the amount of money that you have to pay out of pocket for an insurance claim before your insurance company starts paying for it. For instance, if you have a $500 deductible and you get into a car accident that causes $1,500 damage to your car, then your insurance company will only pay $1,000 because you have to pay the first $500. On the other hand, if your deductible was only $250, then your insurance company would pay the remaining $1,250. The lower your deductible, the more the insurance company has to pay. The higher your deductible, the less the insurance company has to pay. So why would we tell you to buy the highest deductible you can afford if it means that the insurance company will have to pay less? Because the higher the deductible, the cheaper the insurance.

Keep in mind that the more risk you present to your insurance company, the more they will charge you each month. If you have a small deductible, then that means you present more risk to the insurance company because each claim will cost them more money. In addition, you are more likely to file a smaller claim if you have a smaller deductible. For instance, if you have a $500 deductible and cause $650 worth of damage, then you may decide to just pay the $650 and not have your insurance company get involved at all. After all, is it worth it to file a $650 claim just to get an additional $150 from the insurance company, and then take the risk that they may raise your monthly insurance costs now that you have a record of accidents? Deductibles exist to prevent you from making claims on small items, such as hail storm damage, or a small scratch caused by backing into your mailbox.

The bigger the deductible, the more money you will save on your monthly premiums. The key is to only go as high as you can afford. A $1,000 deductible on your car insurance may save you more money, but if you only have $300 in the bank, then where are you going to find the other $700 to pay the deductible should something happen? You probably begin to see that this concept ties back in with your net worth statement. As you increase your net worth, particularly in your savings, checking, or nonretirement investment accounts, you have more cash available to you. The more cash you have available, the more you can increase your deductibles. The more you increase your deductibles, the less money you have to spend on insurance each month. The less you spend on insurance, the more you could be saving in your emergency fund. The more you save in your emergency fund, the higher your net worth. The higher your net worth, the more you can increase your deductibles. The cycle continues until you see that being responsible with your money can help you save money, which will help you accumulate even more money.

Each insurance policy has its own type of deductible. With health insurance, you have a copayment as well as a deductible. The higher your copay amount, the less likely you are to go to the doctor's office for small health issues such as the common cold. In addition, each time you do visit the doctor, your insurance company pays less. If you also have a large deductible, then it may take several visits or more than one small medical procedure before your insurance company has to pay anything. You are presenting less risk, so they are willing to charge you less for your monthly insurance premium. Disability policies have their own deductible. The amount of time after your disability and before your insurance company has to start paying for your loss of income is the deductible. If you can wait 30 days without an income, then your monthly disability insurance will be lower than not waiting at all. If you can wait 60 days instead of 30 days, then your monthly payment will be even less. The point is the same across all types of insurance policies. The less risk you present to the insurance company, the less they will charge to insure you from loss.

## Buy the Broadest Coverage Available

You want to purchase coverage that protects you no matter what the circumstances. Insurance policies that have multiple restrictions and few opportunities to redeem the policy or only cover very specific circumstances should be avoided in most cases. For example, vendors at airports may offer flight insurance. Why would you pay money for one specific event when you should have a life insurance policy that covers nearly all possible events? The amount of money you spend for the limited coverage opportunity results in very little coverage per dollar spent. There are thousands more deaths resulting from drunk drivers than from plane crashes. Buy an insurance policy that pays your beneficiaries no matter what the circumstances are of your death.

Be skeptical of anyone who tries to talk you into a cancer insurance policy. Instead of purchasing something so specific that only covers one type of ailment, you want catastrophic health-care coverage that pays for all sicknesses. The purpose of catastrophic insurance is to pay when bills get so large it would simply destroy your finances if you had to pay them yourself.

When buying broad insurance policies be prepared for riders. A rider is simply extra coverage that is in addition to the coverage you receive with the main insurance policy. And there are many different kinds of riders. Why would the agent try to get you to buy all these extra riders? Because the more you have to spend on insurance the more commission the agent receives. For example, your auto insurance agent may try to convince you to purchase a rider for towing. If your car breaks down your insurance company will reimburse you for towing expenses. It's much cheaper to join an automobile club that includes towing and other roadside assistance. Keep in mind why you are buying car insurance in the first place. You are trying to protect yourself from large losses resulting from some type of accident. If the rider is not part of your overall goal for purchasing the insurance, then it is probably not a good idea to buy it.

However, there might be an exception to the rider rule. For example, many homeowners' policies limit the reimbursement for jewelry. Other items such as art collections might require a rider to be adequately protected. These examples require a rider because a basic homeowner's (or renter's) policy limits the amount of coverage. Although your insurance policy may cover a full $50,000 worth of personal items, you may see a restriction in your policy that limits total reimbursement for jewelry or art to $500 or some other inadequate dollar amount.

## Shop Around

Remember, it is your money so shop around. You do not necessarily have to use the same insurance agent or the same insurance company that your family or friends use. In fact, it may be cheaper for you to have your own insurance policy now than for your parents to pay the additional cost of keeping you on their policy. You should shop around anytime you make a purchase, but especially when you are making a large purchase. Insurance can be a very large purchase over time. For instance, if you pay $100 per month for car insurance, then you are paying $1,200 per year or almost $5,000 if you spend four years in college. Anyone should compare prices before making a $5,000 purchase.

Look for discounts for combining multiple types of insurance coverage. If you have homeowner's insurance and car insurance with the same company, make sure you get your multiple policy discounts. If you have renter's insurance and car insurance, ask if they offer any type of discount as well. If your car, apartment, or house has an alarm system, make sure the insurance company knows about them. If your house has a sprinkler system or if your car has OnStar[35] or LoJack[36] or some other system that can help police locate a stolen vehicle, then you should be eligible for some type of discount. There are literally dozens of discounts available to you, so be sure to take advantage of them all. When comparison shopping, give each company the same information so you can be quoted a price that reflects the same discounts for each.

Take advantage of group plans that are available to you if the price is less than you could get on your own. Most midsize or large employers have group plans for medical insurance and life insurance, and some even have plans for car insurance and disability insurance as well. If you are a member of an organization or a credit union, then you may be able to participate in their group plans. The key is to still shop around and ask questions. In many instances, life insurance plans through an employer still cost more money per $1,000 of insurance coverage than you could purchase on your own outside work as a young college graduate. In addition, you still need to keep the other two principles in mind when deciding which insurance policies you need and how much coverage is appropriate for your situation.

Do not be afraid to purchase your insurance directly from the insurance company as opposed to going through a local agent. For instance, you can purchase certain types of insurance directly through GEICO, Progressive, Traveler's, or USAA, and many more.[37] If you are like some people, you may simply feel more comfortable dealing with a local agent. You just have to determine how much that comfort level is worth each month. You can also use an independent agent, who will shop around for you, instead of an agent that can only represent one insurance company. An independent agent may find that it is cheaper to get your renter's insurance from one company, your car insurance from another, and your life insurance from yet another.

Ultimately, the most important thing to ask is, "How is this insurance agent being compensated?" Most insurance agents are salespeople, so it is in their best interest to sell you an insurance policy. In fact, it is in their best interest to sell you the most expensive policy they can, and perhaps to sell you more coverage than you need or policies that are not a good fit for you. Even an independent agent could steer you toward the companies that offer the largest commissions. You are your own best advocate when it comes to shopping for insurance.

Follow this simple advice, and you will be less likely to purchase the wrong types of insurance, less likely to overpay for insurance, and more likely to have the right amount of coverage. Now let's discuss specific insurance needs.

# Automobile Insurance

In almost every state, drivers are required to carry some minimum level of automobile insurance. Automobile insurance policies can be difficult to understand because they are usually expressed as a series of three numbers such as 30/60/25. For most consumers the numbers do not mean anything. The only number most people pay attention to is the monthly or semiannual cost. In this example, the 30/60/25 policy happens to be the minimum required coverage for drivers in North Carolina. The numbers represent the amount of financial coverage the insurance provides.

A policy written as 30/60/25 provides the following coverage:

> **30**—The coverage numbers are written in thousands of dollars, which means that "30" stands for $30,000. The $30,000 represents the maximum amount paid to any one person for injury from an accident.

> **60**—The "60" means that $60,000 is the maximum amount paid to all parties for injury from an accident.

> **25**—The "25" means that $25,000 is the total amount of property damage from an accident.

Some people believe they should only buy the absolute minimum amount of insurance the state requires. However, if you consider how much it costs to repair a car, particularly if you crash into a $50,000 car, you may realize that the minimum may not be enough coverage. Keep in mind the goal of insurance is to protect you from large losses. If you cause $50,000 worth of damage and you only have $25,000 worth of property damage coverage, then you may have to pay the difference out of your own pocket. For instance, look at the 30/60/25 minimum required by North Carolina. If you were to hit another vehicle and injure the person in the other car who then sues you for $500,000, your insurance company only pays the first $30,000. Any money owed after your insurance company pays their share will become *your* problem. Even if nobody is physically injured, consider what happens if you are responsible for an accident that damages more than one car, or if your car slips out of gear and drifts down the hill into the front window of a Starbucks restaurant.

Because your goal is to protect yourself against large financial losses, you really want to consider having enough coverage to protect you from lawsuits. For instance, consider purchasing a policy with 100/300/50 coverage. This will protect you up to $100,000 per person or $300,000 per incident for bodily injury as well as up to $50,000 for property damage. As you start building your own wealth, you will have more assets to protect and you will have more to lose, so eventually you may want to increase your policy to 250/500/100 coverage.

## *Bodily Injury Coverage*

The first part of your insurance policy includes the personal and total bodily injury limits, which covers the risk of financial loss due to medical and legal expenses, lost wages, and other expenses associated with the accident and injury. If you have ever watched television between the hours of 10:00 AM and 3:00 PM, you are undoubtedly aware of the numerous attorneys who make a living helping the injured sue those who have caused the injury. If you consider how much the medical expenses could end up costing, you quickly realize why the state minimum is usually too low. In addition, you may have to pay for any legal expenses, which could range anywhere from a few hundred dollars to an amount even greater than all the medical bills. If the person you injure is unable to work for a period of time, you are also responsible to compensate them for their lost wages. If you injure someone who earns $52,000 per year, you would be responsible for $1,000 per week until they are able to return to work. Now imagine if you cause a permanent injury. You could be responsible for hundreds of thousands of dollars in compensation. Keep in mind the first number on your policy refers to the total maximum amount of money that can be paid to any single individual and the second number refers to the maximum dollar amount that can be paid to all the injured people combined.

## *Property Damage Coverage*

The third number on your policy refers to the total amount of property damage, which covers damage to another person's car when you are at fault. It also covers damage to other objects such as street signs and buildings. Any property that is damaged because of your car will be paid via the property damage coverage portion of your automobile insurance policy. Keep in mind the maximum dollar amount applies no matter how many cars you may have run into and how expensive the property is that you damage. If you cause more damage than your insurance will cover, the property owner is likely to sue you for the difference.

## *Collision Coverage*

In many instances your insurance policy may also include collision coverage. In fact, if you do not have a clear title, meaning you still owe money to a lender from when you purchased the car, you are required to have collision coverage. Collision coverage covers *your* car when it is involved in an accident. If you do not owe any money on your car, then collision is optional. That means the property damage coverage mentioned previously will not pay to repair your car. It only pays to repair damage you cause to other people's property. If you want to be able to fix your car without having to pay for all the repairs out of your own pocket, then you need collision coverage. Generally, as your car ages, its value continues to decrease. At some point your value will decrease to the level that it no longer makes sense to pay for collision coverage.

To understand when it makes sense to stop paying for collision coverage for your car, you first have to understand how insurance companies will compensate you for any damage. If you get into an accident with your 10-year-old car that is currently worth $2,500 and it will cost $4,000 to fix the car then your insurance company will simply give you a check for $2,500 and consider your car "totaled." In other words, it does not take a lot of damage for an older car or less expensive car to be considered "totaled," whereas it may take a lot more damage before a brand-new car is considered "totaled." If someone else damages your car and their insurance has to pay for your car, the same rules apply. They will only pay to repair damage if the repairs cost less than your car is worth. Once the repairs cost close to the value of your car, they consider it "totaled." Make sure you research the **retail value** of your car and demand you are paid accordingly. Although your car may only be worth $2,500 as a trade-in, the retail value may be $4,500 or $5,000, which is how much you should be paid. After all, the point of the insurance payment is to allow you to purchase a replacement, which would be a car valued the same as the one that was "totaled." Because you will have to pay retail to purchase a car from a dealer, you need to be paid retail to cover your loss.

## Comprehensive Coverage

There are many ways your car could become damaged without being in a collision. Comprehensive coverage allows you to protect against loss for most causes of damage that are not related to a collision. If your car catches fire, is stolen, or gets vandalized, your comprehensive coverage will pay for the damage. If a hailstorm, sandstorm, or windstorm causes enough damage to your car, your insurance policy may cover such losses. Also, if your car rolls downhill into a tree while nobody is driving it, your comprehensive coverage will pay to repair the damage to your car. If the tree then falls over and lands on somebody else's car, your property damage coverage will then pay for the other person's car.

## Premium Factors (How Insurance Is Priced)

Several factors are considered by an insurance company when pricing your automobile policy. The type of automobile including the make, model, and year will influence the overall price. One of the largest considerations is which cars are most frequently stolen. Currently, the Toyota Camry and Honda Accord are the most stolen vehicles in the United States, so a portion of the premium for these cars includes the higher probability that they will be stolen. Of course, the newer a car, the more expensive it may be to replace or repair. Your zip code (or rating territory) can also make a big difference in insurance rates. You may be able to save money on car insurance while you are in college if you can prove that your car spends most of its time in your college town instead of your hometown if the college town has lower insurance rates. Generally car insurance rates tend to be higher in more metropolitan or urban areas because of the increased rate of theft and vandalism as well as the fact that traffic is much heavier and accidents are more likely.

Your driver classification will also have a large impact on determining your rates. Driver classification includes age, sex, marital status, and driving record. A newly minted 16-year-old driver is much more of a risk to an insurance company than a 40-year-old married individual. If you have been in three accidents over the past few years, then the insurance company will either drop your coverage completely or they will make you pay more for the same coverage than someone who has not been in an accident for the past 10 years. Unfortunately for women, one of the areas where they have achieved full equality is in automobile insurance rates. Many years ago, men had to pay much more for automobile insurance than women. Now the rates are very similar with no obvious savings for women compared to men. Finally, your credit score can make a difference in how much you will have to pay for automobile insurance. Insurance companies have been able to demonstrate a correlation between those who are not responsible with their credit and those who are not responsible in other areas of their lives as well, including their driving habits.

# Renters Insurance

If you are a renter and you do not have any renter's insurance, then you are at risk. If you believe that your landlord has insurance for your apartment, then you are correct. The landlord has insurance for the apartment building, but that does not include any personal property that you own. The landlord's insurance will pay to rebuild or repair after fire or water damage, but your computer, your clothes, your iPod, and your school books will not be covered. You are responsible to pay to replace everything that you own. Renter's insurance will pay for property replacement in the event of fire damage or theft, as well as other causes of loss. Because each policy is different, you will have to look at the individual policy to determine if there are any gaps in coverage such as flooding.

Renter's insurance will probably cost as little as $10 per month ($120 per year). You get a lot of protection for very little money. Imagine you decide to cook some french fries the old fashioned way by using grease in a skillet. The next thing you know your cell phone rings, and it happens to be the cute classmate who finally got the hint and gave you a call. You step away from the skillet for just a few minutes, and the next thing you know the smoke detector is going off because some of the grease splashed onto the nearby dish towel, and now you have a fire. Think about how much damage you could be responsible for if you start a grease fire, especially one that requires a fire department to respond. Your landlord's insurance may pay for the damage, but his or her insurance company will then come after you because it was your fault. Legally, you could be held responsible and end up with a judgment against you. When you also consider all the smoke and water damage, the costs could add up quickly.

Your renter's insurance may also provide some personal liability coverage. If you have a friend hanging out at your apartment and he or she falls off the balcony or slips on your kitchen floor, you may be held responsible for their injuries and medical expenses. Having the personal liability coverage through your renter's insurance policy could cover your expenses. In addition, just hiring an attorney could be expensive if you have to defend yourself, but with renter's insurance personal liability coverage, it is in the insurance company's best interest to send their attorney to try to minimize any lawsuit or expenses because they are now on the hook for the coverage you purchased. Of course, anyone who owns a pet such as a dog or a ferret should absolutely purchase some type of liability coverage in case your furry friend bites or scratches someone or if they decide to try to chew through the wall.

Renter's insurance can also provide for additional living expenses. Even the small grease fire example with the smoke and water damage could result in weeks of repairs. During that time, where are you going to stay? Your renter's insurance may pay for your temporary housing, such as a hotel, for a couple of weeks.

When comparing different rates for renter's insurance, first check with your parents' home owner's policy to see if it extends to you to cover your property and liability. If your parents' names are on the lease, then you may be covered, but not in all circumstances, so check with the policy and the agent. After considering the low cost of renter's insurance compared to all the various risks that can be shifted, it is surprising that only about 40% of renters actually have renter's insurance.[38] This is another instance where following the crowd can lead to a financial disaster.

# Homeowner's Insurance

Similar to renter's insurance, homeowner's insurance covers your personal property, provides liability protection, and pays for other incidental expenses. In addition, it also covers the structure of the house, whereas when you are a renter, your landlord's insurance covers the building. You have to be careful of the type of policy you purchase because there are several different kinds. One of the key differences between policy types is what is covered by each. In nearly all instances if you want to protect yourself from losses due to flooding, you will have to purchase separate flood insurance.

Several factors affect the price of your home owner's policy. The primary factor is the location of the residence. Where the house is located brings into consideration many factors that influence your premium such as the crime rate, distance to a fire department and fire hydrant, likelihood of various natural disasters such as hurricanes, and overall property values in the area. The type and age of the structure are also important. A brick home is less likely to be completely destroyed in a storm or even by a fire, which could keep your costs down. An older home may not have been built with as many of the safety standards as newer homes, it may have older wiring, which is more likely to spark a fire. The amount of coverage and the deductible are obviously significant factors. The amount of coverage is based primarily on the value of your home but also includes other variables including any additional structures on your property (such as a detached garage) and how much liability coverage you get.

You can keep your costs lower by increasing your deductible, just as you can with the other forms of insurance. If you have a $250 deductible, then you may be less likely to make smaller claims such as damage to your vinyl flooring from a refrigerator that leaked. If you increase your deductible to $500, then you will see even greater savings, as all smaller claims will likely be handled out-of-pocket by you, so the insurance company has no risk until the losses are large. You should also take advantage of all discounts that you can. If your home has an alarm system or a fire sprinkler system, then you could save some money. In addition, if you have a car or other insurance policies with the same company, then there may be multiple coverage discounts.

## *Umbrella Policies*

So far we have discussed various causes of loss or lawsuits, including what could happen if you have an automobile accident and cause some type of serious injury or someone is permanently injured on your property and sues you. As your personal wealth grows, you gradually have more and more at risk. One of the cheapest ways to protect your wealth in the event of a personal liability lawsuit is to purchase a megaliability insurance policy, sometimes referred to as an umbrella policy. Purchasing an umbrella policy allows you to protect yourself for more than the maximum automobile policy. The umbrella policy is very inexpensive because it only kicks in after your homeowner's or automobile insurance liability limits have been exceeded. Because the policies are only used in the event of large losses, the insurance company immediately provides legal assistance because they are on the hook for a large dollar amount.

# Health Insurance

In general, the way insurance works is large numbers of people purchase policies, and the risk to the insurance company is spread across all participants. That means that although some large claims are paid, there will be plenty of people who have no claims or very small claims, which keeps the insurance affordable for all involved. Health or medical insurance works the same way. The issue is that health insurance has become so expensive that not everyone participates in the insurance pool. Those less likely to participate are young, healthy people who make the financial decision to spend their earnings on other goods or services, such as houses, cars, vacations, or dining out. That leaves us with the older population, those who are already sick, or those with other health issues. As the customer base for insurance companies shifts so that only those who are most likely to use the insurance are the ones who purchase it, then the costs will continue to get prohibitively expensive.

Health insurance should be part of your overall risk management plan to safeguard your family's economic security. The lack of health insurance could lead you to postpone your treatment of an illness until it becomes so severe that it could result in larger costs and longer recovery time. For instance, if you get the flu and do not get treated properly because of your lack of health insurance, it may progress into pneumonia. If you get pneumonia, you will likely miss more work and could end up hospitalized, resulting in thousands of dollars of medical bills instead of $100 for a doctor's office visit and $75 for some antibiotics.

A good health insurance plan should offer basic coverage for hospitals and doctor bills. It should cover at least 120 days for a hospital stay. It should also provide at least $1 million lifetime coverage per person in your family. You want the policy to pay at least 80% of your out-of-hospital expenses. In addition, you want to make sure it does not impose any unreasonable exclusions. You also want your policy to limit your out-of-pocket expenses to no more than $5,000 per year excluding dental, vision, and prescription costs. Following these guidelines should result in a reasonably priced health-care plan that protects you enough to keep you from going bankrupt due to medical expenses.

Keep in mind that the first few days on your new job after graduation will involve making all types of decisions, some of which have lifelong consequences. One of the first decisions you may have to make is selecting your health insurance plan. Now that you have a set of criteria to use as a guide, you can compare plans to find the one that fits your needs or the bare minimums as we have suggested.

# Life Insurance

The purpose of life insurance is to protect someone who depends on you financially from financial loss related to your death. When making the decision on how much life insurance you will need, if any, keep this concept in mind to keep you from making a bad decision or one that is too costly. If anyone depends fully or partially on your income, then you need life insurance. Ask yourself if your spouse, your children, your parents, a disabled relative, or anyone else depends on your income. You also have to ask if anyone would need an income to replace your contributions to your family or household. For instance, if you are a nonworking spouse, then your family would need to replace your contributions by hiring assistance for such activities as day care or general help running the household.

Life insurance is one of the most abused and oversold financial products. Most people either purchase too little coverage with a policy that ensures greater commission for the salesperson, or they end up purchasing too much coverage, which again helps pad the pockets of the salesperson. There are many ways to determine your life insurance needs. You may want to evaluate several different approaches to see what makes the most sense for your situation. Just do not combine all the various ways, otherwise you could end up spending more on insurance than you should.

One approach to calculating life insurance needs is to look for your insurance to provide a lump sum payment to replace your income or your service to the family. With this approach, proceeds from life insurance should not be used to save for retirement, college, or any other reason. You want to have enough life insurance so that you can invest the payout and withdraw enough money each year that it replaces the income that was lost from the working spouse or enough to pay for the services provided by a nonworking spouse. The other approach is to look at the surviving family's needs and add up all the large expenses. For instance, you may want to pay off the mortgage, provide college education for your children, and contribute to a retirement account. You may still need to provide some income to help pay for regular expenses if the surviving spouse's income will not be sufficient. The key is for you to determine your need; do not let the salesperson determine your need for you.

When trying to determine how much life insurance you should purchase, keep in mind that your needs will change over time. After graduation you will likely incur some debt, but over your lifetime you will continue to acquire wealth. Early on in life your need for life insurance will be very high as you have very little wealth and large quantities of debt including student loans, car debt, and possibly a mortgage. Over time you will see your debts decrease and your wealth increase as your mortgage is paid off and your retirement account and other investments grow. By the time you retire you should be in a great position with savings, no debt, a well-funded retirement account, etc. Why would you want to be paying for life insurance when you no longer need it? Prudent financial planning will slowly eliminate your need for life insurance.

So how much life insurance do you really need? As mentioned, there is more than one way to make that determination. If you simply want to replace lost income, then you will need enough to recreate your income if invested wisely. In other words, the recipient of the life insurance payout will receive a lump sum amount that he or she will need to invest to receive enough interest to replace most of the income of the deceased person. For example, if you make $50,000 per year, then $750,000 in life insurance, wisely invested at 7%, would replace the full $50,000 worth of income annually.

The other approach would be to add up your mortgage, childrens' college expenses, and any other major debt or future obligation. So, to pay off a $200,000 mortgage, send both children to college for $100,000, and fund the retirement account at $150,000 would result in a $450,000 need. If the surviving spouse will not be able to live off his or her salary even after the major debts are covered, then some of the income lost would also have to be replaced. In this instance, if the family will still need $20,000 per year, then $300,000 invested at 7% will provide enough income. In both instances above this particular family will need $750,000, even though the income being replaced is only $50,000.

How can the average person making $50,000 per year afford $750,000 in life insurance? They purchase term life insurance. In fact, the only type of life insurance that you should purchase is term life insurance. There is no reason to purchase any type of cash value insurance. Cash value is too expensive. In fact, it was probably designed by a marketing department. Cash value insurance confuses savings with life insurance. These are two completely different things. It is a great marketing tactic to stop policyholders from canceling their policy and keep them paying their high insurance premiums for many years.

## *Term Life Insurance*

Term life insurance provides protection for a specified period of time. The coverage stops at the end of the term (such as 10 or 20 years) or when you stop making payments. Term insurance only provides a death benefit. There is no cash value to your term policy, which means that you cannot cancel the policy and cash it in and expect to receive any money for doing so. Once you stop paying for the insurance, it has no value.

Most term insurance policies have some type of renewability option. If the policy you are considering does not have the renewability option, then you need to select a different policy. You do not want a situation where you become uninsurable at some point in your life while you still need life insurance. With the renewability option you will not have to worry about that situation. You also do not want a term policy that lists what situations it will pay out. You want a life insurance policy that will pay a death benefit no matter how you die.

The premiums that you will pay each month or each year depend on your age. As you get older, you present more risk to the insurance company. Each year you live means you are one year closer to dying. Because your chances of dying increase each year, the premiums can also increase. You can purchase a level term policy that will have slightly higher premiums in the beginning, but they will stay the same for the entire term of your policy.

## Cash Value Life Insurance

Cash value life insurance comes in many different flavors such as whole life or universal life. They are all basically the same general concept with some variations of the details. The distinguishing feature of a cash value policy is that it combines a death benefit with a savings vehicle. The cash value policy actually builds a cash value, which means at some point you could turn your policy in and receive a specified amount of cash or you can stop paying the premiums and the policy is still in effect. The premiums for cash value policies are considerably higher. They combine and confuse two completely different objectives: retirement and life insurance.

For the same amount of benefit, cash value is up to eight times more expensive than term insurance. It is almost impossible to afford enough life insurance if you try to purchase cash value. You can expect to receive a lot of pressure from your insurance agent to convince you to purchase cash value. If you argue your point enough about how much you need and the overall cost, they may concede somewhat and then try to sell you a portion of your needs with cash value and the rest with term insurance to sell you two policies. If cash value was the best one, then you should purchase the whole amount with cash value, but if term is the best option then you should purchase the whole amount using term life insurance. Because we already explained that cash value is a bad idea, do not let the insurance agent convince you to unnecessarily spend *your* money. If cash value policies are such a bad investment then why is there so much pressure to buy them? Remember the golden rule? Always ask how the person helping you is being compensated. Cash value policies are very expensive, and the commissions that the insurance agent earns are much higher. Keep in mind that insurance agents are salespeople, not objective advisors.

Don't fall victim to what seems on the surface to be very logical reasons for buying cash value life insurance. An agent will tell you the premium will be paid up in 10 years, so you no longer have to make payments. True. What is really happening is the total premiums are paid over a 10-year period. The insurance company crams 30+ years of payments into 10 years making the monthly payment very high. Plus the cash value decreases. Not a good deal for you.

An agent may argue that most people cannot afford term insurance as they get older. Of course, the cost of term goes up as you get older because the risk of dying is greater. But if you plan wisely, you will not need life insurance later in life. You need life insurance while you are young and have a mortgage and kids. Once you are old, retired, and have a 401(k) plan, you do not have a need for life insurance. Financial success later in life is about making smart financial decisions while you are young.

One of our favorites is when agents tout that you can borrow against the cash value. The insurance company gives you the opportunity to borrow your own money and pay the insurance company interest; a very good deal for the insurance company.

The cash value of the policy grows tax deferred. True. However, Individual Retirement Accounts (or IRAs) are better. They grow tax deferred plus, and this is a big plus, they provide an immediate tax deduction as well.

Our all-time favorite is when agents push how cash value life insurance forces you to save. If you need a little help to be disciplined when it comes to your savings there are better ways to go about it. There are plenty of ways to force one to save that are much less costly such as payroll deductions, automatic transfers from your checking to savings account, etc.

Bottom line is that cash value policies pay the highest commission among life insurance policies. Thus most insurance agents to try to sell you this type of policy. Our advice is to always, always, always buy term insurance.

## Credit Life Insurance

Often when you purchase a car and finance it, you will be offered the "opportunity" to buy credit life insurance. Credit life insurance is designed to pay off a specific debt in the event that you die. Basically you are buying a life insurance product that only pays what you owe on your debt when you die. Considering that your debt decreases every year as you continue to pay it off, you are paying for a product that gets less valuable every year, yet your payments stay the same. In addition, based on our earlier advice, you quickly realize that this insurance is too narrow because it only covers one specific item. Instead you should have a comprehensive life insurance policy. The proceeds can be used to pay off all your debt, not just your outstanding loan balance.

Credit life insurance is more expensive per dollar of benefit compared to your overall life insurance policy. The policy marketing pieces are designed to play off your emotions because they try to guilt you into thinking you are not protecting your spouse or your family. Any time you borrow money to make a purchase, you need to account for that new debt obligation in your term life insurance needs. It should not be covered by buying credit life.

## Accidental Death and Dismemberment Insurance

Likewise, you should not purchase accidental death and dismemberment insurance. We have already established that you are no more or less dead whether you die because of an accident or not, so your regular life insurance policy will suffice. You will receive offers to purchase AD&D insurance in the mail, through your bank or credit union, and through your employer. The reason everyone is peddling these policies is because they are usually small dollar amounts but they return high margins. This means for every dollar you spend on the policy, the insurance companies can afford to pay a fee or commission to the bank, credit union, or other organization for every policy sold.

# Disability Insurance

We spend much time and energy worrying about, discussing, and purchasing life insurance, but at any age you are more likely to become disabled than you are to die. Becoming disabled is a double-edged sword because your income goes down when you can no longer work, and your expenses tend to go up because of new medical expenses associated with your disability. Disability insurance provides regular cash flow in the event that you are unable to earn a living due to specific conditions such as illness, injury, or even pregnancy. While being pregnant is not legally considered a disability, you (or your spouse) could be forced into bed rest for an extended period of time, particularly toward the final months or weeks of the pregnancy.

Typically, your disability insurance policy will pay about 60% to 80% of your salary.[39] Most policies will not replace 100% of your income because the insurance company wants to make sure you have some incentive to get better and get back to work if at all possible. If you are deemed to have a catastrophic injury such as becoming paralyzed from the neck down with no chance of recovery, some policies have a clause that states the insurance company will replace 100% of your income. There is no need to encourage you to get better because medically your situation cannot improve.

## Sources of Disability Income

There are four sources of disability income:

### #1 Employer

Your employer may offer a group disability policy. The policy may be specifically for short-term disabilities or for long-term disabilities. Early in your career you will need both short-term and long-term disability coverage. Because you have not had time to accumulate sick leave and you have not established a large emergency fund, you need protection from a short-term disability. Long-term disability is necessary for all stages of your career.

### #2 Social Security

Social Security only covers total disability that lasts more than one year. In addition, the clock starts from the date that you are deemed disabled, not from the time the injury or illness first occurred. Because the payments are not retroactive, you will not receive compensation for the year that you were waiting to receive the benefit.

### #3 Workers' Compensation

Employers are required to pay into a workers' compensation fund. In the event that you are injured while working, you become eligible to apply for workers' compensation. The biggest disadvantage of workers' compensation is that it only applies if you are injured at work. If you slip and fall or get into an automobile accident on your way to work, your way home, while on vacation, on the weekend, and so forth, your workers' compensation will not help you at all. Also, if you become disabled due to some type of medical illness, your workers' compensation will not be of any use.

## #4  Disability Insurance

You can always purchase disability insurance on your own or perhaps through your employer. You want to achieve at least 70% to 80% of your take-home pay with your disability insurance benefits. If you purchase through your employer, you may be given the option to have the premium paid in pretax dollars. This means you don't pay tax on the amount of the premium. The trade-off is that if you collect benefits, they are taxable. Pay the premium in posttax dollars (you pay the tax on the premium) then you can collect the benefits tax-free. The benefit of paying the tax up front far outweighs the benefit of paying with pretax dollars.

It is important to recognize the advantages and limitations of each of these forms of disability insurance. They are not mutually exclusive forms of protection, but in fact should be used as part of an overall strategy.

## Reading the Policy

Although the fine print may not be of concern to you at this moment, it will be very important to you in the event you actually have to use the insurance policy. One of the key terms to look for on your disability policy is the phrase "your job" coverage. You want to avoid policies that say "any job" coverage. Although intuitively it may seem that "any" job is better than "your" job because the term "any" is a broader term, you have to think about what the policy is saying. If you are injured and cannot perform "any" job, then you would be covered under the "any job" provision.

For example, if you are a surgeon and you can no longer perform surgeries because of a hand tremor, but you could still teach classes at a medical school or even work the McDonald's drive-through, you would not receive full benefit, because you can still work "any" job. On the other hand, if the surgeon had "your job" coverage and could no longer perform surgeries, then he or she would receive a benefit because even though the surgeon could still teach courses, he or she could no longer perform his or her job. A policy with "your job" coverage is actually better protection for your income.

You also want to make sure the policy is noncancelable and guaranteed renewable. A noncancelable policy simply means that the insurance company cannot cancel your policy at some point in the future. Although the insurance company is unlikely to be able to cancel your policy while you are collecting benefits, your concern would be if they cancel your policy after you have had it for 10 years, even though you have not used it. When you purchase a new policy from someone else, they may charge much higher monthly premiums or they may determine you are uninsurable due to some condition such as the onset of a disease. A guaranteed renewable policy protects you in the same way. If your policy ends at a certain time, you are guaranteed to be able to renew it, even if you now have an injury or illness that would prevent a different insurance company from writing a new policy for you.

One way to save money on disability insurance is to increase your waiting period (also called an elimination period). The waiting period is the amount of time after you become disabled that you have to wait until your disability insurance begins to pay. Keep in mind the pay is not retroactive, so they do not go back and pay you for the time you waited; they start paying the following month. For instance, if you become disabled on January 1 and you have a 60-day waiting period, then you will not receive any payments until sometime in March. You will have to cover your own bills and expenses for January and February. If you treat the waiting period as a form of deductible you can save money on your monthly payment by increasing the waiting period. From the insurance company's perspective, the longer the waiting period, the less likely you are to use the policy. Since some injuries only result in 30 to 90 days of disability you may not use their policy at all, unless you have a severe or permanent injury. On the other hand, if you have no waiting period, you are more likely to use the policy.

## Choosing an Agent

You always have to ask yourself, "How is the person helping me make this decision being compensated?" We do not mean to imply that all salespeople are slimy liars. In fact, we believe that most individuals are good, honest people who try to be good at their job just like anyone else. Still, you want to know where their allegiances are. A sales agent who earns a salary instead of a commission may be a little more inclined to give objective advice because their ability to eat does not depend on whether or not they sell you a policy. On the other hand, you may be unaware of sales contests or bonuses that the company is running based on the number of policies sold or the type of policies sold. Why do you think so many retail salespeople try to convince you to buy extended warranties? It is because even though they get paid by the hour, there is usually an extra incentive or commission on top of their regular pay for every policy they sell. Keep in mind that just because someone has a license or recommends an agent, does not mean they are any good.

You can do some research on your own before selecting an agent if you are willing to take the time. The Independent Insurance Agents and Brokers of America is an organization that lists members of their organization if you want to go that route. You can also reference the Society of Financial Services Professionals to see if your agent has been approved through their organization. The advantage of using an agent or broker associated with one of the national organizations is they have additional accountability because the national organizations require certain standards to be met and will remove members who violate those standards. Your state may also have a Department of Insurance, which you can contact to make sure your agent is truly licensed and to confirm that no complaints have been filed against your agent.

You can also ask parents, friends, or neighbors for recommendations as a starting point. Once you finally meet with an agent, see if they are willing to take their time and find the policy that is right for you. They should also ask about your financial plan. Because your risk management strategy is one part of your overall financial plan, the only way an agent can truly be sure they have recommended the right coverage is if they understand the big picture. You also want to make sure they are available when you need them. Any agent can seem available to you when they are trying to sell a policy, but you want to make sure they will be there for you when you have questions or when you have to file a claim.

# THE COST OF  FINANCIAL IGNORANCE

Insurance is the one area of our financial lives where a lack of understanding is not just costly, it can be financially devastating. Without understanding what insurance is really supposed to do for us, it would be easy to purchase the wrong type of protection (wasteful), too much protection (costly), or too little protection (devastating).

For instance, many drivers have too little automobile insurance. They buy only the state-mandated minimums under the misguided assumption that they are fully insured; after all, you have purchased what the state requires. But you never really discover that you have too little insurance until it is too late.

It would only take one personal injury or an accident with a new luxury or sports car to far exceed the minimum insurance limits for most states. Those who do understand the need for more insurance generally fail to purchase enough coverage because they believe it is out of reach for them financially. What if we can show you how to easily save $120 per year on your current automobile insurance policy or how to increase your protection by almost eight times for just $93 more per year?

The rates listed in Figure 1 are actual rates from an insurance company that show the minimum coverage for someone in North Carolina. Of course, every policy will be different for each individual because there are many contributing factors such as age, credit score, driving history, location, or type of car. The point is to look at the total amount the insurance costs in one year (see Chart 1) for a 30/60/25 policy. The deductible for collision is a low $250, and the deductible for comprehensive is just $100. Because you really do not want to use your insurance for any type of small claim, as it will simply increase your rates with very little benefit, these deductibles are too low.

In this example we could keep our same coverage, but increase our deductibles. Just increasing the deductible for collision from $250 to $500 and the deductible for comprehensive from $100 to $500, we could reduce that portion of our annual insurance premiums from $1,126 down to $1,003, resulting in a savings of $123 per year (see Chart 2). That extra coverage of $250 and $400 per year was costing us $123. After just two years of not making any collision claims, we would be saving more than the difference in the deductible. After just three years of not making any comprehensive claims we would be saving more than the increased amount of the deductible. The point here is that unless we are likely to file a claim very soon, in the long run it is more cost effective to have a higher deductible because the amount of money we save in premiums over time is much more than the amount of extra deductible we may have to pay when we do finally need to use our insurance.

Now that we have saved some money, let's see if we can put that money to better financial use than say a night on the town. If we increase our coverage from 30/60/25 (the minimum) to 250/500/100 (the highest level) the cost of the coverage would increase from $632 to $848 (a $216 increase—see Chart 2). That increase is almost completely offset by the change in premium from the change in our deductibles. Our combined total

### MINIMUM LIMITS

| Coverage | Cost |
|---|---|
| Vehicle 1—Car Type Here | |
| Liability – Bodily injury<br>$30,000 ea person, $60,000 ea accident | $359 |
| Liability—Property damage<br>$25,000 ea accident | $273 |
| | $632 |
| Damage to your auto (not collision)<br>$100 deductible | $260 |
| Collision<br>$250 deductible | $866 |
| | $1,126 |
| **Total Insurance cost** | $1,758 |

*Chart 1*

| Coverage | Cost |
|---|---|
| Vehicle 1—Car Type Here | |
| Liability—Bodily injury<br>$250,000 ea person, $500,000 ea accident | $562 |
| Liability—Property damage<br>$100,000 ea accident | $286 |
| | $848 |
| Damage to your auto (not collision)<br>$500 deductible | $172 |
| Collision<br>$500 deductible | $831 |
| | $1,126 |
| **Total Insurance cost** | $1,851 |

*Chart 2*

insurance policy has only increased by a total of $93 (take the $216 increase and subtract the $123), yet our total coverage went from 30/60/25 to 250/500/100. For only $93 we were able to purchase several hundred thousand dollars worth of additional protection.

| | |
|---|---|
| Cost to upgrade policy to top of the line | $196.00 |
| Saving from adjusting deductibles to proper levels | $123.00 |
| Additional cost to you | $ 93.00 |
| Cost of an accident that exceeds your original coverage by just 10% | **$11,500.00** |

# CREDIT

## Getting What You Deserve

We always have five or six students approach us after class to ask a question or two. Recently one young lady was asking how the credit card laws were supposed to protect her. She was very upset. She received her first credit card as a freshman. Now as a sophomore she owed more than $3,000 on the card. Even though she was having no trouble making the minimum monthly payments, she was having trouble securing a loan for a used car. We did our best to console her and offered her some advice on what next to do.

A young man standing behind her overheard some of the conversation. Before he asked his question, he smugly touted that he did not have a credit card, nor would he ever apply for a credit card. He had done his homework and knew how damaging credit cards could be. No one, he concluded, should have a credit card. At least no college student should have one. And his parents agreed. Imagine his surprise when we told him what a mistake he was making. Almost everyone should have a credit card, especially college students. Given that credit cards are one of the easiest ways to really screw up your finances, how can we recommend that you need a credit card?

# SO WHAT IS CREDIT?

For most of you, right now, you are borrowing money to attend college. In fact, you may have borrowed money just to buy this book! Whether you took out student loans, personal loans, or used a credit card, you are using credit. Credit is simply money that belongs to others that they are willing to let you use for a period of time. When dealing with credit, the fee is usually listed as an interest rate, which is a percentage. There may be other fees attached to various types of credit, such as loan origination fees, late fees, and so forth, but for the most part we are referring to the percentage that you must pay in interest charges.

Credit is important to our economy as businesses use credit to invest, expand, and hire employees. Consumers use credit to make large purchases such as houses, cars, or a college education. If every student had to go out and earn $20,000 before they could attend college, either the enrollment on campuses would decrease dramatically or the average age of a college student would be much older. If everyone had to save up and pay cash for their car, then the automobile industry would look different than it does today. If people had to save up enough money to buy homes with cash then the housing market would be much smaller, homes would have very few amenities, and the American dream may be reduced to a pitch tent.

If credit helps an economy grow as consumers can spend money on large purchases that keep businesses running, and businesses can then use credit to expand operations to build more big items that consumers can buy, then why would we not want everyone to use as much credit as possible? The more credit we use, the more debt we accumulate. Debt allows an economy to appear very large but debt also creates more risk in an economy. Think about it from an individual level. Suppose you make $2,000 per month and have $100 in debt payments. Then your boss cuts your salary by 20%. Your income would only be $1,600 per month, but you would still be able to make your $100 per month debt payment. Now imagine if you have $1,500 in debt payments every month. You would just barely be able to make your debt payments, but you would not have any money left over for your other expenses such as food. Now imagine that you have $1,800 in debt payments every month. A reduction in salary means that you could not even make your minimum payments. As you can see, there is an upside and a downside to credit, so the key is to balance it at the appropriate level where you are not increasing your risk too much, but you are using credit the right way and for the right types of purchases.

## What Lenders Want

At this stage in your life, you are likely to need credit over the next several years. Because credit is offered by businesses, generally banks, they have the right to make sure you are a worthy customer. They cannot base your worthiness on demographics such as race, religion, ethnicity, and so forth, but they can base it on how likely and willing you are to pay them back, with interest. The financial industry has come up with some standard ways to evaluate whether you can and will pay back your loans. They can use these measurements to determine how much credit they are willing to extend to you and how much they will charge you to borrow their money.

## What Lenders Measure

Lenders want to make sure that you have the ability to repay your loans and that you are willing to use your resources to do so. Both factors are important to a lender because any money you do not pay back results in a loss for the lender. Large losses could cost some people their jobs, could result in higher fees and rates for those who do pay their loans, or could even cause the lender to go bankrupt.

Although you may be the most honest person on the planet, have every intention of repaying a loan, and can even demonstrate your honesty to the bank, if you simply do not have any income they will not lend you money. Or maybe they will lend you money, but they simply will not lend you as much as you want. They have to make sure you have the ability to pay the loan back before they are willing to give you their money.

On the other hand, maybe you make lots of money and definitely have the ability to repay the loan without too much problem. Now the lender will need to make sure that you are *willing* to pay back the loan. Not everyone who has money is responsible with it. If you have a history of missing or late payments, then lenders may decide either to not lend any money to you or to lend it to you at a higher interest rate.

# THE FIVE Cs OF CREDIT

1. Character

2. Capacity

3. Capital

4. Collateral

5. Conditions

*Five Cs of Credit*

**Character** has to do with your willingness to pay your bills on time. Your credit history is the key here. Late payments may be an indication that you are not as serious about your financial obligations as you should be. Most creditors won't report a late payment until it is more than 30 days late. So any late payments will give you a "red flag" to lenders and could impede your ability to get the loan or increase the rate that you have to pay.

**Capacity** deals with your ability to pay the loan. Do you have the financial resources to pay the loan when it is due? Typically this comes from your income. Lenders usually do not like to see your debt payments (home, car, credit cards, and other loans) exceed roughly 36% of your gross monthly income. A debt payment ratio in excess of 36% may be a sign that you won't have the resources to pay the loan on time, even though you may have the desire.

**Capital** looks at your assets (the things you own) and your net worth (the difference between what you own and what you owe). In looking at your assets, the creditor is trying to see if you could sell anything to satisfy the loan in a worst-case scenario. Closely related to this, your net worth helps the creditor understand if over time you are moving in the right financial direction. A negative net worth is not necessarily a bad thing. It depends on the circumstances. A college graduate at age 22 who has a negative net worth of $15K from student loans is in much better shape than a 45-year-old with a small positive net worth.

**Collateral** is something that you own of value that is pledged to the lender that can be taken away by the lender and sold to satisfy the debt if you don't pay the loan. You can typically receive better loan terms when you provide collateral like your house or your car.

**Conditions** take into account the big picture. What economic conditions, typically beyond your control, could affect your ability to repay the loan? Are you working in an industry that is currently downsizing? Did you leave your last job of ten years to go to work for a dot.com company? Do you move or change jobs frequently?

The five Cs of credit take into account both your willingness and your ability to repay your loans. So how exactly can the lenders use these five Cs to make their determination? Put another way, what exactly do the lenders look at or use to determine how much, if any, money they are willing to lend and at what interest rate?

## What Lenders Consider

Almost every lender looks at your credit score. Your credit score is derived from information gathered from your credit reports. Your credit reports are literally reports from credit bureaus or reporting agencies. Although there are several reporting agencies, the three most utilized are Equifax, Experian, and TransUnion. The information that is gathered for your credit reports come from credit and banking agencies voluntarily reporting information about you and your credit habits to one or more of the agencies. In addition, some public record information about you is collected, as well such as any judgments or liens.

Credit reports are like report cards about your financial life. Your name, address, and Social Security number are all collected, which should "hopefully" keep your information from being mixed up with someone else's. In addition, the reports collect your loan amounts, your payment history including on-time and late payments, and when your accounts were opened. In addition, some utility companies may choose to report your information, particularly if you begin to fall behind on your payments.

Because the reporting of your information is technically voluntary, your three credit reports may actually look somewhat different from each other, as not all financial companies report to all three major credit bureaus. It is important, as a consumer, that you check all three credit reports at least once per year to make sure the information is up to date and correct. You can get access to each report for free once per year by going to www.annualcreditreport.com.[40] Although numerous commercials advertise access to free credit reports or free credit scores, the only way to get the reports for free is through the annual credit report Web site. The advertisements are for credit monitoring services to which you pay a monthly or annual fee to use, and as part of your payment, they will provide a report or a score for free. In addition, anytime you are denied credit due to information gathered from a credit report, you have the right to see your credit report to ensure that it is accurate. Please note that you can get free access to your credit reports, but if you want to see your actual credit score, you will have to pay a fee.

The difference between your credit report and your credit score is a credit report has some public information available about you as well as information reported by various financial companies, whereas your credit score is based on a formula that is owned by a private company. The most common credit score used is the FICO score. The score is called FICO because it was created by a company called Fair Isaac Corporation. Your FICO credit score consists of five main pieces of information: your payment history, the amounts owed, the length of credit history, new credit, and types of credit.

Your payment history represents 35% of your score and includes past due items, how long they are past due, and any delinquencies or judgments that are a result of paying late or simply never paying them at all. That is why it is important that if you borrow money, make sure you have the ability to pay it back on time. A credit card is considered delinquent when you are more than 30 days late on your payment and will likely show up on your credit report.

The amounts you owe represent 30% of your score. That means multiple loans and credit cards with large amounts owed can hurt your score even if you are making all the payments on time. Banks understand that the more debt you have, the harder it will be for you to make your payments if something goes wrong, such as the loss of a job or a major unexpected emergency . They also look at the proportion of your credit that is being used. That means if you have two credit cards with a $1,000 credit limit and one card is maxed out and the other is not being used, you are using 50% of your available credit. Some people mistakenly close the unused card, but if you close the unused card, you would now be using 100% of your available credit, and your score will go down.

The length of history represents 15% of your score. Keep in mind you must have credit that is reported for at least six months to even have a credit score. The length of history looks at the time since you opened your accounts and the time since you last had activity on them. Ask yourself would you rather have a surgeon who has 10 years of experience or one who just graduated from medical school? The same concept applies to credit. From the perspective of a bank, if they are going to loan you money, the longer history you have of proving you will repay your debt, the less risky you seem. On the other hand, having never missed a payment over only one year of credit history you have only proven that you can make payments for a short period of time. You may not have had a chance to go through life's ups and downs while still maintaining your payments.

New credit represents 10% of your score. It looks at the number of new accounts and how many times you have asked for credit recently. If you have five accounts, but they are all new, then all that says is that you are either just starting out, or you suddenly found yourself in need to borrow more. This only makes you appear more of a risk to lenders. Each time you apply for credit (loan, credit card, etc.) it is tracked. If you do it too frequently, then it looks like you are desperate for credit, which makes you look like a poor credit risk.

The remaining 10% of your score is made up of the types of credit you have. A mix of different types of credit is good. For example, if you only have four credit cards and nothing else, you only have one type of credit, which is revolving credit. On the other hand, if you have a loan and a credit card then you have at least two types of credit; a revolving loan and a fixed-term loan. This will improve your score as you can demonstrate that you are able to handle different types of debt.

Most lending institutions go through a process called underwriting. During the underwriting process, they are essentially trying to make a decision about how risky you are as a borrower to determine if they will lend any money to you, how much they are willing to lend, and at what rate. During this process they look at your credit score as one of their main sources of information. However, they do consider other elements as well, as demonstrated by the Five Cs of credit such as what industry you work in and whether that industry is stable or not. They will also consider how much available credit you have relative to your income. In other words, if you want to lower your credit utilization ratio by opening up several credit cards, it could help your credit score, but the bank will look at this ratio outside your credit score and may still find that you are too risky.

The point is that banks, credit card companies, and other lending institutions take a look at your financial situation to make sure you are someone they want to lend money. The better you take care of your money to minimize your debt, spend responsibly, and pay your bills on time, the better chance you will have to get a loan at favorable (low) interest rates.

# CREDIT CARDS

Credit cards are a very controversial financial product. Some experts say you should avoid credit cards at all cost. Others say that you should definitely have credit cards for various reasons. Sometimes it is difficult to know whose advice to use. The key to understanding credit cards is to understand how they work, what purpose they serve, and when you should and should not use them.

Credit cards are not evil by themselves. In fact, credit cards are simply a tool. You can use that tool to build or destroy. Going one step further, credit cards are really more like power tools. In high school, when you take a shop class, you are not allowed to use the power tools until you receive the proper training and are supplied with the proper safety equipment such as goggles and gloves. You are not allowed to drive a car, which is a powerful machine, without first receiving training and being issued a license. Yet, we allow people to use a credit card without providing any of the necessary warnings, safety training, or basic instructions. Although credit cards will not hurt you, misusing your credit card will.

Currently, 84% of the overall student population have at least one credit card. For undergraduates, 76% have credit cards and an average credit card debt of $2,200. Half of all undergraduates actually have four or more credit cards.[41] With so many students carrying credit cards, and many carrying debt, it is essential to understand how to properly use the cards. The misuse of credit is not easily resolved after college students graduate and begin to increase their income. In fact, the issue only gets worse as credit limits increase with increased income. The average credit card debt per household is $15,788.[42] Although many adults begin to use credit cards in college, the lack of education on how to properly use them results in more debt issues after graduation.

Historically, credit card companies or their vendors would visit college campuses and college events and offer freebies to students who applied for a credit card. While most students opened credit cards through solicitations received in their mail, the on-campus booths were the most visible form of solicitation.[43] As a result, many students found themselves in financial difficulty within their first few years of college. These direct appeals to college students were outlawed in the 2009 Credit Card Accountability, Responsibility, and Disclosure Act (the Credit CARD Act).

The Credit CARD Act also made it more difficult for college students to open credit cards before the age of 21. Anyone under the age of 21 must have a cosigner or be able to prove their ability to make the payments. Other changes under the law include the elimination of practices such as universal default and two-cycle billing, requiring credit card bills to be sent at least 21 days before the payment is due, allowing payments to be received up to 5 p.m. on the due date, and several other restrictions on fees and rates.[44]

The changes were designed to provide greater consumer protection. The biggest gap in the law was that interest rates were not capped, which means credit card companies are still free to charge whatever rate they want, particularly for adjustable rate credit cards. You do have to be notified at least 45 days before your rate will change if it is a fixed rate card or if your variable rate card will be increased for any reason other than the movement of the index attached to the rate.

All of these practices were used by credit card companies in the past to increase their revenues. They looked for behaviors that occurred frequently and could be used to make money. Although there is certainly nothing wrong with an industry finding ways to make more money, it is only fair if the consumer understands what is happening.

Credit card companies employ PhDs in finance and economics, as well as attorneys, who try to find ways to charge you and to keep you from understanding what they are charging! Now that the laws have changed, it is even more important that you do your research and be aware of what is going on as credit card companies will be looking for new ways to earn more profits off you such as new fees, increased rates, or other approaches that have not yet been discovered.

## Advantages of Credit Cards

There are several advantages to using credit cards. You will not need to carry cash if you make your purchases with credit cards. Whether you are making large purchases or several small purchases, it is difficult to carry large amounts of cash with you. Using your credit card instead of cash means that you will not have to estimate how much cash you will need to carry to go shopping. You have the ability to buy now and pay later. If you do not have enough money in the bank, but find something that is on sale or that you really want to buy, you can make the purchase now and then pay off the card as you earn future income. Your bookkeeping will be much easier because you can always use your monthly credit card statement to see where you spent your money during the previous month. In addition, you are more protected from fraud and poor business practices when you use your credit card compared to when you use cash. If you make a purchase with cash, it may be difficult to return to the store or company that did not deliver what was promised and demand your money back. With most credit cards, you may be able to stop the payment so you will not be charged or defrauded. Perhaps the key advantage to credit cards is that they are simply more convenient.

## Disadvantages of Credit Cards

There are several disadvantages to credit cards as well. The biggest disadvantage is they are simply more convenient. Yes, the key advantage of credit cards is also their key disadvantage. Due to their convenience, you are able to obligate your future income very easily. Your ability to buy now and pay later could mean that you could buy too much now and have too much to pay later and may find it difficult to make your minimum payments. Using credit cards can result in you losing lots of money in high interest rates and other hidden costs. Using a credit card actually results in spending more money. The convenience of having a credit card could result in purchasing items on the spot that you would have otherwise had time to think about and reconsider. In other words, if you have time to go home, get the cash, and think about whether you really needed the item, you may change your mind and not make the purchase. If you have a credit card, you could just make the purchase that instant without giving yourself time to really think about it.

Because interest rates are not capped, you could find yourself paying rates well over 20%, particularly on department store cards. If you are more than 60 days late on your payment your rates could easily go above 30%. Late payment fees and over the limit fees could easily reach as high as $25 or $35 if it is not your first offense (the fees reached $39 before the recent Credit CARD Act).[45] Grace periods (the time between when you make your purchase and when you will be charged interest) are nonexistent if you already carry a balance on your credit card.

Credit cards may offer you to transfer your balance from another card to their card. However, they usually charge a 4% fee, which means if you transfer a $1,000 debt you will now owe $1,040. If the offer came with a 0% introductory rate, it will most likely be for only six months. That means you get 0% for six months, you had to pay 4% to transfer the amount, and then the rate goes to whatever the standard rate is for that card. If you repeated that process again in six months, you would have effectively paid an 8% fee (interest rate) for the 0% interest rate. In other words, you are not really getting much of a deal at all. What can you do?

Let us recap how the financial system works. To get any significant type of loan, such as for a car or a mortgage, the lender will want to look at your credit report. To have a credit report you need to already have credit for at least six months. The longer your credit history, the better your credit score. The better your credit score, the lower your interest rate. Therefore, it makes sense for college students to get a credit card while they are still in college, so their credit score will have a chance to increase before they need their first big loan. If it is in your best interest to get a credit card, yet we have already discussed the disadvantages of credit cards and the warnings about how the credit card companies operate, what can you do to protect yourself?

You need to carefully select the credit card that is best for you. Cards come in all varieties with different interest rates, rules, annual fees, reward points, and so forth. You want to shop around using sites such as www.CardWeb.com.[46] You can look for college student credit cards and see what offers are available from the various carriers or you can see if you are eligible for other credit cards besides those specifically for students.

You should read the offer (which is the contract) to see if there are any restrictions or fees that you do not want. There is a box that summarizes most of the key points of the contract, including the annual fee, the interest rate, the grace period, and other fees.[47]

Once you have a credit card you can always try to negotiate better terms. The first time you are late on a payment you may be able to have the late fee waived. If you make a habit of late payments you will end up paying a lot of money in late fees, see your interest rate rise, damage your credit score, and the credit card company will be very unlikely to work with you. You can also ask for a lower rate at any time as well. Again, if you are in good standing you have a much better chance of getting better terms from the credit card company than if you abuse or misuse your credit.

To keep your credit score high and your rates low make sure you make your payments on time. Use automatic direct draft from your bank account if it is available to you. If not, then make your payments manually online. Rarely, if ever, will you have to mail paper checks to a credit card company. If you do use an automatic direct draft, be aware that your minimum payment may change as your balance changes so you will still want to monitor your card and the payments to make sure you always pay at least the minimum. Keep your e-mail confirmation or print the confirmation page for your files as verification you made your payment. In the event that a credit card company tries to argue that you did not pay on time, you have proof. If they try to do anything you feel is unethical or illegal such as not counting your payments and you are not able to resolve the issue directly with your credit card issuer, then you can make a complaint to the office of the attorney general for your state. You can find your attorney general's contact information at www.naag.org.[48]

# DEBT

After all the discussion about credit cards and debt, you may be convinced that debt is bad. In fact, debt in and of itself is not bad. All debt is risky, but risk is not necessarily bad. Some debt is considered good debt, whereas other debt is considered bad debt. Your job is to first distinguish between the two and then focus on minimizing your bad debt.

## Good Debt

So what is good debt? Good debt can be identified by three common characteristics. Keep in mind, all three characteristics must be present, not just one.

> **Good debt is attached to a purchase that:**
>
> **1. Appreciates (increases) in value AND**
>
> **2. Last longer than the loan AND**
>
> **3. Creates positive financial leverage**

A purchase does not always have to be an actual product. For instance, are college loans a good debt? It depends. First, if you borrow money to attend college, but never complete your degree, then it immediately breaks rule #3. Any education will last longer than your loan, but you are unlikely to leverage some college education to get a substantially better job. On the other hand, if you complete your degree, you may very well have made a great investment. Of course, if you borrow $100,000 to become a public schoolteacher making less than $30,000 per year, then it may actually create negative leverage because you are unlikely to earn enough money to comfortably repay your loans. On the other hand, if you borrow $25,000 to become a civil engineer, then you may have made an investment that will result in a great income for years to come.

## Bad Debt

Because you can now identify good debt, it should be simple to identify bad debt. Although good debt had to display all three characteristics, bad debt only has to demonstrate one of the following three characteristics as it relates to the purchase.

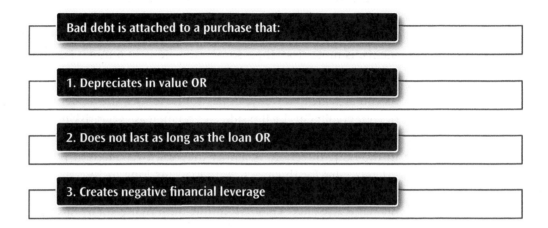

Bad debt is attached to a purchase that:

1. Depreciates in value OR

2. Does not last as long as the loan OR

3. Creates negative financial leverage

When you borrow money to purchase a car, you have immediately bought an item that depreciates in value. A car is worth less each year, even if you bought it used. The good news is that cars will generally last longer than the loan, although new cars will likely lose their warranty during the last year or two of your payments. Even so, it does not matter because it only has to meet one of the rules to be considered bad debt.

As a reminder, all debt is risky. Any time you are in debt, you are taking on some level of risk, even if your only debt is good debt. The main reason debt is risky is because it takes away your choices. If you buy a car your last year in college, and then decide you would like to spend three months in Europe after graduation before starting a full-time job, you may not be able to make that choice because you have a car payment. Maybe you borrowed $100,000 to get a medical degree so you could become a doctor. Arguably, borrowing for a medical degree is a good debt. However, if you decide you do not want to practice medicine, or you would rather open a free clinic to help the economically disadvantaged, you may not have that option because you have to make the payments on the $100,000 you borrowed.

When you borrow money, you are essentially making purchases on credit. Credit purchases come in many different varieties, such as mortgages, car loans, personal loans, and credit cards. The real danger is if you fail to understand what it really means to borrow money and fail to understand how much you could end up paying for the privilege of borrowing that money including interest payments and any additional fees.

## Credit Costs

By referencing your cash flow statement you can calculate your own bad debt ratio. First, add up all your bad debt payments and divide that total by your total income. Any ratio greater than 25% is an indication that you could be in financial difficulty, and you could possibly find yourself in financial trouble. As your ratio exceeds the 25% threshold, it may limit your ability to handle short-term obligations, such as paying the utility bill or making a credit card payment. Remember the more risk we present to the lender, the more debt will cost us. It is the same concept that insurance companies use to justify how much they charge us in premiums. A person who gets into fender benders every couple of years is more risky than someone who has never been in an accident. Likewise, someone who misses a few payments or even someone whose financial picture indicates they are likely to miss a few payments, is more risky than someone who is in a much better cash position and can easily make their payments.

As you are able to lower your risk to the lender, the lender is willing to lower the cost of your credit. On the flip side, as you increase your risk to the lender, the lender will increase the cost of your credit. So, the lender's risk and your cost (interest rate) move in the same direction. A lender may ask two different people to pay two different interest rates for the exact same loan. As long as they are asking the riskier person to pay more than the stable person, they are not discriminating and they are not breaking any laws. They are simply employing smart business practices.

Risky behavior will have ripple effects across your finances. For example, it will end up costing you in credit costs when you borrow money. It could also cost you in insurance costs because automobile insurance rates can be adjusted based on credit scores. Of course, how much credit will cost you only matters if you have credit or if you plan to borrow any money in the future. Because it is unreasonable to think that you will not have some type of debt at some point in time, especially within the first few years after graduation, you need to consider the consequences of debt and interest rates. Even if you do not plan to borrow any money, you have to be realistic and assume you will at least borrow if you plan to purchase a house or if you plan to buy a car as well.

# SHOPPING FOR CAR LOANS

For car loans, you want to keep the financing portion separate from the price of the car and the value of your trade-in. Keeping the pieces separate will allow you to truly achieve the best rate possible for your circumstances. It is critical that you shop around for rates, as the dealership may not necessarily offer the best rate. A 1% difference on a $25,000 car loan would be $12 per month for a total of $720. Another way to look at it is 1% difference equates to an extra 1.5 monthly payments. For someone making $30,000 per year, you would have to work more than one hour per month just to pay the interest on the extra 1%. If your favorite restaurant kept overcharging you by $12 every time you visited, you would likely complain and stop eating at the restaurant.

While shopping for a car loan, keep in mind that everything is subject to negotiation. Maybe the used car needs new tires so you can negotiate for the tires to be replaced at the current negotiated price. If there is any part of the contract you do not understand, make sure you get clarification. For example, you want to make sure there is no prepayment penalty. You do not want to be charged an extra fee just for paying off your car loan early.

When it comes to financing a car, anything longer than five years is too long. If you need to finance longer you are buying too much car. You should step down in the type of car price or switch from buying new to used. With a longer loan you will be upside down on the loan much longer, which could get you into financial trouble. Being upside down on the loan means that you owe more than your car is worth. You should try to pay off the loan before the warranty on the car ends if at all possible. Otherwise you could find yourself in the tough financial position of making car payments and huge repair bills at the same time.

# SHOPPING FOR MORTGAGES

At some point in the not-too-distant future you will need to shop for a mortgage. You may not want to consider buying a house immediately after graduation so you can remain mobile in your career. After a few years of getting comfortable in your career and your location, then you can settle down and purchase a home.

Home loans, or mortgages, come in two major varieties; fixed rate and adjustable rate mortgages (ARMs). You need to consider the risks and the rewards with each, depending on your situation. ARMs have lower rates during the early months or years of the loan, then adjust upward periodically at predetermined times and a predetermined percent in some instances. ARMs were really designed by the marketing departments of mortgage companies and banks as a way to lure buyers in with low teaser interest rates that would adjust to a specified financial index. They were designed during periods of high interest rates so banks could take less risk and they could offer lower rates.

The issue with ARMs is evident in the present financial crisis. One of the contributors to the housing crisis was the number of home buyers who held ARMs that began adjusting upward. The problem was that the home buyers could just barely afford the payments based on the low teaser rates, so when the rates increased (as everyone knew they would), causing the monthly payment to increase by hundreds of dollars in many instances, the home owner simply could not afford the payments. The home owners originally planned to simply refinance their mortgage into a new fixed-rate loan when the ARM began adjusting; however, once housing prices dropped and the home owners owed more than their house was worth, the banks would not lend them money to refinance. Now the home owners were stuck with mortgages they could not afford and a house that had decreased in value that would not cover the mortgages if they sold it.

The other problem home owners experienced was the fact that they were buying ARMs with low teaser rates during a period of time when rates were at historic lows. If rates were already at historic lows and a person held a rate that adjusted, then the only place the rate could go was up! ARMs rarely make sense today unless we find ourselves in another period of high interest rates, such as what happened in the 1970s. Of course, if you do get an ARM, then at least make sure there is still room in your budget in the event the rate creeps upward and your monthly payment increases along with it. Otherwise you could end up losing your home to foreclosure.

## Points

When purchasing a mortgage you may have the option to pay points. Points are nothing more than prepaid interest. One point is equal to 1% of the loan value. Most mortgage rates are quoted with the assumption of one or two points paid up front.

# (ALL THE WRONG) REASONS WE GET INTO DEBT

Because debt takes away our choices and we know there is such a thing as bad debt, why are so many people in debt? What causes us to get into debt? There are seven key reasons why people get into the kind of debt that destroys personal finances.

### #1  Keeping up with the Joneses.

It is human nature to compare ourselves to those who are better off than we are. If you were in a room with 100 other people and you were better off than 95 of them, your only focus would be on the five people who had more than you. No one person can have everything. You cannot expect to have the best house, the best car, the best deck, the best pool, the best clothes, the best furniture, and the best vacations compared to everyone else in your neighborhood. One person may have the best car, while another may have the best clothes. Even if you do not have the best of anything, it does not mean you are failing in some way. You do not know your neighbor's financial situation. Maybe they are living off a family trust fund, receiving structured settlement payments from a medical injury, or perhaps they simply have large amounts of debt and all of the stress that goes along with it.

### #2  The use of money to punish.

Couples have a tendency to use money to punish each other. It is easy to go spend money that your spouse does not want you to spend to punish him or her. For instance, if your husband is saving to buy a new truck and he makes you mad, it is easy to go on a shopping spree causing him to not have enough money for his truck. Of course, he may buy the truck now out of spite, taking on larger monthly payments than the two of you had originally agreed on. As you can see, this spiteful spending can lead to a vicious cycle that will eventually lead to bankruptcy or divorce or both.

## #3  Emotional problems.

The need for instant gratification is a huge part of our debt crisis. We are unwilling to simply wait and save until we can afford an item. We also use spending as a means to celebrate happy occasions (such as a new job or an anniversary) as well as a way to elevate our mood during sad occasions (such as a bad day at work or after a marital fight). The point is that we use shopping and spending as a way to mask the symptoms of a deeper emotional issue.

## #4  Unrealistic expectations of young couples.

Most young couples who come from a home with means expect to start their first home with the same level of amenities as their parents' homes. For example, you may expect that your first home must have a dining room. Now you have to buy a dining room set and a china hutch to fit into that dining room. Of course, if you have a china hutch then you are going to need china. At the end of the day you have a small monthly payment for your china hutch, a small monthly payment for your dining room table, a small monthly payment for the china, a small monthly payment for that new big screen 3-D LED high-definition television, and a small monthly payment for all the curtains you had to buy to cover the windows. Although each small monthly payment is affordable to the young couple, the combination of them all is too much for their finances to handle. You cannot expect to start off where your parents left off. Your parents have had 20+ years to earn income, get pay raises, pay off debt, and learn a little about their finances. Your parents should have a nicer car, nicer vacations, and nicer stuff in general than you. You should hope that you will have nicer stuff in 20 years as well!

## #5  Lack of communication among family members.

When a couple is not communicating about their finances and goals, they are likely to overspend significantly and usually by accident. For instance, if the couple receives a tax refund or a bonus paycheck, both spouses may make a joint spending decision based on the extra money that was deposited into their checking account. However, if both spouses spend the same money independently from one another you could end up even further in debt.

## #6  The amount of finance charges is too high.

As you continue to borrow more money or take on additional loans, your minimum monthly payments become higher and higher, which makes it that much harder to make ends meet. Add to that a missed credit card payment, which results in increased interest rates and more of your money will be used just to pay the interest with very little being applied to the actual balance. In addition, an interest rate spike will cause your minimum monthly payment to increase as well, which could further cause you to slip behind.

### #7   Overindulgence of children.

Babies only require and desire three things: to be loved, fed, and changed. Any indulgence above those three are really for the parents and not the child. Do you really think a baby knows what brand of shoe he or she is wearing? Does a child really need 80 boxes of Christmas gifts under the tree? Most parents experience a January hangover when the credit card bills arrive and they realize how much they spent. Sadly, the payments last longer than most of the toys.

# THE COST OF  FINANCIAL IGNORANCE

The young woman at the beginning of the chapter with $3,000 of credit card debt wanted to buy a used car. She found a three-year-old car in great shape and needed a loan of almost $12,000. She did not realize that because of the balance on her credit card, the car loan would put her at the maximum total debt any lender would consider safe. It wasn't that she could not get a car for the loan, but because of the additional credit card debt the loan would be more expensive. Lenders would lend her the money, but at a higher interest rate.

| | | |
|---|---|---|
| Car loan with the credit card debt | $12,000, 8.6%, 5 years | = Total Interest $2,807 |
| Car loan without the credit card debt | $12,000, 6.9%, 5 years | = Total Interest $2,223 |
| Total Cost of Financial Ignorance | | $ 584 |

# MARRIAGE

## Till Debt Do You Part

Just after we finished the marriage topic for our class a young woman asked if she could meet with us in private. Once in our office she wanted to know how she could talk to her new husband about their finances. They had been married less than a year and were struggling when it came to communicating about money. Their most recent fight was when her husband spent the $650 they received from a tax refund on a gym membership without telling her about it. To compound the problem she had spent the $650 on a new dinette suite for their apartment without telling him about it. Now, not only did they not have an extra $650 dollars, but they were $650 overdrawn on their account. What should they do?

# IN US WE TRUST

They say that love is blind. In that case, some may argue that to get married, you must lack all of your other senses as well. Watch any late night comedian, and you will hear an endless number of jokes about marriage and relationships. Books abound on the shelves that talk about how men and women are so different from each other. If we know that we are different and there are enough crazy moments during a typical marriage to fill an entire HBO comedy special with material, then why do people get married? There are many reasons why people get married, and there are many more reasons why people get divorced. How is it that two people who claim to love each other, build a life together, and often have children together end up in divorce? More often than not, we fail to simply realize that marriage is not just about love and happily ever afters but that it is the biggest financial decision we make in our lives.

We talk more openly about sex in our society than we do about money. Experts agree that the number one cause of divorce is not infidelity (cheating) but rather arguments about money that strain a marriage to the brink of no return.[49] Keep in mind the arguments are typically not about the lack of money, but about how to handle whatever money we do have. The key to minimizing the damage from those arguments is communication. The purpose of communication is not to convert your spouse to your way of thinking. The purpose of communication is to understand how each other thinks so you can make your decisions together, openly discussing any issues within the context of each other's needs and wants and your shared financial goals.

## Communication Is Key

You are different from your spouse emotionally, spiritually, and physically. Each bring their own set of values and biases to the marriage. We also bring different money personalities. Do you know your money personality? Do you know your spouse's money personality? If not, then you may be in for a very rude awakening. You will face all kinds of difficulties in marriage. By recognizing and understanding that the two of you are very different, and that is okay, you can begin to minimize struggles over money. So how do we marry two money personalities?

The first step to bringing together two different money personalities is to first understand and accept each individually. The next step is to bring the money personalities together so the two of you can grow together over time and not grow apart. For any marriage to be successful it will take constant and continual work. You are different now than you will be five years from now. You will be different in your 30s than you are in your 20s and so forth. The two of you can learn to grow together and keep your marriage strong as the two of you change over time.

Of course, there are some things that we will simply never understand about each other. Men and women are hardwired differently. We each have to accept things about our spouses that we will simply never understand. We need to take it on faith that if something is important to them then they deserve our understanding and support. A couple who communicates will quickly learn each other's needs and will be able to respond appropriately to each other.

# Financial Togetherness

You expect to merge lives and households when you marry, but nowhere in the marriage vows does it spell out how—or how much—to merge your financial lives. So how much financial togetherness is good for a marriage? Is it one checking account or separate checking accounts? Do you divide expenses or combine your money? The right approach is whatever works best for you and your spouse. The key is to have regular conversations about money.

The hard stuff is not over when you say "I do." Although it may be a relief to finally be done with the wedding, the real hard work is just beginning. You must plan to protect yourself financially in a marriage. Financial protection can mean any number of things from having a prenuptial agreement to having the right amount of life insurance. There are a number of strategies in between that we will discuss later in the chapter. The point is that marriage is for better *and for worse*. It is also for richer *and for poorer*. Be prepared to encounter all kinds of scenarios that will strain your relationship over the course of your marriage.

So what is the best way to "marry" your financial lives? No single system is best for everyone. The method you adopt should accommodate how each partner feels about financial independence and fairness, and each method has its pros and cons. For example, should you have one, two, or three checking accounts? Who will be in charge of paying the bills? How much money can each spouse spend on items they want without consulting their partner? These and many more questions will be addressed in every marriage. You must decide if you will talk about them ahead of time to minimize conflict or if you will allow the tension to build until the issues erupt into a battle.

# How Many Accounts?

A single account certainly makes the bookkeeping part of money management simple and accountable. However, it can lead to scrutinizing every dollar spent and, more important, what it was spent on. Because you both have different money personalities what is a frivolous purchase to one spouse may be one of life's necessities to the other. In addition, with both spouses using debit cards and making ATM withdraws all from the same account, the bookkeeper may get blamed for mistakes that are a result of not having all the information. The flip side is to keep everything separate. Each spouse is responsible for their own purchases and debts, including the debts that were brought into the marriage, such as student loans, car loans, and credit card debt. You will still have to work together to determine who pays for the "community" bills such as the rent or mortgage, utilities and food. For instance, if she pays the utilities and he keeps turning the air up, she may get frustrated because "he" is spending "her" money on utilities. The other issue with keeping everything separate is that it may undermine the entire purpose of being married; merging your lives and working toward common goals. So given all the possible choices, which method should you choose?

With one-half of marriages ending in divorce, maintaining some separation may be a prudent strategy. On the bright side, you may find a few degrees of financial separation can reduce fights, especially when each spouse has a designated amount of "MAD" money to spend as he or she wishes. Basically, each spouse gets to spend their "MAD" money without regard for how the other spouse would choose to spend it. Amounts not spent may be carried forward but you can never take an "advance" against future amounts. The point is for each spouse to be able to spend some amount of money on himself or herself without feeling guilty or without comment or rebuke from the other spouse.

Ultimately, each married couple will need to discuss their options and decide what is right for their marriage. You want to make sure that whatever you decide, you are working toward building your wealth as a couple and not toward maximizing individual happiness at each other's expense. For many married couples having at least two joint accounts may be the best approach. With two joint accounts, each person primarily responsible for one of them, you are both active in marital finances. You will be more likely to discuss money openly with each other and neither of you will feel that too much of the burden has been shifted on one person.

When you first start out and money is extremely tight you may need to start with one account. You may be able to move to two accounts after a few years. One account could be specifically for all your bills such as rent, utilities, car payment, and insurance. The other account could be dedicated as your spending account for groceries, dinner out, and household expenses. This system will at least prevent you from accidentally spending part of your rent payment on movie tickets and popcorn.

Some couples even prefer to have three accounts. A joint account is used for all of the common bills and common goals while each spouse maintains an entire account of personal spending "MAD" money. If you do decide to own any nonjoint accounts in your marriage, make sure to have a transfer-of-death notice put on your account with your spouse's name. Otherwise your spouse may not be able to access the account immediately on your death.

Be careful not to get into the wrong types of money discussions. If you do not set up your system properly, you may end up arguing about one spouse owing the other money for the mortgage payment or the utility bill. Money issues among family members, particularly when one owes another, or one *feels* owed by another, rarely end well. Suddenly your marriage has turned into nothing more than two college roommates arguing about whose food is on the top shelf of the refrigerator. Keep the lines of communication open and be open to whatever system works best for both of you as a couple and keeps both of your levels of stress at a minimum.

## Switch Places

To avoid resentment from one spouse carrying all the burden of maintaining the books, plan to switch places once in a while. This could be a real eye-opener as the other spouse suddenly understands the burden or the stress of the other. If your household is running a very tight budget, the spouse not managing the money may not realize the stress he or she is causing the other every time the credit card or debit card is used. In addition, switching duties will protect the other spouse in the event they are forced to take over the duties for one reason or another. Try this method for other chores and duties around the house as well. As a couple you will appreciate each other more and learn to work together to improve each others' lives.

### Allow Personal Spending Money

You have spent most of your life up to this point as an individual. Now you live together and see each other and spend a lot of your time together. That is a lot of togetherness forced on a couple in a small period of time. A little "me" time and a little "me" money could be better and less expensive than a therapist. Each spouse should have some amount of personal spending money; money that they can spend on whatever they want without complaint or scrutiny from the other spouse. Even if you can only afford $10 each, at least it gives you some autonomy. Let the account grow as your income grows or as your finances improve.

### Hold Financial Summits

No matter what method you choose for bookkeeping, bill paying, and money sharing, you must meet regularly to discuss your finances. You cannot assume that your spouse shares the same goals as you. Talk about where your money has gone, where you would like your money to go, and what steps you are going to take to get there. If you have accumulated a lot of debt, then discuss what happened, how you will prevent it in the future, and how you will both work to reduce it. You also want to discuss any major purchases or expenses in the coming year such as the need for a new car or vacation. Do not assume that everything will work itself out because with money and marriages, it never does without communication.

## Who Pays the Bills?

Who should be in charge of the money? The spouse who earns the most or the one who earns the least? The one who works fewer hours or the one with the business degree? Again, no single system is best for everyone, so you are on your own to try a few different ways until you see what works best for the relationship. The key is to balance independence, fairness, and convenience. Keep in mind there is a big difference between paying the bills and making the decisions. Paying the bills is nothing more than a bookkeeping task. The person paying the bills is not necessarily the person spending the money. If one person pays the bills it is critical that both still know what is going on with the daily finances.

Too often one spouse knows absolutely nothing about the money. Not only is this an unfair burden on the spouse that must take care of everything, but the other spouse is often shocked to see where the money is going. Completely giving up control of the household finances to your spouse is no different than ignoring any other household chore. Not having regular financial summits leads to unnecessary stress on the marriage. So how do you have a financial summit?

# 8 TIPS ON HOW TO TALK ABOUT MONEY

So how do you talk about money with your spouse? When is a good time to mention you did something wrong or when do you ask your spouse about something you think he or she did wrong? The fact is, as a couple you absolutely have to talk about money no matter how unromantic it sounds. The key is to make it part of your routine and make it fun. For instance, if the two of you agree on a goal to buy your first home or take a tropical vacation, keep that goal in mind whenever you talk about money. There is nothing sexy about looking at a utility bill that is way over your budgeted amount, but discussing it in the context of "what can we do to reduce this bill so we can take that vacation sooner" will certainly help. As a couple, when you begin to understand that money is part of the relationship and it will be there to help you achieve your goals together, you can look at it differently. Here are eight tips from MSN Money[50]:

1. **Take a hike. Or a walk.** "Men don't like to open up about this, so having the discussion while you're relaxed, out in the fresh air, will help."

2. **'Fess up.** Start by telling your partner what your own family's attitudes and behaviors toward money were. (HINT: If you haven't spent much time mulling over your family's financial dynamics, do that first.)

3. **Be humble.** "Never assume your way is the right way." Listen to what your partner says and take it in. Their outlook may differ wildly from yours, but they hold their views as dearly as you hold yours, so be respectful, even if you disagree.

4. **Establish common goals.** The worst fights couples have boil down to the fact that they haven't planned their Big Picture goals yet. "You need to think about the various milestones in your life that will require money, having kids, buying a house, caring for a parent—and discuss them."

5. **Quantify your goals.** Once you've established even a small goal, like saving for a vacation, start to work toward it together.

6. **Get help.** Talking to a financial planner together can help ease money tension because it's easier to address tough issues with an objective party. Or take a financial seminar together.

7. **Don't lay blame, take action.** Let's say your partner is in debt. Rather than fight about it (NOTE: Arguing will not reduce your monthly payment!), force yourselves to focus on a game plan. Taking steps to address the problem will remind you that you are, and always will be, a financial team.

8. **If at first you don't succeed. . . .** Talking about money is hard, much harder than fighting. So if it takes a while to replace debates with discussions, don't sweat it. "Even if you do it wrong, it's better to communicate than to not say anything."

# EVERYBODY FIGHTS OVER MONEY

They say "All is fair in love and war," but in marriages nothing is ever fair about the way we fight about money. Arguments about money may be the most volatile of all arguments in a relationship. After all, we work very hard for our money, and there is little left over after all the expenses. That little bit of money left over is all we have to show for the years of studying and stress and suffering we endure at our jobs, so how dare our spouse not handle money the same way we want them to!

At times you may start to think that you and your spouse are the only couple who argues about money. Relax, *everybody fights about money*. You need to accept it. The difference between money arguments and many other arguments is that we are less likely to share with our friends that we had a money argument than many other topics. For instance, let us assume a couple is arguing over whether or not to purchase a new car, and the argument boils down to money. What does the couple tell their friends? "He thinks he knows everything about cars and won't let me get a new one." Or, "She is never happy with anything we have and always wants more." The root of the problem is a disagreement about how to spend money, but the couple dances around the issue when discussing the problem with their friends. That is why every couple in society fights about money, yet has no idea that everyone else is also fighting about money.

So, if every couple fights about money, and money is the number one reason for divorce, is there anything that can be done about it? Of course, there is a solution to every problem. The key is to understand how to fight about money. You need to do it the *right* way.

## The 5 Rules for Fighting about Money

Most money arguments among couples involve more than just money. In fact, the entire argument may have little to do with money itself and more to do with other areas of our lives. Because money is such a tangible object, we find it easier to slip into an argument about money than about other areas of our lives. To avoid destroying your marriage when fighting about money follow these five simple rules:

### #1  Keep it about money.

Do not use money as a weapon in your marriage. When you are arguing about money, whether it is spending too much by one spouse or making payments late by the other keep the argument about that particular money issue. You will never resolve a money issue by bringing unrelated topics into the argument. The other topics do nothing more than cloud the issue and make an emotional argument more intense. On the other hand, if she has a problem with him watching too much television or he has a problem with her texting during dinner then those are the topics that need to be discussed as well. Arguing about how much the cable costs or how expensive the cell phone bills are is not getting to the point of the problem.

If the problem is not about money, then do not talk about money in that argument. If the argument is about money, then argue only about the money issues and don't bring other things into the discussion. Gentlemen, that means you do not bring her mother into the argument (and *never* say, "You are acting just like your mother.")

Ladies, that means you do not bring stuff from the past into the current argument (sure, he may have forgotten about the third anniversary of the first time you went to the movies, but that is not relevant to the topic at hand.)

### #2  Work as a financial couple.

You are still two people but you are working together as one financial couple. Look for those areas where you do agree and bring those up in the argument. If your only goal is to win the argument then you have already lost. In a marriage the only way to really win an argument is to find a way to end it where both spouses calm down and they agree on a resolution. Even if you are completely right, what good is it if your spouse resents you for it? Find common ground, look for ways to agree with some of what your spouse is saying, and try to de-escalate the argument into a conversational voice. The most important task any couple can undertake is to stop thinking like Two and start thinking and acting like One. For that, you need to agree on a set of shared goals and, hopefully, a few shared values. You may always have values that differ from your mate's, but you need to see eye to eye about certain aspects of your financial life so that your priorities are aligned.

### #3  Fight for your marriage, not against it.

Most couples immediately look for where they are different when fighting about money; one is a saver and one is a spender. One is trying to get out of debt and the other does not care. Instead of immediately trying to prove to each other that you are on different teams, think about how you are simply serving two different positions on the same team. Just as a football team cannot have all quarterbacks and no receivers, a marriage will have two people that differ. Start thinking about how you can each work together, using each others' strengths to make a winning financial team. The purpose of the argument should be about getting both of you to refocus on how to achieve the common goals you already set together.

### #4  Address the issues as they occur.

Do not artificially suppress your frustration over the last rule and perhaps the most critical: Don't wait for the issue to disappear simply hoping that it will go away. It is much better to discuss the issue with your spouse while you are simply frustrated than to wait until it evolves into anger. Otherwise, you will blow up and pitch a fit like a two-year-old because your spouse went to the wrong gas station and overpaid by two cents per gallon. You start fighting over an issue that is an irrational reason to get so upset because you did not address the real issue when it occurred such as the new pair of shoes you saw in her closet or his new golf clubs you saw in the garage. The point is to talk about it when it happens, otherwise it will continue to boil like a pot of water with the lid on it until it reaches a point where the steam literally blows the lid off the top.

### #5 Do not go to bed angry.

Some couples allow the frustration to build to anger and still choose not to address it. Then they go to bed angry, lose sleep while lying in bed justifying their anger, and wake up even angrier. The next morning their spouse has no idea what is about to hit them and is unfairly attacked. In addition, with your lack of sleep, you are now on edge emotionally and you are angry at your spouse for two reasons: The money issue and the fact that *they* caused *you* to lose sleep. Using the other four rules, you should be armed with enough knowledge to protect yourself and your marriage during a money argument. There is no excuse to take your anger to bed with you. Discuss the issue with your spouse. Perhaps the shoes were simply dug out from the closet and the golf clubs were borrowed from a friend. Or maybe not. But at least you will know and you can work through it before going to bed.

Now that you are fully aware that couples argue about money, and you are prepared with the rules on how to argue properly, you are well on your way to being able to have a successful and fulfilling marriage.

# GETTING TO "I DO"

For most men, marriage is not something they think about too much until well after they have fallen in love with the woman they want to spend the rest of their life with. For most women, marriage is something they think about from the time they are old enough to dress up in their mother's high heels and pearls. In fact, most women already know where they want to hold their wedding and their reception, and they have probably already decided on what colors, flowers, and centerpieces they will use. Like a Chia Pet that just needs water added, the wedding just needs a groom added. So how do you go about finding that perfect someone in today's wired and connected world? Very carefully.

Do you remember the *Highlights* magazines from early elementary school or the ones lying around the doctors' offices? One of the features in every magazine was a picture with hidden items where the reader had to look around the picture in great detail to find all those hidden items. In today's online world where we post pictures, profiles, and updates about what we are doing every three minutes of the day, there are plenty of predators online who are still looking for hidden parts of pictures, but their goals are to harm others.

For example, you may post a picture of your new apartment but what you may not think about is whether a street sign is in view or if your car is also in the picture. Predators now know what car you drive and where you live, so it is easy to identify when you are not home. Add to that your tweets or Facebook updates, and your home is a sitting target for thieves . . . or worse. In addition, smart criminals look for other clues, such as a chipped pot on the porch or a fake looking rock in the shrub garden, which may indicate where you keep your "hidden" key. Unfortunately, not everyone lives their life with the same positive intentions that you do. Some are only looking for ways to hurt or take advantage of others.

What about the online dating services? There are several from which to choose. How do you know which one is right for you, and what is the best approach when using the online services? Matching for each site is different. Although some sites require you to sift through the singles on your own, others automatically match you with others based on criteria that you provide. There are many features to choose from when deciding which site or combination of sites to use. Your best approach is to "date" the sites first and see which aligns more closely with your personality and goals. Consider the matching ability, ease of use, cancellation policy, screening process or policy, if any, cost, and any other factors that are important to you.

There are two very important things you need to know about online dating. First of all, you need to go in with your eyes wide open and realize that there are sharks in the water. According to MSNBC, nearly one-third of people using online dating services are married![51] Anybody can claim to be single on an anonymous Web site. Many others claim they are "getting a divorce." Keep in mind that there is a big difference between "getting a divorce" and "divorced." For some individuals, the phrase "getting a divorce" simply means that they are seeking some sort of thrill outside their marriage, and if they get caught by their spouse, then they will likely have to get a divorce, but otherwise have no intentions of leaving their marriage.

Second, once you upload information to one of these sites, you no longer own it. Once you do manage to cancel your service your profile is still owned by the site. So for a very long time expect to receive e-mails and solicitations even after you are no longer a member of a site.

## The Ring

Once you are finished swimming the shark-infested waters of the dating world and have your soul-mate, it is now time to get engaged. One of the biggest traditions of the engagement process is the presentation of the ring. For years men have approached the presentation of the ring from many different angles. Examples include the traditionalist (down on one knee), the sports fanatic ("Will you marry me?" on the JumboTron), the extremist (while skydiving), the outdoorsman (while at the top of a mountain or near a waterfall), or the romantic (proposing at a location with special meaning). Regardless of your approach, to have a ring to present to her, you must first purchase one. The diamond industry will have you believe that you should spend three months' salary on a ring. How did they come up with that figure?

As we discussed with cars, sometimes prices are set up by the marketing department and not by the finance department. The concept of three months' salary is more of a marketing ploy. Of course, if you are in college making $6,000 per year, then you are looking at $1,500. On the other hand, if you are several years out of school earning $60,000 per year, then you are looking at a $15,000 ring. Does it make sense just because you start a new job the ring should be significantly more expensive?

Like an MSRP for cars, the three months' salary is a fake number. Besides, are they talking about how much you make or how much you actually get to keep from your paycheck? It only matters to you how much you actually get to keep. By the time you deduct taxes, insurance, and retirement contributions, you are left with a much smaller number. What about your other expenses such as rent, college loans, car loans, and credit card payments? Should your food, fuel, and utilities also be deducted first before looking at how much money you have left over for a ring? With this approach you may only be able to afford an empty ring setting with no diamond. The point is, do not let the diamond industry's marketing cause you to go into more debt than you can handle just to make them rich.

The industry also emphasizes the four Cs of ring buying that actually do help with your purchase. The four Cs are a guide to help you decide which ring to purchase for your special someone:

◆ **Cut**—The cut of the ring refers to the shape. Keep in mind that women have planned almost every detail of their wedding, even before they have met the groom, so a specific cut may be her favorite. At some point she will start dropping hints. You will need to pick up on these hints or plan to take her ring shopping at some point.

◆ **Color**—Diamonds come in various colors, particularly clear through yellow. The clearer the color, the more expensive the ring and the more it sparkles. The closer to yellow, the more ring you can get for your money, but the ring will appear cloudy or dirty, so look for a good balance.

◆ **Clarity**—The clarity refers to imperfections or "inclusions" in industry terms. The scale runs from VS1 to I3, where VS1 is the best quality (VS means very small inclusions) and I3 is the lowest clarity, as inclusions will be visible to the naked eye.

◆ **Carats**—The size of a diamond is measured in carats. A single diamond may be anywhere from a fraction of a carat to multiple carats (such as ¼ carat or two carats). Rings with multiple diamonds including small diamond chips that accent the main diamond are measured in total carat weight, which includes the main diamond along with the various smaller ones. A one carat total weight diamond ring is much less expensive than a single one carat diamond ring.

Is anything missing from the four Cs? Yes, the fifth "C". Women are interested in maximizing the four Cs, but most men try to minimize the fifth "C", which is cost. In reality there are five Cs but the industry only wants you to focus on the first four. As a responsible adult it will be up to you to make a responsible financial decision for the ring purchase. Although women may appreciate a much larger or more expensive ring, your inability to resist the urge to spend more money than you have on a ring just because you can may be a sign of future money problems if it becomes a pattern. On the other hand, the ring is your presentation to your future wife when asking her to marry you and will be the one piece of jewelry she will wear forever, so your unwillingness to spend a little extra on her could also indicate future money disagreements. You need to look at your budget and decide on a reasonable amount to spend on a ring. If you want to spend more, then look for ways to either earn extra money before purchasing the ring or ways to cut some expenses so you can set more money aside.

## The Prenup

After the ring, but long before the big day, you have to decide if a prenuptial agreement is necessary or right for you. A prenuptial agreement is not for everyone, and in most cases you can expect the conversation to be uncomfortable. Most young couples considering marriage have very few assets and have little need to spend the money on a prenup. However, if you are coming into a marriage with significant assets, whether yours or your family's, you want to make sure that those assets are protected in the event of a divorce.

## The Big Day

Your wedding is a very special event, but it can be expensive. In fact, the average wedding costs around $20,000.[52] Marriage is very difficult, especially the first few years as you are adjusting to all your major life changes such as starting a new career, relocating, and sharing your life with someone new. Add to that debt from a wedding, and you could be dooming your marriage before it even begins. However, with a little creative financing it is possible to have your cake and eat it too, without sacrificing your fairytale wedding.

The first step is to set a realistic budget and stick to it. Once you determine the amount you are willing to spend, start listing your top priorities and work your way down the list. Then everything else will fall into place. Go through the list and see where you run out of money and determine if you really need everything that comes after that point. If so, look for ways to reduce each of the other items on the list. For instance, if you always dreamed of a horse and carriage to deliver you from the white steeple church, then go ahead and splurge but make the open bar a cash bar instead. If a custom-made designer gown is a must, then go for it, but opt for a D.J. instead of a live band.

To determine your budget, take a look at how much money you have available, how much you can save for the wedding between the time you get engaged and the actual wedding day, and how much money, if any, your families will contribute. Do not take any amount for granted. It is important to be responsible enough to ask the families if you have any hope or expectation of money from them. It is better to know ahead of time and budget accordingly than to start spending and have awkward or contentious conversations a few days before the wedding.

Unfortunately, most of us do not budget nor plan well for a wedding. The costs quickly spiral out of control. Young couples and their parents can make very poor financial decisions as they get caught up in the emotions of the wedding. To pay for unplanned expenses young couples will take out additional credit cards and parents will use home equity loans or withdraw money from their retirement accounts. The point is that large amounts of debt are being acquired that will have long-term consequences.

Again, communication is the key. You have to involve both sides of the family to determine who is willing and able to contribute to the wedding and how much. The last thing you want to do is cause unneeded stress between the families by not communicating and assuming it will work itself out. With the average wedding costing nearly $20,000, there is the potential to do long-term harm to your personal finances as well as your relationship with your in-laws. There is also opportunity for savings. By planning and shopping around, you can have a champagne wedding on a beer budget.

# Big Savings

Creating a wedding budget and sticking to it will prevent you from going into debt. However, if your budget does not allow for the extravagances you dreamed of as a child, there are many ways to save on your big day.

1. **Avoid the wedding season**—The wedding season begins in May and lasts through October. This is when limousines, florists, photographers, reception halls, etc. are in greatest demand. By getting married in an off-month, you can save a significant amount of money. As a consumer you are in a better position to negotiate a lower price. You may still get everything you wanted, but at a much lower price simply by getting married in the off-season.

2. **Avoid primetime**—The most expensive time to have a wedding reception is Saturday evenings. The reception halls and catering will both cost more during this time. You will be able to get a much better price by holding your reception on a Friday evening, or on a Saturday or Sunday afternoon.

3. **Fake the cake**—Instead of spending hundreds of dollars on a three-tier cake big enough to feed all 100 guests, why not choose a well-decorated smaller cake for presentation. The guests can actually be served from a much larger sheet cake that is kept in the kitchen and served. The guests will never know the difference, and you save a lot of money.

4. **Flowers—less can be more**—Instead of finding flowers that you like and then asking how much they cost, start with a set floral budget and have the florist show you a variety of arrangements in that price range. Using fewer blooms and more greenery can be just as festive at a fraction of the cost. You can also focus your decorations on the reception hall and use fewer flower decorations at the church. The guests will spend most of their time at the reception anyway.

5. **Say yes to the *other* dress**—You do not need a designer gown if it is not in your budget. You can save a significant amount of money by buying off the rack. In addition, last year's designs are available for a fraction of the cost. You can also find wedding dresses in consignment shops, if owning a new one is less of a concern. Some brides may decide on tradition and have their mother's gown altered for their special day.

6. **Uncle who?**—It is not unusual for the guest list to spin wildly out of control. One of the quickest ways to reduce your wedding costs is to control the

number of guests. This will be a delicate discussion as you decide where to draw the line. You can also choose a destination wedding where only the closest handful of family and friends travel to some exotic location for the wedding.

7. **Go greener**—The first thing you pull out of a wedding invitation envelope is another envelope. Inside the second envelope is a fancy invite with an invitation liner. By simplifying your wedding invitation, you can cut your printing costs in half and you may even save money on postage. You can also save money by having the RSVP printed as a postcard that saves on printing and postage.

No matter how hard you may try or how much careful planning you do and, most important, no matter how much you spend, your wedding day will not be perfect. In fact, the more you try to control every detail of the day's events the greater the likelihood that something will not go as planned. Adopt a flexible attitude, roll with the punches, and remember the reason for the day.

## To Have and to Hold

Now that the big day has passed, the real work begins. Marriage is hard. It is a lifelong journey. For a marriage to be successful it requires constant work by both spouses. You must be attentive not only to each other's emotional needs, but also to each other's financial needs. You will need to know a little bit about the laws and regulations in the state where you marry and reside. Knowing the laws and handling your assets correctly will help keep you financially protected.

First, recognize that in some states it only takes one spouse to obligate both to debt. In addition, each spouse is held responsible for the total debt. It's not that each of you is responsible for half the debt, rather either one of you can be held responsible for the entire debt.

Second, how assets are titled can make a big difference during divorce, retirement, and death. It is essential for a young couple to list their assets and determine what you want to happen to each asset if you divorce or either of you die. In some states, your inheritance would remain yours alone, but once you combine your money or ownership, you are entitled to only half in the event of divorce.

Third, not only do you want to protect yourself, but you also want to protect your spouse. Now that you're married you both need wills. You must designate what is to happen to your assets should one of you die. Newly married, young couples with little assets can do just fine with one of the "do-it-yourself" or online will services. You want something that says if something happens to me then all that we own becomes yours. You also need to determine your wishes should one of you become incapacitated. A living will provides clarity and gives you undisputed authority to make medical decisions on behalf of your spouse, in what will be a very difficult and emotional time.

Fourth, you will retire some day. As you make decisions at work and at home you must think as a financial couple. Retirement accounts should not be treated separately, but rather should be viewed in the context of your overall financial picture. You must consider your spouse's money personality in relation to your own as you develop common financial goals and objectives.

Finally, divorce is ugly and expensive. Despite your best efforts, your marriage might end in divorce. Even if it is unavoidable you can take steps to reduce the financial impact to you. Each spouse should have their own attorney. Hiring a good attorney is expensive, but is a must to make sure your interests are represented and protected. One caveat is that the more issues you want to slug out the more billable hours you'll run up. The only people that win in a divorce are the lawyers.

There are many pressures on newly married couples. In the interest of marital harmony, we tend to avoid conversations that make us or our spouse uncomfortable. Money is one of them. Yet the lack of communication about those uncomfortable topics is what leads to problems between two people that care about each other very much. No matter what approach you take to build a successful marriage, ultimately, communication is still the key.

# THE COST OF  FINANCIAL IGNORANCE

By not communicating and setting common financial goals our young couple at the beginning of the chapter found themselves in a financial hole. Not only did they not have an extra $650 to save for something on which they both agreed, by each of them spending $650 separately their cash flow statement took a hit for $1300.

| | |
|---|---|
| Gym membership | $  650 |
| Dining suite | $  650 |
| Total Cost of Financial Ignorance | **$1,300** |

# INVESTING

## Make Your Money Do the Walking

One of our best students stopped by the office about three years after he graduated to tell us about his promotion to senior recruiter for his company. He was on campus recruiting for his company and wanted to know if he could speak to our class about opportunities with his company. He was very complimentary about our personal finance class he had taken when he was a sophomore. He credited us with helping him get ahead in his career. He thanked us for helping him better understand how to buy his car insurance, how to evaluate his lease, and even how to buy his first car. Although we suspect that he would have done just fine by himself, we thanked him anyway.

We were starting the investment topic in class and asked how his savings accounts had fared for the past three years. "What?????" was his answer. "Uh oh," we said.

# NOT YOUR TYPICAL INVESTMENT CHAPTER

Reading this chapter will not make you a successful day trader or a Wall Street tycoon. In fact, we will barely even scratch the surface of all the ins and outs involved with trading stocks and bonds and real estate investing. You are not going to learn the difference between a put from a call or a bull from a bear. You will not even learn how to select individual stocks or how to get rich quick.

What you will learn from reading this chapter is how to make sound financial decisions when it comes to investments. You will be able to distinguish between good and bad investment advice, and avoid getting ripped off by those in the financial industry who try to take advantage of your financial ignorance. As we have stated throughout this book, understanding how those who are helping you are being compensated is the first step to being a savvy consumer. If you wait until you think you are ready to start investing, you have already missed your best opportunities.

## Investing Begins the First Day on the Job

After graduation you are going to find a job at some point (hopefully sooner rather than later). Your first few days on the job will involve sitting in the human resources office signing all kinds of documents. Many of these documents are relatively harmless as they involve verifying your citizenship and your eligibility to work in the United Sates and some basic personal information. Buried within those documents will be the single most important document you will complete, yet nobody will call your attention to it. It will look like all the other forms you completed. It will ask two simple questions: "How much money do you want withheld from your paycheck for your retirement?" and "How do you want it invested?"

Wait, we just snuck something in there about retirement. The point is there are many decisions you will make your first week on the job that will have a strong impact on your personal finances, both immediate and in the future. These decisions will have meaningful impact on the quality of your life. You must understand enough about investing to make sound decisions from the very first day on the job. Early on, your investments will only consist of the money you put into your retirement accounts. Of course, investments involve more than just retirement. People who accumulate wealth throughout their lifetime invest in something. Whether they invest in real estate, a business, bank deposits or stocks, they put their money somewhere to increase their wealth.

There are more investment choices out there than you can count. You must sift through all the garbage and noise so your choices become simple and clear.

All your investment decisions will revolve around three key concepts that are all tied together:

- ◆ The risk/return relationship
- ◆ Goals/time horizon
- ◆ The basic investment types

# RISK/RETURN RELATIONSHIP

In the risk management chapter, we defined risk as the probability or likelihood of an unfavorable event occurring. As it relates to our investments, risk is represented by the probability that we could lose some or all our money. Return is the amount that we can expect our money to grow. If we boil down the risk/return relationship to its most basic principle, it would be the higher the return you want the more risk you must be willing to take.

This risk/return relationship works especially well in the financial world, but it works in real life as well. For instance, if you are looking for something to do this weekend and you really want a great rush or a great sense of thrill (your return) you can choose between playing video games with your friends or going skydiving (your risk). If you choose to play the Wii skydiving video game, you will have a certain level of excitement with very little risk. On the other hand, if you actually go skydiving, you are going to have a much greater level of excitement with a larger amount of risk. The point is that it takes greater risk for the possibility of a greater reward.

The same risk/return relationship holds true for money. If you want to earn 1% or less interest on your money, you can put it all into a typical bank savings account. With an FDIC-insured bank, the federal government will guarantee your deposit (up to a certain amount) so if the bank goes . . . well . . . bankrupt, you still get your deposit back so there is no risk. On the other hand, there are no guaranteed 10% returns with zero risk. You have to increase your risk to move away from that 1% return. You might do this by investing some money in the stock market, which can go up significantly (the return), but can also go down (the risk). The point is the higher the return you hope to earn, the higher the risk you must be willing to take.

Once you determine what level of risk you are willing to take, you can find numerous opportunities to invest your money within your risk level. At any given time your particular investment may go way up or way down compared to the average, but over a long period of time, such as 20 years, your investment will end up averaging about the same return as other similar investments. It becomes less important *where* you invest your money and more important that you invest your money.

Each year East Carolina University holds an event called "ECU Pigskin Pig-out." Vendors and businesses from all over meet under the football stadium to spend all night grilling pigs to a mouth-watering perfection. Each grill master uses their own combination of seasonings and marinades for the perfect roasted pork. The next morning judges taste the various flavored pork and decide which individual or business has the best tasting pig. Regardless of who is chosen as the current year's winner, the true winners are the people attending the next day's event where they sell the combined pork for a few dollars per plate. All the pork from all the pigs (usually around 100 pigs in total) is combined. That means more than 100 different flavorings of pork are combined to form the best-tasting pulled pork you can imagine. Why is it so good? Because while no one individual can make the best possible pulled pork flavoring, when you combine the seasonings from that many people into one, you now have an amazing flavor.

In finance we have something called the efficient market theory, which works the same way. No single investor can possibly know everything on their own. By combining the knowledge of millions of people, it results in the best "flavored" or accurately priced investments. That means stocks, bonds, real estate, and any other investments are priced correctly according to their associated level of risk. So, if something sounds too good to be true, it is. An understanding of the relationship between risk and return prevents someone from taking advantage of your financial ignorance. This includes everyone from investment advisors to swindlers and con artists and even you choosing the wrong investment for your goals.

# Unnecessary Risk

Smart investors avoid unnecessary risk. Although you have to be willing to take more risk to get greater returns, only necessary risk counts. For instance, if you were to flip a coin you know there is a 50% chance the coin will land on heads. If you want to make some quick money, you could bet someone $100 that you will flip the coin and it will land on heads. If they take the bet and you win, congratulations; you just turned $100 into $200. If they take the bet and it lands on tails, then you lose your $100. You had a 50% chance of winning, but you also had a 50% chance of losing. If repeated enough times you will have an equal number of heads as you do tails. Your total return is zero. That is because you have exactly as much chance of winning as losing and your return exactly mirrors your risk.

Now assume the bet changes so you only win $100 if your coin lands on heads two times in a row. Now you only have a 25% chance of winning. The coin could land as heads/heads, heads/tails, tails/heads, or tails/tails. You have a 75% chance of losing. You just increased your risk, yet you did nothing to increase your payout. You are taking unnecessary risk for no additional return. You should only take on additional risk if you receive additional compensation. Unnecessary risk is, by definition, unnecessary.

## *Acceptable Risk Levels*

Your goal when choosing investments is to understand your tolerance for risk. Ask yourself how much money you can stomach losing, and also ask yourself how long you can handle losing money. In other words, you have to look at both the dollar amount of your risk tolerance as well as the time horizon. If you have $10,000 in an investment and it drops to $9,900, most people can handle a temporary setback.

However, what happens if it drops to $7,500 or lower? At what point will you get so frustrated from that investment that you pull your money out and hide it under your mattress? At the same time, what happens if it simply drops to $9,999, but stays that way for three years in a row? You are not earning any money on your investment. What about five years in a row? At some point each of us will question our investments and want to get out or lose sleep in the meantime. You have to decide where your tolerance level is and then find investments to match. Remember, anyone can say they have a high risk tolerance while their investments are going up. The true test is when their investments actually start going down.

## Goal/Time Horizon

In the financial planning chapter we learned how to develop SMART goals. When it comes to investing, we must first establish what we want to do and when. The time horizon is how long before the money is needed for that specific goal. For example, you are 22 years old and decide you want to retire by age 67. By making that decision you have just established a time horizon of 45 years to achieve your retirement goal. We further refine the goal to determine how much money we will need to achieve it. Now we know what we want to do, how long before we want to do it, and how much money it will take.

# TWO TYPES OF INVESTMENTS

Of all the hundreds of thousands or maybe even millions of investment options there are to choose from, they all fall into one of two categories: debt or equity.

Debt is nothing more than a loan. When it comes to investing, debt for us means we are loaning money to someone else. We are acting like a bank. When we use debt as a form of investment, that means we are the ones lending the money. Whoever we lend money to must pay us back with interest. There are lots of ways we can lend money to companies, governments, and organizations. To the investor, debt provides a fixed return for a fixed period of time. It comes with lower risk and lower returns because the probability of losing our money is less.

Equity, on the other hand, is ownership. When it comes to investing, equity for us means we own all or part of the asset. For instance, if we open up a lemonade stand by ourselves we are 100% owner in the company and we keep 100% of the profits. If we decide to partner with our friend for an equal 50/50, we each own half the company and are entitled to half the profits. To the investor, equity provides a variable return for an unspecified period of time. Equity investments come with greater risk and greater expected returns because the probability of losing our money is greater.

## Tying the Basic Concepts Together

Risk and return are tied together by your time horizon. The longer your investment horizon, the greater the level of risk to which you are exposed because the future becomes increasingly more difficult to predict. Would you lend your roommate $10 for lunch if they promise to pay you back $10 tomorrow? Assuming you like and trust your roommate, of course you would. What if they promise to pay you back next month? What about next year? Although you will lend it to them for a day you probably will not lend it to them for a month and certainly not for a year. What if they promise to pay you $15 next month? What if they promise to pay you $50 next year? The amount your roommate is willing to pay you back changes your decision. At some point your roommate can offer you enough money to get you to lend them the $10. The extra $5 or $40 is your return. The further in the future you "invest" in your roommate the greater the return you require to compensate you for the additional risk that you may not get paid at all.

The type of investment you choose should be linked to your time horizon. If you have a short time horizon you cannot afford the luxury of higher returns. As mentioned earlier equity pays higher returns than debt but is more risky given the higher probability of loss. Therefore, your short time horizon forces you to accept the lower return of the debt investment in exchange for lower risk. If you have a longer time horizon, you can afford the higher risk associated with earning higher returns.

Assume you and your best friend are both 25 years old and you both plan to retire at age 75. Both of you received a $1,000 signing bonus at work, and you each decide to invest your $1,000 for your retirement. Your friend decides to invest in stock funds (equity) that average 12% over the next 50 years.

Because you do not like risk very much you decide to invest your $1,000 into a bond fund (debt) that ends up returning 5% over the next 50 years. When the two of you retire, your friend's account has grown to $289,002. Your friend's account has increased 289 times the original investment of $1,000! You are excited to find out that money can grow so much that the two of you decide to use your retirement funds to spend your first year of retirement traveling around the world. You go to withdraw your funds and discover that your conservative 5% investment has grown to a paltry $11,467. So what was the real risk here? The risk was not aligning your savings goal to your time horizon with the proper investment choice.

Now that we have a basic understanding of debt versus equity, let us take a closer look at each to see how we use them to achieve our financial goals.

# WHAT IS DEBT?

Now that we know debt is nothing more than a loan where we act as the bank, how do we make a loan to companies, governments, and organizations? We use something called a bond. A bond is a long-term debt instrument that pays a fixed rate over a specified period of time. Unlike a typical loan where each month you make a payment that includes the interest, plus some of the principle so that at the end of the loan you owe nothing, bonds generally only pay the interest until the bond matures or comes due.

At the time of maturity, the bond issuer must pay the entire amount that was originally borrowed. For instance, a 10-year $1,000 bond that pays 5% interest only makes payments of 5% per year ($50 per year), but at the end of 10 years, the bondholder will receive their $1,000 back.

The advantage of investing in debt is that debt must be repaid ahead of owners. If a company earns $1,000 in revenue and they are supposed to pay the bondholder $50, then they first have to make that payment before the owners get to take any profit. What happens if the company only makes $50? The company must still pay the bondholder their $50, so that leaves no money for the owners. On the other hand, what happens if the company makes $5,000? They still have to pay the bondholder $50, but that would leave the owners with $4,950 in profits to split. The point is that bondholders get paid first so the risk is lower. That also means the return is less for bondholders because no matter how much money the company makes, the bondholders still only get the specific amount of money they were promised.

# WHAT IS EQUITY?

Now that we know equity is ownership, how do we own assets such as companies? To own part or all of a company we typically buy shares of stock. Thus a stockholder is an equity holder. Let's take a look at investing from the ownership or stockholder's point of view. The stockholder as owner must wait until the debt holders have been paid. Only if the company earns more than what is required by the debt holders will the stockholders receive any money.

This means the stockholder is taking on more risk than the debt holder because they are last in line. Because more risk should equate to greater return, how can the equity holder be compensated? Once all the debt holders are paid, every dollar of profit from that point forward is shared by the stockholders distributed based on the amount of shares each stockholder owns. As we saw earlier, the bondholders never received more than the $50 return regardless of how much profit was earned by the company. Meanwhile if the company was highly profitable the stockholders had very high returns. If the company was not profitable the stockholders received nothing. The stockholders accepted more risk for the possibility of greater returns.

# RISK, RETURN, AND VOLATILITY

So far we have explained that risk and return move in the same direction. As risk goes up so does the expected return and as risk goes down, so does the expected return. But exactly how do we measure return? In other words, what makes up a return? Your return is actually made up of two components; the increase or decrease of the value of the asset and the interest earned along the way. The risk of the asset affects both components of the total return.

For example, take a look at a $1,000 bond paying 5% interest that will mature in 10 years. Why is the bond paying 5%? The rate is based on the level of risk. A financially strong company, such as Microsoft, can pay very low interest on their bonds because there is little risk to the investor that the company will go bankrupt or will not be able to make the payments. On the other hand, a riskier company such as a new Internet start-up may have to pay a much higher interest rate because they are perceived to be risky. In addition, if you own a $1,000 bond from a company, such as an internet start-up company, and they start doing really well, the market may perceive the Internet company's bonds to be less risky, and you may be able to sell your bond for more than $1,000. Of course, if the company starts performing poorly, the bond may be worth less than $1,000.

What makes one investment riskier than another? Several factors are involved in determining the amount of risk of an investment, but one of the key factors is the change in value, or volatility, of the investment. For example, if you purchase a share of stock and the price remains $20 every day for two consecutive years, then it is not considered a high risk. If the price increases by 10% each year for several years it is also considered not to be a high risk. On the other hand, if the stock increases by 5% one year, then decreases by 10%, then increases by 17%, then decreases by 8%, the stock would be considered volatile and be of high risk. What makes it risky in this scenario? The stock could have large gains but also large losses. If you look at the average return over the four years you would have a 1% gain. However, the difference between the average of 1% and each of the actual returns is very drastic. When comparing the average of 1% to the 17% gain and then comparing the 1% to the 10% decrease, it seems that you just cannot tell where the stock price may end up. That is what makes it risky.

We have already discussed that equity is riskier than debt and that holders of equity can expect to receive greater returns than holders of debt. We have also explained the most common forms of equity holdings is stock and bonds for debt holdings. So it stands to reason that stocks should average larger annual returns than bonds. In fact, from 1928 to 2009 stocks have averaged an annual return of 11.27%. Over that same time period bonds have averaged an annual return of 5.24%.[53] During that same period inflation has averaged 3.02%. (Source: www.inflationdata.com and TVM calculation.)

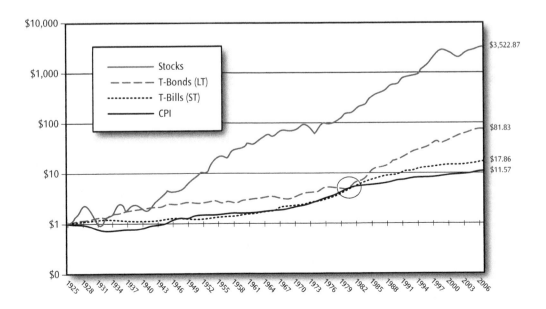

While the long-term return for stock has been significantly higher than the return for bonds, not everyone invests in stock all the time. Why would anyone invest in bonds if the long-term returns are expected to be only 5% while stocks can expect to return about 11%? The answer is simple; because stocks have higher short-term price volatility, when compared to bonds. Not everyone needs their money invested for several years, so they may choose to invest in bonds, which tend to have more predictable pricing from year to year. In addition, some individual investors simply cannot handle the thought of losing 20% or more in any given year, even though the long-term expectation is to earn a positive 11%. Because stock investments have been known to have some very bad years, some investors do not want to deal with, or they cannot handle the stress of, these large drops in price.

Because bonds are less volatile, why would anyone take the added risk to invest in stocks just to gain a few percentage points on their investment returns? Wouldn't it be better to sleep well every night knowing that your investments tend to be relatively safe and constant as opposed to worrying about how far down the investment might go? Look at how the interest rates can make a big difference over time.

With our understanding of interest rates, risk, and volatility, we are ready to maximize our returns and minimize our risk.

# MANAGE YOUR INVESTMENT RISK

To maximize our returns we have to get comfortable with risk. If we are not willing to take any risk, then we cannot really expect any return. We do not want to take any unnecessary risk because there is no added reward. Because we need to embrace risk and it cannot be eliminated, we need to learn how to manage it. Risk is going to become our friend.

How can we manage our investment risk? We do so through diversification. What does diversification mean? It is a fancy way of saying, "Don't put all your eggs in one basket." Diversification simply means we do not want to put all our money into one single investment.

You do not want to invest in a single asset because you are taking unnecessary risk, risk that will not be compensated by the market. What happens if you invest all your money into a single stock? If the stock price goes up you could earn a lot of money, but if the company goes bankrupt you would lose all your money. What if you put half your money into the bank and the other half in a stock? Again, if the company goes bankrupt you only lose half of your money. Now what if you put one-third of your money in the bank, in a stock, and in a bond? I don't know about you, but I would rather lose one-third of my money than lose it all.

If you invest in stock from a single company and that company goes bankrupt or simply starts performing poorly, then your investments will drop in value or possibly even be reduced to nothing. Likewise, if you have all your money in bonds with a single company and that company goes bankrupt you can also lose all of your investments. What if you have some of your money in 10 different companies? If one of them goes bankrupt you only lose 10% of your money. But, if one company goes bankrupt but the other nine companies increase in value just over 11%, then you would not have lost any money whatsoever. More important, if they were to increase by 12%, your return would still increase despite the total loss of one of your investments.

The point is that you need to spread your money around in different investments to best protect it from companies that do poorly. To better diversify, it is suggested to invest in companies in different industries. For instance, if you invest in five different retail companies (such as Walmart, Kmart, JCPenney, Kohls, and Target) you are still poorly diversified. What happens if the retail industry has a bad year? All five companies decrease in value. Meanwhile technology and energy companies are doing quite well. You missed an opportunity for positive returns.

Properly diversifying across companies, industries, and markets protects you from any single investment bringing down your portfolio. A portfolio is what we call all the different investments we own.

## Change Your Mentality

You are in this for the long haul. As you begin to build your portfolio one of the things all new investors have to guard against is fear. Prices will go down. That is no reason to sell. You will be choosing quality investments, which will increase in value over the long term. When prices fall take a shopper's mentality; everything is on sale.

Would you rather pay full price for something or buy it on sale? Everyone wants a bargain so of course you would rather get it on sale. Your goal in this situation is to fight the herd mentality. When everybody is selling you want to be buying. You do this by having cash at your disposal to take advantage of buying opportunities. By making the right decision your first day on the job you have set up a system to automatically deposit money regularly into your retirement account. This is the secret to successful investing.

If you wait until you get advice from your friends or even most brokers, it is too late. By the time information starts spreading from person to person, all the professional investors have already snatched up the bargains. This is why having money regularly deposited into your investment account works best.

## Who Is Helping You?

Any time you seek professional advice ask how the person advising you is being compensated. One of the ways to maximize your returns is by minimizing your fees. All companies, including investment companies, are in business to make money. There are many reputable companies to choose from that can assist you with your investments. Your job is to choose a firm that will help you select investments that most closely align with your goals with the lowest fees. Some investment companies make their money by getting you to buy and sell stock frequently because they charge commission, or fee, on each transaction. They may be tempted to push products that have high sales commissions because it is in *their* best interest not in *your* best interest. You want to avoid these types of companies because they are contrary to your investment strategy.

In addition to avoiding investment companies that would have you buy and sell frequently, you must also work to minimize your fees. While a 2% fee may seem like a small amount, consider the following example: If an investment company charges 2% of your portfolio in management fees and you earn a 10% return in one year you only get to keep 8%. But if you lose 6% the following year they still get to take their 2% fee off the top resulting in a total loss of 8% to you. So a 10% gain one year and a 6% loss the next gives you a two-year return of zero, yet your investment firm earned money from you both years. You have earned nothing and the investment firm still made money.

Investment companies do have to charge some fees for their service to stay in business. It is your responsibility to make sure you are not being overcharged. A reasonable fee is less than one percent.

There is a huge difference between a reputable investment company and an investment guru. Beware of these so-called experts. Nobody can predict the future, not even an investment guru. Most investment gurus are all about marketing their "unique" strategy. The problem is they never give you the complete picture. It is easy to demonstrate 300% returns if you ignore commission, taxes, losses, and risk. There is no such thing as high returns without high risk. So do not be fooled by the paid celebrity endorsements, the late-night infomercials with the large swimming pool and bikini models in the background, or even by personal testimonials most likely from paid actors. For all you know the guru told 10,000 people what to do with their money and guessed right for five of them. The guru then asked those five investors to talk about how great that investment advice was. What you do not hear is that the other 9,995 people lost all their money based on the guru's advice.

It is up to you to be an intelligent and well-informed investor. Fully understand exactly what you are investing in. If you do not understand, keep asking until you do. Do not invest your money based on solicitations or emotions. Even with investments, if the salesperson can get you to make an emotional decision you are less likely to make the decision that is in your best interest.

# WHERE TO INVEST

The key to investing is to align your investment vehicles with your SMART goals. You have identified short-term, medium-term, and long-term goals. You have also identified how much you will need to achieve those goals. Now you must select your investments, aligning risk with your needs and your time horizon. There are different investment vehicles best suited for different time horizons.

# Short-Term Investments

For short-term savings goals you want something that is very secure and has little chance of decreasing in value because you will use the money soon. Interest-bearing checking accounts, savings accounts, and money market accounts pay small returns but rarely decrease in value. That makes these investments appropriate for our short-term goals.

# Medium-Term Investments

For medium-term savings goals most investors consider debt investments such as bonds. Bonds do not provide as easy access to your money as most bank or money market accounts, but pay a slightly higher return in exchange. You can purchase bonds that will result in a certain level of return for when you need the money. For example, if you want a down payment for a new home in five years you can purchase bonds that will mature, or pay you, in five years.

# Long-Term Goals

When you are saving for long-term goals, including retirement, wealth building, or college education you want equity investments. Equity means ownership, and the easiest way to own companies or businesses is by purchasing stock. Investing in the stock market is the only way to see aggressive gains.

# The Problem with Stocks

You are going to hear "Stock Market," "Stock Market," "Stock Market," and think you need to go out and buy stocks. Yes, you do need to invest in stocks, but to be true to your investment strategy you should be properly diversified. The problem with stocks is that diversification is expensive. Stocks are traded in 100 share blocks. For example, if you purchase stock of five different companies in five different industries you would have stock in 25 different companies. At 100 shares per company that would be 2,500 shares of stock. At an average price of $50 per share you would need $125,000 just to be minimally diversified. The bad news is we cannot diversify if we only have $100 to invest this month. The good news is there are thousands of other investors out there with exactly the same problem. This problem can be overcome through the use of mutual funds.

## *Mutual Funds*

The way most of us diversify our portfolio is through the use of mutual funds. So what is a mutual fund and how will it help you diversify?

A mutual fund brings us together to pool our resources. The mutual fund takes our $100 and the $100 from 1,000 other people giving us $100,000 to invest just this month. Because we invest $100 each month, by the end of the year our $1,200 is now part of a $1.2 million mutual fund. With that much money, a professional fund manager can properly diversify. As an individual, we do not personally own stock of any individual company; the mutual fund does. Our ownership comes from owning a piece of the mutual fund. Investing in mutual funds allows us to take advantage of the large gains that are possible in the stock market, while managing our risk through diversification without having to be wealthy.

So how wealthy do you have to be to invest in mutual funds? You can invest with as little as $25 per month. If you are not ready to make monthly contributions,, you can make a one-time investment (perhaps with graduation money) of as little as $500.

With mutual funds you get immediate diversification. In addition, the funds are professionally managed so you do not have to become a full-time investor doing research on thousands of companies to decide which stocks to buy or sell. Mutual funds come in a variety of shapes and sizes. A mutual fund is not limited to only investing in stocks. Because a mutual fund is nothing more than a way for many people to pool their resources together and invest in something bigger than they otherwise could afford or diversify beyond what they could do on their own, the mutual fund could invest in many different types of assets. There are many types of mutual funds, each designed with specific time horizons and risk tolerances in mind.

## Money Market Funds

Money market funds are relatively low risk and best suited for short-term time horizons. Many money market funds allow check writing privileges so you can use this type of account in place of, or in addition to, a checking account. While the fund buys short-term investments that constantly change the fund itself is continual. This is a convenient, low-cost place to invest your money for the short term.

## Bond Funds

A bond fund is simply a mutual fund that invests in bonds. The fund may invest in any mix of short-term, intermediate, or long-term bonds, depending on the risk level and objectives of the fund. Although there is slightly more risk associated with bond funds, they provide a slightly higher return. Typically these funds do not provide the ease of access to your money like the money market funds. Bond funds are best suited for short to midterm savings goals.

## Stock Funds

Stock funds invest in shares of stock from multiple companies. These funds carry considerable more risk than your other investment options but offer the opportunity to earn greater returns. The value of these funds can fluctuate widely over short periods of time. Stock funds are best suited for long-term savings goals.

Stock funds come in all shapes and sizes including company size, growth potential, expected income, specific industries, geographic regions, or even social awareness. You will find stock funds that focus only on the size of companies, some that only look for companies that pay high dividends, and others that only look for companies with expected rapid price appreciation. Then there are funds that only invest in international companies and right around the corner are funds that concentrate on a specific region or industry. You can find hybrid funds that do any combination of these or even socially responsible funds to support your specific values or beliefs.

If you choose to invest in a specific mutual fund, you will be bombarded with even more decisions. Several pieces of critical information are needed to make an informed decision. The first is to read the first few pages of the prospectus to make sure the fund manager's investment philosophy is aligned with your savings goals and objectives. Keep in mind that your objectives are dependent on your age and personal life circumstances and are constantly changing. The second thing to consider is whether the fund is front-load, no-load, or back-load. Load refers to the commission and when it is paid. The third, look at administrative expenses and fees. Remember, every company needs to make money to stay in business. Finally, you need to understand the fund's past performance. Any fund can have large returns for a very short period of time by getting lucky once or simply taking on large amounts of risk. Are you investing in a quality fund and one that is aligned with your interests? This gets extremely complicated.

If you are feeling overwhelmed, you are not alone, and the feeling is perfectly normal. Just as every other industry out there works to confuse you so does the mutual fund industry. Fortunately there is a solution. Perhaps one of the easiest and least expensive ways to begin investing in mutual funds is through an index fund.

## Index Funds

Index funds appear complicated, but are not. An index fund is simply a type of mutual fund that works to give the same return as a particular market index. A market index is nothing more than the average price of a group of stocks as determined by a financial institution. The Dow and the S&P 500, for example, are market indices. Index funds try to mimic a specific market index by purchasing the same stocks that make up the index.

Unlike regular mutual funds managers that constantly buy and sell stocks to try and beat the index, the index fund manager only has to mirror the market index. Because index fund managers do not do extensive research of the stocks they are purchasing, the fund's administrative costs and associated fees are much smaller. Not only do index funds have lower fees, but over time they provide higher returns.

In a given year only about 25% of professionally managed mutual funds ever actually provide a higher return than their market index.[54] This means 75% of the time the market index is better than the professionally managed mutual fund. Because there are index funds that mimic a market index at a lower cost why not just buy index funds? An index mutual fund gives you a greater chance to maximize your returns at the lowest cost.

### Real Estate

What if you want to invest in real estate? It can be a good investment, but rarely provides a positive return until sold, yet has many monthly costs and cash outlays. In addition, being a landlord is like being any other small business owner, all of the problems are yours. One way to get around becoming a landlord is to use a Real Estate Investment Trust (REIT).

A REIT is a mutual fund for real estate. By investing in a REIT you are able to pool your money with other investors so you can each own a small piece of many different properties. Investing in real estate is simply another way to diversify your portfolio.

### Small Businesses

Investing in or starting a small business can be the most personally rewarding of all investment types. All the customers are *your* customers. All of the decisions are *your* decisions. All the profits are *your* profits. Having something you own, grow, and nurture makes owning a small business like no other investment.

However, even the smallest new business can require significant cash and other resources. You do not just invest a few dollars and sit back to watch your investment grow like a mutual fund. You do the work and run the business. All the problems, decisions, and, most important, the risks are *yours* to manage. Changing regulations, changing customers, changing technology, and the changing economy all have to be juggled on a regular basis.

Owning a small business gives the greatest probability of high returns, but also carries the most risk. Yet, owning a successful company and doing something you love to do carry rewards that you cannot measure in dollars or returns.

# WHAT NOT TO BUY

There are many good investments that align well with almost everyone's goals. There are also investments that almost everyone should avoid. For most of us there are three common investments that rarely align with the most common SMART goals: limited partnerships, time-shares, and second homes.

Limited partnerships are okay if you want to be part of a small business as a limited partner. On the other hand, buying into a limited partnership as part of your long-term investment strategy is a terrible investment. Most limited partnerships carry relatively high fees and commissions and can be extremely difficult to sell.

Time-shares may be a good vacation decision but tend to be bad investments. Most are sold as part of a high pressure sales presentation with tremendous markups and large commissions. There are continuing homeowners' fees and maintenance costs and rarely are resold for as much as the original purchase price.

Second homes, like time-shares, may be good quality-of-life decisions, but rarely work out to be a good investment decision. Just as with a first home, second homes rarely provide a positive return yet have all the costs and cash outlays for maintenance, utilities, taxes, etc. They may make a great vacation retreat, but not a good investment.

# SUMMARY

It should be clear to you now that unless you are prepared to invest considerable time, effort, money, and risk that you are never going to become an investment expert. We barely scratched the surface of the complexities involved in investment decision making. Yet you are armed with enough information to distinguish between good and bad investment advice, and avoid being ripped off by those in the financial industry who try to profit from your financial ignorance.

# THE COST OF  FINANCIAL IGNORANCE

The most important thing you can do to advance your savings goals is to start early. For our student from the beginning of the chapter he waited three years before he started saving for his retirement by taking advantage of the retirement plan offered by his employer. Let's be very conservative and assume a long-term rate of 8% and that he will need his retirement savings when he is 67. He was 22 years old when he graduated but waited until he was 25 before putting $100 per month into his employer's retirement plan. By waiting just three years he cost himself:

| | |
|---|---|
| Retirement starting at 22 years old | $525,454 |
| Retirement starting at 25 years old | $412,049 |
| Total Cost of Financial Ignorance | **$113,405** |

# REFERENCES

[1] Trends in College Pricing, 2009. Table 1a. Average Published Charges for Undergraduates by Type and Control of Institution, 2009–10. (Enrollment Weighted). Accessed 5/28/10. http://www.trendscollegeboard.com/college_pricing/1_1_published_prices_by_sector.html?expandable=0

[2] *Percentage of undergraduates receiving financial aid and the average amount received, by type and source of aid and selected student characteristics:* 2007–08. SOURCE: U.S. Department of Education, National Center for Education Statistics. (2009). 2007–08 National Postsecondary Student Aid Study (NPSAS:08) Student Financial Aid Estimates for 2007–08, Selected Findings. Accessed 5/28/10. http://nces.ed.gov/fastfacts/display.asp?id=31

[3] Average of high and low Stafford Loan rates as of 6/10/2010. Payment based on 10 years, monthly payments at 5.1% using Excel payment calculator. http://www.salliemae.com/get_student_loan/apply_student_loan/interest_rates_fees/

[4] *Earned degrees conferred by degree-granting institutions, by level of degree and sex of student: Selected years, 1869–70 to 2013–14.* Table 247. SOURCE: U.S. Department of Education, National Center for Education Statistics, Earned Degrees Conferred, 1869–70 through 1964–65; Projections of Education Statistics to 2014; Higher Education General Information Survey (HEGIS), "Degrees and Other Formal Awards Conferred" surveys, 1965–66 through 1985–86; and 1986–87 through 2002–03 Integrated Postsecondary Education Data System, "Completions Survey" (IPEDS-C:87–99), and Fall 2000 through Fall 2003. Accessed 6/13/2010. http://nces.ed.gov/programs/digest/d04/tables/dt04_247.asp

[5] *Petrecca, Laura. Toughest test comes after graduation: Getting a job.* USA Today. May 21, 2010. Accessed 6/13/2010. SOURCE: A CollegeGrad.com poll. http://www.usatoday.com/money/economy/employment/2010 05 19 jobs19_CV_N.htm

[6] *One-Quarter of College Class of 2010 Have Jobs Waiting (5-6-2010).* National Association of Colleges and Employers. Accessed 6/13/2010. http://www.naceweb.org/Press/Releases/One-Quarter_of_College_Class_of_2010_Have_Jobs_Waiting_(5-6-2010).aspx?referal=pressroom&menuid=273

[7] *College Enrollment and Work Activity of 2009 High School Graduates.* SOURCE: Bureau of Labor Statistics. Accessed 6/13/2010. http://www.bls.gov/news.release/hsgec.nr0.htm

[8] National Center for Education Statistics. Graduation rates of first-time postsecondary students who started as full-time degree-seeking students, by sex, race/ethnicity, time between starting and graduating, and level and control of institution where student started: Selected cohort entry years, 1996 through 2004. http://nces.ed.gov/programs/digest/d09/tables/dt09_331.asp

[9] National Center for Education Statistics. Graduation rates of first-time postsecondary students who started as full-time degree-seeking students, by sex, race/ethnicity, time between starting and graduating, and level and control of institution where student started: Selected cohort entry years, 1996 through 2004. http://nces.ed.gov/programs/digest/d09/tables/dt09_331.asp

[10] College Board. What It Costs to go to College. http://www.collegeboard.com/student/pay/add-it-up/4494.html

[11] CNNMoney. Four myths about college costs: The true price of that B.A. may not be as high as you think. January 20, 2005. Penelope Wang. *Money Magazine*. http://money.cnn.com/2005/01/20/pf/college/myths_0502/index.htm

[12] U.S. Department of Education, Federal Student Aid, Student Aid Awareness and Applicant Services. *Funding Education Beyond High School: The Guide to Federal Student Aid 2010–2011*, Washington, D.C. 2010.

[13] IRS.gov. Tax Benefits for Education. http://www.irs.gov/newsroom/article/0,,id=213044,00.html. December 28, 2010.

[14] Student loan debt exceeds credit card debt in USA. *USAToday*. Susan Tompor, *Detroit Free Press*. September 10, 2010. http://www.usatoday.com/money/perfi/college/2010-09-10-student-loan-debt_N.htm

[15] Sources: http://www2.ed.gov/offices/OSFAP/DirectLoan/RepayCalc/dlentry1.html. http://www.finaid.org/calculators/ibr.phtml. Accessed 04/25/2011.

[16] The Income-Based Repayment has many variables. You will have to use the online calculator and enter your information for a more accurate estimate. For this example the following variables were used, based on the default settings of the finaid.org income-based repayment calculator: Table Year = 2009, Family Size = 1, Discount Rate = 5.8%, CPI = 3%, State of Residence = Continental U.S., Income Growth Rate = 4%, Poverty Level Change Rate = 3%. In addition the following variables were used for this example: Loan Forgiveness = 25 years, Adjusted Gross Income = $30,000, First Loan = $35,000, Interest Rate = 6.8%, Minimum Payment = $10.00, Interest Rate Reduction = 0%. In this example payments begin at $172 per month and increase each year until year 19 where the payment reaches $403 per month and remains constant for the remaining three years (except the final payment which is $313).

[17] Robert, Johnnie L. *The King's Ransom*. Newsweek. June 26, 2009. Accessed 08/06/2010. http://www.newsweek.com/2009/06/25/the-king-s-ransom.html

[18] Palmer, Kimberly. *Lindsay Lohan: Cash-Strapped and Unemployed*. U.S. News and World Report. March 23, 2009. Accessed 8/06/2010. http://money.usnews.com/money/blogs/alpha-consumer/2009/03/23/lindsay-lohan-cashstrapped-and-unemployed.html

[19] Murray, Sara and Conor Dougherty. *Personal Bankruptcy Filings Rising Fast*. Wall Street Journal, January 7, 2010. Accessed 06/13/2010. http://online.wsj.com/article/SB126263231055415303.html

[20] *Divorce Statistics in America*. Accessed 08/06/2010. www.divorcestatistics.org

[21] Sallie Mae Student loan interest rates and fees. Accessed 06/13/2010. http://www.salliemae.com/get_student_loan/apply_student_loan/interest_rates_fees/

[22] *The Real Costs of Car Ownership*. Bikes at Work. Accessed 5/10/2010. http://www.bikesatwork.com/carfree/cost-of-car-ownership.html

[23] *2009 Honda Civic Ownership Costs*. Automobile Magazine. Accessed 5/10/2010. http://www.automobilemag.com/am/2009/honda/civic/ownership_costs.html

[24] Edmunds provides True Market Value® pricing, car reviews, ratings, & advice to help you get a fair deal. Edmunds. Accessed 5/10/2010. www.edmunds.com

[25] Consumers Union (CU) is an expert, independent, nonprofit organization whose mission is to work for a fair, just, and safe marketplace for all consumers and to empower consumers to protect themselves. Consumer Reports. Accessed 5/10/2010. www.consumerreports.org

[26] CARFAX Report contains information that can impact a consumer's decision about a used vehicle. CarFax. Accessed 5/10/2010. www.CarFax.com

[27] A registered collective membership mark that identifies a real estate professional who is a member of the National Association of REALTORS® and subscribes to its strict Code of Ethics. Realtor.com. Accessed 08/04/2010. www.realtor.com

[28] http://www.google.com/earth

[29] Home Sellers Can Haggle Broker Commissions. Consumer Reports. August 4, 2008. Accessed 10/04/2010. http://pressroom.consumerreports.org/pressroom/2008/08/consumer-reports-survey-home-sellers-can-haggle-on-broker-commissions-paying-less-may-not-hurt-service-or-sale-price.html

[30] The price of new homes increased by 5.4% annually from 1963 to 2008, on average according to US Census data. MichaelBluejay.com. Accessed 10/04/2010. http://michaelbluejay.com/house/appreciation.html

[31] *Federal Income Tax Rates.* Money-zine.com. Accessed 10/4/2010. http://www.moneyzine.com/Financial-Planning/Tax-Shelter/Federal-Income-Tax-Rates/

[32] Lorren, Brooke. *HGTV Dream Home Winners Don't Always Live Happily Ever After.* Associated Content. Accessed 5/13/2010. http://www.associatedcontent.com/article/1353888/hgtv_dream_home_winners_dont_always.html

[33] *HGTV Grand Prize 2010.* HGTV.com. Accessed 5/13/2010. http://www.hgtv.com/hgtv-dream-home-2010-giveaway-rules/package/index.html

[34] Based on 6.8% APR and 10 year payback period

[35] OnStar is the world's most comprehensive in-vehicle safety, security and communication service. OnStar.com. Accessed 11/13/2010. http://www.onstar.com

[36] LoJack Corporation is the premier worldwide provider of tracking and recovery systems. LoJack.com. Accessed 11/13/2010. www.lojack.com

[37] Companies that provide automobile, homeowners or business insurance. Sites accessed 11/13/2010. www.geico.com, www.progressive.com, www.travelers.com, www.usaa.com

[38] Romano, Jay. *Why Renters Need Insurance.* The New York Times. October 7, 2007. Accessed 7/19/2010. http://www.nytimes.com/2007/10/07/realestate/07home.html?_r=1

[39] *Personal Disability Insurance.* © Steve Crawford 2001. Accessed 09/26/2010. http://www.about-disability-insurance.com/

[40] The official site to help consumers to obtain their free credit report. AnnualCreditReport.com. Accessed 09/27/2010. www.annualcreditreport.com

[41] *Study finds rising number of college students using credit cards for tuition.* Sallie Mae. Apr 13, 2009. Accessed 09/27/2010. https://www.salliemae.com/about/news_info/newsreleases/041309.htm

[42] *Credit card statistics, industry facts, debt statistics.* CreditCards.com. Accessed 09/27/2010. http://www.creditcards.com/credit-card-news/credit-card-industry-facts-personal-debt-statistics-1276.php

[43] Silver-Greenberg, Jessica. *Majoring in Credit-Card Debt.* Business Week. 09/04/2007. Accessed 09/27/2010. http://www.businessweek.com/bwdaily/dnflash/content/sep2007/db2007093_443488.htm

[44] *FACT SHEET: REFORMS TO PROTECT AMERICAN CREDIT CARD HOLDERS.* May 22, 2009. Accessed 09/27/2010. http://www.whitehouse.gov/the_press_office/Fact-Sheet-Reforms-to-Protect-American-Credit-Card-Holders/

[45] New Credit Card Rules Effective Feb 22. http://www.federalreserve.gov/consumerinfo/wyntk_creditcardrules.htm Accessed 03/30/2011

[46] CardWeb.com, Inc.® is a leading publisher of information pertaining to the payment industry, including, but not limited to, credit cards, debit cards, smart cards, prepaid cards, ATM cards, loyalty cards and phone cards. CardWeb.com. Accessed 09/27/2010. www.cardweb.com

[47] What is a Shumer Box? Credit.com. http://www.credit.com/products/credit_cards/schumerbox.jsp

[48] National Association of Attorney's General. Accessed 11/13/2010. www.naag.org

[49] *Why Money is the Leading Cause of Divorce.* Jet. FindArticles.com. Accessed 09/27/2010. http://findarticles.com/p/articles/mi_m1355/is_n1_v91/ai_18930297/

[50] Dunleavey, MP. *12 Biggest Reasons We Fight over Finances & 8 Tips for Money Talks.* MSN Money. December 4, 2009. Accessed 08/15/2010. http://articles.moneycentral.msn.com/CollegeAndFamily/LoveAndMoney/The12BiggestReasonsWeFightOverFinances.aspx?page=2

[51] Bailor, Kelli. *Online Dating: How to stay clear of married men.* Online Dating Magazine. Accessed 7/6/2010. http://www.onlinedatingmagazine.com/features/marriedmen.html

[52] *8 ways to Cut Wedding Costs.* June 11, 2008. Accessed 09/27/2010. http://www.smartmoney.com/personal-finance/marriage-divorce/theyll-never-know-eight-hiddenways-to-cut-wedding-costs-13918

[53] *Annual Returns on Stock, T.Bonds and T.Bills: 1928–Current.* New York University. Accessed 10/11/2010. http://pages.stern.nyu.edu/~adamodar/New_Home_Page/datafile/histret.html

[54] Salmon, Felix. *Yes, Fund Managers Really Do Underperform.* November 18, 2008. Accessed 10/11/2010. http://seekingalpha.com/article/106685-yes-fund-managers-really-do-underperform